# Consumer Behavior

## FOR

# DUMMIES®

**by Laura Lake**

WILEY

Wiley Publishing, Inc.

**Consumer Behavior For Dummies®**

Published by
**Wiley Publishing, Inc.**
111 River St.
Hoboken, NJ 07030-5774
www.wiley.com

WILEY

# Consumer Behavior For Dummies®

Cheat Sheet

## Segmenting the Marketplace into Target Markets: A Quick How-To

The goal of segmentation is to enable yourself to create marketing messages that speak directly to your consumers. The process of segmentation goes like this:

1. **Identify your core market.**
2. **Determine whether your core market qualifies for segmentation.**
3. **Evaluate your core market for potential success.**
4. **Identify potential customer needs.**
5. **Identify submarkets within your core market.**
6. **Identify segment dimensions.**
7. **Evaluate the market segment.**

## Reaching Consumers through Their Decision-Making Process

When consumers look to buy your products, they engage in a decision-making process. When you understand that process, you can walk them through each step, thereby increasing the chances of them purchasing from you. Here's a quick rundown of the process:

✔ **Phase 1: Recognition and Awareness of a Need**

In this phase, it's your job to position your product or service as a solution to a problem or need that a consumer may be encountering.

✔ **Phase 2: Search for Information**

In this phase, you must make sure that your information is available to potential consumers. If they watch television, you need to produce a few commercials. If they often use the Internet, you want to make sure you have a Web site and are participating in search-engine marketing. Make yourself available where your potential customers go to find information about your products or services.

✔ **Phase 3: Evaluating the Alternatives**

Provide information about your product in a way that it's easy to understand and that explains why you're better than the competition. In other words, make sure it's easy for consumers to understand why they should buy from you.

✔ **Phase 4: Purchase**

Make your products available to consumers or they'll go somewhere else to make a purchase. Also be sure to make the purchase process easy and enjoyable for the consumer.

✔ **Phase 5: Post-Purchase Evaluation**

Service, Service, Service! Sure you need to provide your consumers with service before the purchase, but did you know that you also need to provide service after the purchase? Extraordinary customer care after the fact can help diminish feelings of buyer's remorse.

*For Dummies: Bestselling Book Series for Beginners*

# Consumer Behavior For Dummies®

## The Relationships among Consumers, Their Behavior, and You

The following figure is a pictorial summary of this book; it shows you how consumers' purchase decisions are influenced by personal and social factors as well as by your marketing mix.

For more information about Wiley Publishing, call 1-800-762-2974.

**For Dummies: Bestselling Book Series for Beginners**

# *About the Author*

**Laura A. Lake** has been involved in the marketing industry since 1997. She brings a fresh, easy-to-understand perspective to consumer behavior. Despite popular belief, the understanding of consumer behavior can even benefit small companies, because it enables them to market more effectively by meeting the needs of the buyers in the marketplace. The end result is a higher rate of success; this is where Laura finds her passion.

Laura has helped many companies understand consumer behavior and the management and implementation of the findings within. Understanding why consumers purchase, consume, or dispose of products is invaluable as the battle for customers intensifies day by day. Laura consults with companies to emphasize the importance of investing in research to determine why customers think, feel, reason, and ultimately purchase from among alternative products or services.

Laura serves as the current marketing columnist at About.com, a New York Times Company. She shares her extensive marketing knowledge in more than 600 articles published on some 4,000 Web sites and in various publications. She's also a featured writer in several magazines. As if that weren't enough to keep her busy, Laura has served in director and vice president positions for well-known advertising agencies in previous years. In 2008, she founded her own successful marketing agency and sales training company. She now advises companies on how to create and implement effective marketing strategies that help them grow their businesses.

# Dedication

As most authors will tell you, it takes much more than just them to write a book. It's a collaborative effort between you and those who encourage you to do the work it takes to get the book done. I had several people by my side along the way, and without them the possibility of finishing would have been impossible.

First and foremost I must thank my mom and dad, Jack and Jill Brown, for pushing me to live my dreams and follow my heart. Even if it seemed at times I wouldn't make it, you always believed.

A special thanks goes to my son Taylor. You've always believed and stood by me, even when change was difficult. You are my daily inspiration and the person who creates the drive to keep me moving forward. You never complain when it comes to the long hours that I work, and throughout the entire process of writing this book you were patient and understanding. We've come a long way, and your sacrifices have not gone unnoticed. Your patience, your love, your hugs, and your encouragement made the long hours spent in the office a little easier to bear.

Also, a big thanks goes to Abby. You made me smile when you understood that the hours locked away in the office would one day produce a book that you would see in the stores. Here it is! Thank you to my business partner Jamie Verkamp as well. You held down the fort and made things happen when my attention was elsewhere. You kept our business going and growing without skipping a beat. You were always encouraging during sharp deadlines, and you never complained when you had to pick up the slack. I couldn't have picked a better partner. To you I am grateful, and I couldn't think of a better person to share success with.

Last, but not least, thank you to my circle of friends: Hilda, Lori, Vicky, Kay, Rhonda, and Angel. You have pushed me through the trying times and encouraged me to keep moving forward. Your words of encouragement, e-mails, and telephone calls always came at the right times. Thank you for sharing your knowledge, your experiences, and your lives with me over the years.

To those who were affected by my crankiness, absenteeism, and requests for silence: I finally did it! Thank you all. You will never know the impact you had and the important roles that you played in the completion of this project. Not even words could express my gratitude.

# Author's Acknowledgments

I must acknowledge the people who made this book possible and who made writing easier. Of course, no one ever said this would be easy.

Huge thanks goes to my project editor, Kristin DeMint, from Wiley Publishing. Thank you for the support, encouragement, guidance, and patience during the course of this project. Just the mere fact that you had to read every page of this book and make sense of it in its initial draft form means that you deserve a Medal of Honor!

And to my literary agent, Barbara Doyen, thank you for keeping me on track, answering my questions, and guiding me through the process of writing this book. I couldn't have done it without you!

## Publisher's Acknowledgments

We're proud of this book; please send us your comments through our Dummies online registration form located at http://dummies.custhelp.com. For other comments, please contact our Customer Care Department within the U.S. at 877-762-2974, outside the U.S. at 317-572-3993, or fax 317-572-4002.

Some of the people who helped bring this book to market include the following:

**Acquisitions, Editorial, and Media Development**

**Project Editor:** Kristin DeMint

**Acquisitions Editor:** Mike Baker

**Copy Editor:** Jessica Smith

**Assistant Editor:** Erin Calligan Mooney

**Editorial Program Coordinator:** Joe Niesen

**Technical Editor:** Russell G. Wahlers, DBA

**Editorial Manager:** Michelle Hacker

**Editorial Assistant:** Jennette ElNaggar

**Cover Photo:**
© artpartner-images.com / Alamy

**Cartoons:** Rich Tennant (www.the5thwave.com)

**Composition Services**

**Project Coordinator:** Kristie Rees

**Layout and Graphics:** Reuben W. Davis, Stephanie D. Jumper, Melissa K. Smith, Christine Williams

**Proofreaders:** Bonnie Mikkelson, Dwight Ramsey

**Indexer:** Sherry Massey

**Special Help**

   Elizabeth Rea, Victoria M. Adang

---

**Publishing and Editorial for Consumer Dummies**

   **Diane Graves Steele,** Vice President and Publisher, Consumer Dummies

   **Kristin Ferguson-Wagstaffe,** Product Development Director, Consumer Dummies

   **Ensley Eikenburg,** Associate Publisher, Travel

   **Kelly Regan,** Editorial Director, Travel

**Publishing for Technology Dummies**

   **Andy Cummings,** Vice President and Publisher, Dummies Technology/General User

**Composition Services**

   **Debbie Stailey,** Director of Composition Services

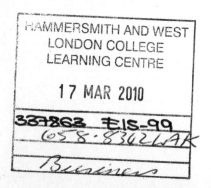

# Contents at a Glance

# Table of Contents

# Introduction

. . . . . . . . . . . . . . . . . . . . . . . . . . . . . . . . . . . . . . . . . . . . . . . . . . . . . . . . . . . . . . . . . . . . . . .

Consumer behavior is way more than just a guessing game; it's crucial to a successful marketing plan. A clear understanding of the consumer usually makes the difference between companies that succeed and those that fail. By understanding the behaviors of consumers, you can make more informed business decisions; these decisions alone can raise bottom-line revenues, lower customer acquisition costs, and increase customer retention and profitability.

The study of consumer behavior tells you why consumers act the way they do, why they buy what they buy, and why they buy from who they buy from. It's the study of the external and internal influences that affect consumers in purchasing decisions. Consumer behavior also shows the marketing influence that businesses have on consumers.

Consumer behavior is a subjective topic, so there are no absolutes. The only absolute is the fact that consumers are influenced by psychological and sociocultural factors. However, not all consumers are affected in the same capacity. Luckily, by understanding a few processes, you can gain the type of insight about consumers that helps your business market succeed and stand out from the competition.

If you want to succeed in your marketing, you have to understand why a particular consumer thinks, acts, and responds in the way that he does. Then you create an effective marketing strategy that accommodates those feelings, actions, and responses.

When you hear of consumer behavior, you probably begin thinking of big words, hard-to-understand formulas, and dry explanations of research methods. My approach is different. I show you how to take a look at a consumer as an individual and evaluate the influences he may be experiencing. I then teach you how to direct your marketing strategy so it's effectively based on the influence the consumer may be experiencing. Plenty of books on consumer behavior are available, but they're written in textbook style. My goal with *Consumer Behavior For Dummies* is to bring consumer behavior to you on a level that's easy to understand and applicable to your business. I don't talk theories. I talk actionable items that you can put into place today.

This book can be used as a tool to not only gain the knowledge of consumer behavior, but also to better understand and "speak" to your customer.

# About This Book

*Consumer Behavior For Dummies* is an easy-to-understand guide to consumer behavior. I've written it for anyone who wants to understand what consumer behavior is, how it affects the purchase process, and how it can be used to better market a product or service. My goal with this book is to explain consumer behavior in simple terms so anyone can pick it up and read it without getting a headache. And everyone will benefit from its contents. Consider the many uses:

- ✔ **If you're a marketing student,** this book can help you better understand consumer behavior and why it's so important to marketing.

- ✔ **If you're a business owner,** you can use this book to evaluate your marketing techniques, target market, and marketing message. Evaluating and tweaking these items helps you increase sales and revenue.

- ✔ **If you're an aspiring entrepreneur,** this book gives you a road map to consult when creating and marketing your business. You'll have a clear idea of who your target market is and how best to cater your message to that market.

- ✔ **If you're in sales,** you can use this book to transform your sales message. I show you how to identify customer need and create a message that satisfies that need, helping you close more sales. I provide a road map of the buying process so you can identify the phases that your prospect is in. This knowledge helps you restructure your sales message to meet your customers' needs and move them to decisions.

- ✔ **If you're a sales manager,** you can use this book to train your sales team to better understand consumer behavior. They'll be able to read their prospects like a well-written book.

- ✔ **If you're in customer service,** this book can serve as a guide to help you understand your customers. In return you'll offer them top-notch service that creates loyalty and returning customers.

# Conventions Used in This Book

To help you navigate the complex waters of the fluid nature of this book's topic, I use the following conventions consistently throughout the book:

- ✔ When I talk about *marketing,* I'm referring to any of the following aspects of business: advertising, publicity, customer service, direct mail, direct response, online advertising, or telemarketing.

- ✔ I use *italic* for new, important terms that are followed with a definition.

- ✔ I use **bold** text to highlight key concepts within bulleted lists as well as the action-oriented parts of numbered steps.

# What You're Not to Read

The gray-shaded text boxes throughout this book are what the *For Dummies* folks affectionately refer to as *sidebars,* and they contain helpful or interesting information that you don't *need* to know in order to understand the important concepts at hand. I wrote them, of course, so I recommend that you do read them. But if you're pressed for time or just not in the mood for extras, feel free to skip on over them.

# Foolish Assumptions

When I was writing this book, I kept a few assumptions in mind about you, the reader. These assumptions kept me on track so that I provided the most useful and pertinent information. Here's what I assume about you:

- ✔ You have an interest in why consumers behave the way they do, and you have a desire to understand the influences that affect consumers when it comes to their purchase patterns.

- ✔ You want to use that knowledge to influence consumers in an ethical way to purchase from you or the business you work for.

- ✔ You have an interest in marketing because you have your own business, you're studying marketing in school, you work in a marketing department at a company, or you desire a career change where you will have the ability to influence consumers.

- ✔ You have an interest in psychology either to understand your own purchasing behavior or to people watch and understand why consumers act the way they do.

# How This Book Is Organized

This book is chock-full of information, research techniques, marketing tips, and easy-to-understand advice that helps you understand the power of consumer behavior and how you can use it to not only better understand your market but to better market your own business. The six parts in this book are organized so you can find the information you need quickly. Determine what you need to know and head to that part. Here's a rundown of the different parts.

## Part I: Introduction to Consumer Behavior

Part I fills you in on the basics of consumer behavior. I outline the consumer decision-making process and show you why consumer behavior is important to your marketing strategy. You find out how to use the knowledge of consumer behavior to determine your ideal segments and target market. I also explore the different research methods with you.

## Part II: Delving Into the Psychology of the Individual Consumer

In this part, you take a deeper look into the individual customer. You get the scoop on the internal influences that affect the way consumers behave, and you discover how to work with those influences. I show you the power of perception and motivation and explain how attitude and intentions affect the purchasing decision. You can even read about how self-concepts, situation influences, and lifestyle change the behavior of your customer.

## Part III: Consumers in Their Social and Cultural Settings

Social and cultural settings have an effect on your customer. So in this part, I discuss the external influences that affect consumers and their purchasing patterns. These influences include those from cultures, subcultures, groups, family life cycles, and household structures. I also delve into the misbehaviors of consumers and show you what you can do to protect yourself against those misbehaviors.

## Part IV: Crafting Your Marketing Strategy

In Part IV, you get to make your consumer knowledge applicable to your business. This is the part where you put the knowledge you've gained regarding the influences of consumers to work. I show you how to focus on the core pieces of your marketing strategy by taking a peek at market research, identifying your key segments, and successfully finding and launching into untapped markets.

## Part V: Implementing Your Strategy with a Marketing Plan

In this part, I help you put all the pieces together. You create your marketing plan by using the consumer behavior knowledge that you've discovered. This isn't just any ordinary marketing plan, however. This is a plan that's created by understanding your customer more than you ever have before. You find out how to influence the perception of your consumers, educate your consumers, and create positioning strategies that are effective and successful. I also show you the process of new product adoption and help you encourage your customers be loyal and to come back often. Finally, I round out this part with some information on marketing ethics.

## Part VI: The Part of Tens

The chapters in this part are short, but full of great info. For example, because customer communication is key when it comes to consumer loyalty and repeat buying, I give you ten easy ways to communicate with your customers and ensure their satisfaction. These tips won't require much time to implement, but they will definitely bring an increase in business if you follow through. In another chapter, I explain the ten considerations you should keep in mind for business-to-business marketing.

Don't forget to take a look at the glossary at the back of the book, just before the index. It helps you find definitions for key marketing and consumer-behavior-related terms.

# Icons Used in This Book

Throughout this book, I highlight specific types of information with pictures called icons; the icons flag information so you can more easily access it if you want to flip back to it. They also help you to know what's crucial to remember and what isn't. Here's what each one means:

I use this icon when I want to remind you of essential and critical information regarding consumer behavior and its effect on your business.

This icon flags advice that can make a task easier or more successful.

This icon warns you of things that can cause you trouble.

# *Where to Go from Here*

The great thing about *Consumer Behavior For Dummies* is that you can thumb through it and read the chapters that interest you. You can go through it at your own pace in whatever order you desire. It's easy to use as a reference as you're beginning to explore consumer behavior in your own daily situations. I suggest that you start with the basics of Part I to gain a general understanding of consumer behavior. These chapters give you a foundation that you can use when thumbing through the other chapters.

If you want to focus on how consumers are influenced internally and externally, check out Parts II and III. With the chapters in these parts, you'll gain a greater understanding of why consumers behave the way they do when faced with particular influences.

Parts IV and V provide you with information regarding your marketing strategy, but without reading Parts II and III you won't gain the knowledge you need to create an effective marketing strategy and implementation process.

This book equips you with the knowledge and information that you need to create a consumer-generated marketing plan. It's like getting an MBA in a book. Okay, maybe not, but you *will* feel confident when it comes to understanding your customer and putting together a marketing plan that focuses on that customer.

# Part I

# Introduction to Consumer Behavior

"It's for people who have been using 'Obsession' too long."

# In this part . . .

Here I uncover the mystery behind consumer behavior and why it's important for you to understand. Consumer behavior is no longer just for the sophisticated corporations and multimillion-dollar businesses. Small- to medium-sized businesses will find the knowledge in this part just as useful.

By understanding consumer behavior, you can better understand your customers and gain insight into how they make decisions to purchase products. In this part, I give you an overview of the many variables involved in the study of consumer behavior. Then I walk you step-by-step through the consumer's decision-making process and show you how to help customers if they become stalled. If you can help your customers this way, you're more than one step ahead of most of your competition.

In this part, you also discover why incorporating the knowledge of consumer behavior is important to your marketing strategy. I discuss the different pieces of product strategy, placement strategy, pricing strategy, and promotion strategy. Adding the knowledge of consumer behavior to your marketing strategy sets your business up for success.

# Chapter 1

# Consumer Behavior: The Basics

. . . . . . . . . . . . . . . . . . . . . . . . . . . . . . . . . . . . . . . . . . . . . . . . .

## In This Chapter

▶ Understanding the basics of consumer behavior

▶ Considering the decision-making process and the influences that can affect it

▶ Examining your marketing strategy and crafting a marketing plan

▶ Testing your knowledge of consumer behavior

. . . . . . . . . . . . . . . . . . . . . . . . . . . . . . . . . . . . . . . . . . . . . . . . .

Consumer behavior is often misconceived as only useful to the sophisticated and bigger corporations. Nothing could be farther from the truth. After all, consumer behavior can teach companies of all sizes about the consumption patterns of their consumers as well as the internal and external influences that affect those customers.

When you understand the behavior of consumers, you can create products and services that provide the consumers with more value. And then you can market those products and services in ways that the consumers understand. The whole point of studying consumer behavior is to motivate customers to purchase.

In this chapter, I explain the basics of consumer behavior and show you how you can use it to better your marketability, explain your value, and increase your sales.

## What Is Consumer Behavior, and Why Is It Important?

Consumer behavior represents the study of individuals and the activities that take place to satisfy their realized needs. That satisfaction comes from the processes used in selecting, securing, and using products or services when the benefits received from those processes meet or exceed consumers' expectations. In other words, when an individual realizes that he has a need, the psychological process starts the consumer decision process. Through this process, the individual sets out to find ways to fulfill the need he has identified. That process includes the individual's thoughts, feelings, and behavior. When the process is complete, the consumer is faced with the task of analyzing and digesting all the information, which determines the actions he will take to fulfill the need.

To simplify the explanation even further, you can think of consumer behavior as the process that determines the why, what, who, when, and how of what a consumer purchases. Consumer behavior answers the following questions:

- ✔ **Why do consumers buy?** Consumers make purchases for a variety of reasons. These reasons include the following:

  - • To reinforce self-concepts

  - • To maintain their lifestyles

  - • To become part of a group or gain acceptance in a group they already belong to

  - • To express their cultural identity

- ✔ **What internal and external factors influence their purchases?** Each consumer is influenced internally by his own attitudes, personality, perceptions, self-concepts, and emotions. He also must deal with external influences, such as household structure, group association, and cultural beliefs.

- ✔ **Who do they buy from?** Consumers purchase from businesses that fulfill their psychological needs by making them feel welcome, understood, important, and comfortable.

- ✔ **When do they buy?** Consumers buy based on their consumption patterns, which are determined by their family life cycles and household structures.

- ✔ **How do they purchase?** Consumers go through a decision-making process that guides them in their purchases. This process takes into account both internal and external influences of the consumer.

Consumer behavior provides a wealth of information about the individuals that purchase your products and services. When you understand a consumer, you can speak directly to him and his needs. This special communication not only increases the consumer's ability to understand the value in your product, but it also increases sales. Consumers buy what they understand and what they see value in. Consumer behavior also provides you with insight on how to create an effective marketing strategy. After all, if you don't understand your consumers, how can you market to them?

Companies often fail to gain an understanding of what their consumers want and need before they actually create their marketing strategies. They lack knowledge of what influences their consumers. So remember that evaluation and understanding of consumer behavior should always come before the development of a marketing strategy or plan.

Today consumers are faced with an array of product selection, and competition is fierce among companies. This is why your understanding of consumer behavior is vital to the success of your business. When you understand your consumers better than your competition, you have a greater chance of winning their business.

When you're equipped to speak and market directly to consumers and the needs they're facing, you can help walk them through the decision-making processes and counteract any negative influences they may encounter in the process. Throughout this chapter, I explain both the processes and the influences that affect individuals when it comes to consumer behavior.

# Getting a Glimpse of the Consumer's Decision-Making Process

The consumer decision-making process consists of five steps. I focus on this process in detail in Chapter 2, but I want to give you a brief overview here. This overview will help you understand how consumer behavior impacts the decision a consumer makes on purchasing a product or service. Here are the steps in a nutshell:

1. **A consumer becomes aware of a need.** This need is triggered either internally or externally.

2. **After the need is identified, the consumer goes through a process to search for solutions that will fulfill that need.** This search involves identifying criteria that's important to her. Then she begins to search for a location where she can find her solution.

3. **The consumer evaluates the alternatives or options.** She takes the information she collected in Step 2 and processes that information in order to evaluate her options and arrive at a decision.

4. **The consumer makes the purchase based on the information processed in Step 3.** In this step, the consumer determines where to purchase and how to purchase as well as when she should purchase.

5. **The consumer evaluates the purchase.** This step focuses on the psychological response of the buyer regarding the purchase. It's in this phase that buyer's remorse often pops up.

Many factors can influence the individual throughout this process. But by understanding consumer behavior, you can help a consumer move through this process smoothly. You can even assist the consumer if for some reason a step keeps her from making a decision. As a business owner or marketer, you can influence the entire process and not just the purchasing decision.

# Recognizing Factors that Influence the Purchase Decision

Consumer behavior is subjective. Even though you won't find many absolutes, one thing always remains true: When it comes to the consumer decision-making process, many factors play a part. There are two categories of personal influence regarding the purchase decision. They include the following:

- ✔ **Internal influences:** These influences include perceptions, attitude, lifestyle, and roles.
- ✔ **External influences:** These influences include cultures, subcultures, household structures, and groups that have an effect on the individual.

Every situation and influence is different. You can change some influences and others you can only deal with as they happen. Sometimes you'll even find that you can counteract the way the influences affect a consumer. It's important to understand that while you can categorize internal and external influences of consumers into two groups, they're actually interconnected and work together to assist the consumer in making a purchasing decision.

Throughout this book, I dig deep into how consumers are influenced, why they behave the ways that they do, and how you can use these influences to work to your advantage. For now, in the following sections, I give you a peek at each category and show you how they can affect your consumer.

## Internal influences

*Internal influences* come from inside the consumer. They're the personal thoughts and feelings, including perception, self-concepts, lifestyle, motivation, emotion, attitudes, and intentions. You could call these the *psychological influences*. These influences describe the ways consumers interact with the world around them, recognize their feelings, gather and analyze information, formulate thoughts and opinions, and take action. You can use consumer internal influences to better understand the why and how of specific behaviors. The following sections help you gain a better understanding of each of these influences.

### Motivation and emotion

Motivation and emotions serve as the emerging forces within consumers that activate certain behaviors. *Motivation* is the persistent need that stirs up and stimulates long-term goals within a consumer. *Emotions* are temporary states that reflect current changes in motivation. They also often trigger changes in behavior.

Motivation and emotion often work together to impact consumer behavior. Motivation drives a consumer through the consumer buying process, and emotion drives that motivation. You can apply your knowledge of motivation and emotion to your marketing strategy by finding ways to stimulate consumers' emotions and motivate consumers to fill the need aroused by those emotions.

### Perception

*Perception* is representative of how a consumer processes and interprets information. You could describe perception as the way that consumers see the world around them — the world that includes your products and services. Perceptions are unique and determine purchasing behavior in every consumer differently.

Perception is important to you because it represents the way the consumer views your product or service. You can influence the perception of your consumer by understanding the current perception consumers have of your product and making changes so your product is recognized, interpreted, and stored in their memory (rather than simply ignored). See Chapter 5 for the basics on consumer perception.

Familiarize yourself with perception, sensory thresholds, and the process that consumers go through to construct their perception. You can then use this information to tailor your marketing stimulus — such as ads, packaging, and pricing — for each particular segment that you're trying to attract.

Perception is such an important part of getting consumers to purchase your product or service that I've dedicated Chapter 16 to explaining how you can influence perception of whatever it is that you're selling while educating consumers about your particular offering.

### Attitude

*Attitude* is that lasting general evaluation of something. It represents how consumers feel about products, services, and companies. Attitudes can tell you a lot about your consumers and how well you're accepted in the marketplace. Just remember that consumers easily screen information that conflicts with their own attitudes.

A consumer's attitudes are learned. They're formed by direct personal experiences, and they're influenced by the individual's ideas and personality, the experiences of friends and family members, and media exposure. The good news is that you can influence attitudes. In fact, when you combine knowledge with a positive or negative attitude about a specific object or product, you drive the perception of that consumer. In Chapter 6, I share with you the attitude models and their functions and strategies. These models can help you influence and change the attitudes of your consumers.

### Self-concept and lifestyle

A *self-concept* represents how an individual sees herself. Four self-concepts typically impact individuals and their consumer behavior. Here they are:

- ✔ **Actual self,** which is reflective of how the individual actually is today
- ✔ **Ideal self,** which represents how the individual would like to be
- ✔ **Private self,** which is the self that's intentionally hidden from others
- ✔ **Public self,** which is the self that's exposed to the public

Self-concepts explain why consumers wear certain fashions, purchase particular products, and drive specific cars. They determine a consumer's behavior, because they represent how a consumer sees herself and how she thinks other people see her. When you understand the roles of self-concepts, you can use them to better target your marketing message and advertising to reach potential customers. In Chapter 7, I explore self-concepts in detail.

Self-concepts often translate themselves into a person's lifestyle, which is why I discuss them together here. Technically, a person's *lifestyle* is determined by a mixture of both internal and external influences; it's a function of her motivations, learning, attitudes, behaviors, beliefs, opinions, demographic factors, and personality. Lifestyle also represents a consumer's income level, culture, social class, and buying power.

Lifestyle is reflected by the outward appearance of both internal and external influences of consumers. When you look at all the factors to gain a greater grasp of the lifestyles of your consumers, you can target promotional plans to those consumers. You also can identify market opportunities.

## External influences

Consumers are faced with many external influences, including an individual's culture, subculture, household structure, and groups that he associates with. Marketers and business owners call these *external influences* because the source of the influence comes from outside the person rather than from inside (which would be internal, or psychological, influences). You also could refer to them as *sociocultural influences,* because they evolve from the formal and informal relationships the individual has with other people. In the following sections, I introduce you to each of the external influences and show you how and why they affect consumers.

### Culture and subculture

The culture of an individual shapes her values, beliefs, attitudes, and opinions, which in turn shape her attitude toward products and buying decisions.

Culture also meets many of the emotional needs of individuals, so they strive to protect the beliefs and values of their cultures. This protection is reflected in their behavior as consumers.

In fact, culture can create a consumer need, influence the satisfaction of needs, and dictate how an individual meets that need. Products and services that resonate with the priorities of a specific culture have a much better chance of being accepted by consumers. Cultural values are transmitted through the family, religious organizations, and education institutions. You can use this information to gain a better understanding of the values that specific cultures teach.

*Subculture* represents a group of individuals within a culture that have unifying characteristics. A subculture is often representative of a particular nationality, religion, racial group, or geographic group. You can use these unifying characteristics to market directly to a subculture. You can target consumers more directly with your marketing and create messages that are more appealing and enticing when you understand the subcultures of consumers. In Chapter 8, I show you why it's possible that a subculture can create a distinctive market segment on its own.

### Groups

*Groups* represent two or more individuals who share a set of norms, values, or beliefs. Examples include peer groups, school groups, business groups, and clubs. Individuals identify with groups to the extent that they take on the values, attitudes, and behaviors of that group. You need to understand the groups that consumers belong to because groups carry significant weight when it comes to the influence they have on consumers. You can also benefit from identifying the opinion leaders within groups and informing them of the products you offer. By gaining their support, you market to the mass of a group by using the leader's endorsement.

Chapter 10 walks you through the reasons that people are attracted to groups and tells you everything you need to know in order to market effectively to them.

### Household structures

*Household structure* represents how many live in a home, what the ages of the occupants are, and what the household income is. Household structure is important to consumer behavior because the structure affects the consumption and purchasing patterns of the individuals within the home. Each member of the household structure also has a role in the decision-making process, and when you understand those roles, you can be more effective in helping those consumers make decisions on whether to purchase your product.

It's also important to understand the difference between traditional and non-traditional households. Doing so helps you determine each household's needs, thereby marketing to those needs in a way that's appealing to the consumers. Finally, you need to take into account family life cycles, because they too have an effect on consumers and their consumption patterns and needs.

Marketing to families isn't as easy as it use to be, because there are a variety of situations and changing roles that need to be considered. However, consideration of these issues puts you ahead of your competitors and enables you to gain sales that you may be missing out on.

Chapter 9 walks you through the various types of households as they apply to marketing strategy. I describe in depth the ways that these households affect purchasing behavior and how you can target particular individuals within a household.

# Accounting for the Unpleasant: Consumer Misbehavior

*Consumer misbehavior* is behavior that violates laws and generally accepted norms of conduct in today's society. Examples include shoplifting, fraud, and abusive consumer behavior. Consumer misbehavior can disrupt consumption activities and can cause loss to your business both in revenue and in the loss of other consumers. All businesses are at risk of experiencing consumer misbehavior.

By being aware of consumer misbehavior, you can watch for the warning signs and be proactive at protecting your business. Just as you can use your marketing strategy to gain consumers, you can also use it to detour those consumers who are involved in misbehavior.

In Chapter 11, I discuss the effect that consumer misbehavior has on businesses. I share with you the warning signs and the reasons behind the behavior. I also provide you with ways to detour misbehavior by using proactive steps and your own marketing strategy.

# Seeing How Consumer Behavior Can Guide Your Marketing Strategy

Many components come into play with consumer behavior, but the power is in knowing how to understand and influence that behavior. The knowledge of consumer behavior actually allows you to improve your marketing strategy.

It helps you understand the way your consumer thinks, feels, reasons, and selects between alternatives. You can use the knowledge you gain from studying consumer behavior to create effective marketing campaigns that speak directly to specific consumers. In this book, I show you how to do just that. By the time you're finished, you'll see the works behind a consumer's decision process, buying behaviors, and consumption patterns.

In the following sections, I outline the major steps involved in creating a marketing strategy, and I show you how to use your understanding of consumer behavior to work through each phase.

## Researching the market to find commonalities

*Market research* is the key to understanding your consumers and their behavior. It's the systematic collection, recording, analyzing, and distributing of marketing data. It ensures that you produce what your consumers really want and need — not just what you think they need. Market research is the function that links the consumer and the public to the marketer. You use the information that you gather in research to identify marketing opportunities as well as problems.

In Chapter 12, I help you evaluate the different marketing research options and determine whether primary or secondary research is best for you. I discuss their advantages and disadvantages, and by the end of the chapter, you'll have a good grasp on where to begin your market research. I also give you an in-depth look at how market research helps you identify new trends, develop long-running marketing strategies, identify external threats and opportunities, evaluate the potential of diverse markets, select a target market, establish realistic goals, and formulate a strategic plan. Finally, I look at the process of market research from defining a problem to analyzing your findings and presenting them in a report.

## Breaking the overall market into the segments you'll target

*Segments* are market groups within the total market that are made up of people who have similar needs. When you can recognize a segmented group, your marketing opportunities increase and you gain the highest return on your marketing. That's because segmenting enables you to focus on the customers that are most likely to purchase your products or services — those individuals that are most interested in what you have to offer.

Segmenting, which is cost-effective and makes your marketing easier, allows you to delve into the behavior of consumers. It also assists you in identifying their needs. In turn, you can position your product in a way that shows them how you fulfill an unmet need that they have. Chapter 3 covers the segmenting process and shows you how to better position your product so your offer is attractive to your determined segments.

## Uncovering the untapped markets

Determining new marketing opportunities and identifying untapped markets can help you grow your business. *Untapped markets* represent markets that you haven't yet entered and that your competitors may not be aware of. When you get into untapped markets, you identify new ways to grow your business by opening up doors for consumers who may not be familiar with you yet. You can identify untapped markets by taking the time to examine your consumer base and understand your market.

In Chapter 14, I show you how to recognize untapped markets that you may be missing. I also help you identify product offerings. Finally, I also provide steps you can take to protect your current market share.

# Creating a Consumer-Driven Marketing Plan

Marketing isn't just about flashy advertisements and fancy commercials. And it isn't just about creating awareness; it's about gaining new customers. The only way that you gain new customers is by creating a marketing plan that's intentionally consumer driven.

A consumer-driven marketing plan is developed and created and then practiced with integrity in mind. With a consumer-driven marketing plan, you do all the following:

- ✔ Listen and speak directly to consumers and tell them that you understand their needs.

- ✔ Position your products in a way that shows them that you fulfill their unmet needs.

- ✔ Gain their attention by providing them with the education they need to make good purchasing decisions.

- ✔ Share with them the reasons they should adopt new products and accept the changes that you make to existing products.

- ✔ Gain their committed loyalty and make them want to be a customer for life.

All of these tasks help you create a marketing plan that not only benefits your business but benefits the consumer by creating an awareness that causes them to want to purchase your product. In this section, I show you how to use your knowledge of consumer behavior to market to consumers in a way that they understand and are attracted to.

## Practicing integrity

Marketing ethics impact both the consumer and your business. When it comes to marketing, you must build trust with your consumers. It's your responsibility to embrace, communicate, and practice ethical values that improve the confidence of your consumers. You need to understand the importance of marketing ethics, because deceptive marketing practices can affect consumer behavior.

Unethical marketing behavior affects the emotions, attitudes, and perceptions of consumers — whether it happens to them directly or they just hear about it. In Chapter 15, I discuss the different types of unethical marketing practices and share with you the importance of having your own code of ethics and how to go about creating one. Your integrity is not only what gains new customers; it's also what helps you keep them.

## Inducing need awareness through positioning

*Positioning* is the act of creating a unique identity for whatever it is that you're selling and then targeting a segment of the broader market by fitting your product or service to that segment's wants and needs. In order to get consumers to recognize that your product fits their needs, you must figure out what the consumers in your target market need and want, what you have to offer them, what your benefits are, and who your competitors are (including how you're different from them). You use this information to create a positioning strategy and statement. These tools help you reach out to your targeted consumers. They communicate, identify your company, and differentiate it and its products from the competition.

When positioning your product or service, you proceed through two separate steps. First you have to differentiate your product or service from its competition, and then you address the consumer's need or desire. These steps form the basis for the articulation of what your product does, which is also known as your *positioning statement*. Within each of the two steps are three strategies you can use to reach out to your target market. I explain them all in Chapter 16, where I also guide you in creating your positioning statement.

## Engaging consumers' attention and leading them to purchase

At this point in the process, you really begin working with the influence of perception in order to engage your consumers' five senses and draw their attention to your product or service. In order to do so, you must create value for your consumers to shape and cultivate their perceptions. You create value by focusing on what your consumers believe is essential.

It isn't enough to get consumers to notice whatever you're selling; you must educate them about the value and benefits of your offering in order to overcome any objections regarding the purchase of it. In Chapter 16, you discover how to effectively educate your consumers about your product or service. Successful marketing counters any objections to the prospective purchase.

The key is to present the benefits of your product in a way that consumers understand. You also need to develop a *unique selling proposition* (or USP). A *USP* is a statement that sets you apart from the competition. It paves the way for your positioning strategy and statement. When you identify your USP, you find something meaningful and unique to say about your product that competitors either can't or won't say. Several core steps help you to identify and develop your USP. After you've proceeded through the steps, you can work on drafting a marketing message that will grab their attention. (Check out Chapter 16 for more on USPs.)

## Convincing customers to adopt new products and changes in terms

Do you ever wonder why so many new products fail? Well, the truth is that it's often because business owners don't understand the adoption process. They don't know what it takes for a consumer to adopt a new product.

So you aren't in the same position as those business owners, here's the scoop: Consumers go through a series of evaluation steps when adopting new products. This process often involves the give and take. In other words, they determine what they have to give up in order to take in the benefits of a new product.

Consumers are inundated with new products every day. So when trying to get consumers to adopt a new product, it helps to understand the product life cycle and to identify what phase your products are in. You also need to be able to identify characteristics of the different adopter categories that consumers fall into. This way you can speak directly to any apprehensions they may have and gain a better understanding of their readiness to purchase. Just remember that you can influence new product adoption by simply understanding the adoption process that consumers go through.

Consumers also face a great deal of challenge when it comes to accepting changes in the terms of your existing product. Term changes can be any change that you make to your current products. Examples include a change in benefits, a change in price, or a change in distribution. You can help consumers in the transition of change. One way is to take into account how your consumers will view the change and whether they will see it as a "gain" or a "loss." Then you can develop a marketing strategy that speaks directly to the challenges the consumer may be feeling. This strategy helps to increase the rate of adoption to the change and save you the loss of customers who otherwise may stop buying your product.

In Chapter 18, I show you what it takes to get consumers to adopt your new products and how to overcome adoption challenges. I explain the reasons that consumers are apprehensive to adopt new products and what you can do to soothe those concerns. I also take a look at the challenges that consumers face when being presented with changes to your current products and how you can help them in the transition of accepting those changes.

## *Encouraging customer loyalty*

Success is about getting consumers to continually buy from you, because it's easier to gain loyalty from a current customer than it is to gain a new customer. You can gain consumer loyalty by understanding how consumers learn and by using techniques that help them remember you. Consumer loyalty really comes from meeting the emotional needs of consumers. Those needs include the need to be understood, feel important, feel welcomed, and feel comfortable. You can meet these needs and encourage consumer loyalty by providing consumers with expertise, attention, friendliness, flexibility, patience, and superiority in your products and your services. This is done by communicating and creating relationships with consumers.

Customers carry a great deal of value when they're loyal to you. So it's important to be able to gauge and nurture the relationship that you have with your consumers and to be able to turn satisfied customers into loyal customers. In Chapter 19, I talk about the different kinds of consumer loyalty, and I tell you how to turn your customers into repeat buyers.

# Assessing Your Knowledge of Consumer Behavior: A Quick and Painless Quiz

The quiz in this section can help you gauge your current knowledge of consumer behavior. Take the quiz now and see how you do, and then after studying various part of the book come back and take it again to see if your score has improved.

## The questions

1. **Which of the following factors might influence a consumer's perception of a product, service, or company?**

    A. Cultural beliefs

    B. Social groups

    C. Household structure

    D. All of the above

2. **One of the motivating forces a consumer might experience is**

    A. A desire to get married.

    B. A desire to be accepted by peers

    C. Wanting to be more like one's boss

    D. All of the above

3. **The consumer misbehavior of shoplifting is often a deep-rooted problem caused by:**

    A. Low self-esteem

    B. Compulsive buying/overspending

    C. A lack of funds

    D. All of the above

4. **Consumption factors that change when it comes to the family life cycle include:**

    A. The number of people in the family, the ages of family members, and the number of employed adults

    B. The number of bedrooms in the house, the variety of car models in the garage, and the rate paid to the babysitter

    C. The shopping place, the frequency of pay raises, and the number of kids

    D. All of the above

5. **External influences are called external because:**

    A. They're outside influences

    B. The consumers have no control over the influence

    C. They're based only on outside appearance of the consumer

    D. All of the above

6. **When a consumer considers a purchase, he:**

    A. Calls his best friend

    B. Texts his spouse for advice

    C. Enters into the decision-making process

    D. All of the above

7. **How many strategies can you use to change the attitude of consumers?**

    A. 1

    B. 4

    C. 6

    D. All of the above

8. **A consumer's actual self refers to:**

    A. The self one would like to be

    B. The self that isn't exposed to the public

    C. The self that's a realistic perception of the individual at that moment

    D. All of the above

9. **When a consumer changes her marital status, she:**

    A. Joins different social groups

    B. Changes her spending patterns

    C. Quits spending money on entertainment

    D. All of the above

10. **You can encourage consumer loyalty and repeat buying by:**

    A. Creating an emotional connection with your customers

    B. Changing your prices often

    C. Changing the benefits of your product

    D. All of the above

## *The answers*

**1. D**

Cultural beliefs, social groups, and household structure are all factors that may influence a person's perception of your product, service, or company. All three of these have an external influence on the consumer and provide them with a reference point when it comes to the values and beliefs that they hold. Refer to Chapter 8 for more information on culture, Chapter 10 for social groups, and Chapter 9 for household structures.

**2. B**

The desire to be accepted by peers is a motivating force that a consumer might experience. Motivation comes from an emotion that a consumer may be experiencing, so an emotion to be accepted will provide a motivating force to consumers to make a purchase. See Chapter 4 for more information on motivation and emotions that affect consumers.

**3. B**

The consumer misbehavior of shoplifting is often a deep-rooted problem caused by compulsive buying/overspending. The need to satisfy their compulsive disorders often causes consumers to shoplift. Flip to Chapter 11 for more information on consumer misbehaviors.

**4. A**

Consumption factors that change when it comes to the family life cycle include the number of people in a family, the ages of the family members, and the number of employed adults. Consumption patterns change because there may be more people to buy for. Also, the different age groups need different necessity items. Finally, the number of employed adults in the home determines how much money a family has to spend. Visit Chapter 9 for more information on household structures.

**5. A**

External influences are called external because they're outside influences. External influences come from the outside and don't pertain to the internal or psychological influences of a consumer. Refer to Chapters 8, 9, and 10 for more information on external influences.

**6. C**

When a consumer considers a purchase, he enters the decision-making process. In the decision-making process, he decides to call a best friend or text his spouse, but *first* he must acknowledge that he has an unmet need (the first step in the decision-making process). Check out Chapter 2 for more information on the decision-making process of consumers.

**7. C**

You can use six strategies to change the attitudes of consumers. These strategies include changing the basic motivational function, associating your products with different groups, relating to a conflicting attitude, altering components in your product attributes, changing beliefs about competing brands, and using the elaboration likelihood model. Chapter 6 provides more information on changing consumer attitudes.

**8. C**

A consumer's actual self refers to the self that's a realistic perception of the individual at that moment. To read more information on self-concepts and their impacts on consumers, refer to Chapter 7.

**9. B**

When a consumer changes her marital status, she will change her spending patterns. When a consumer's consumption patterns change, her spending patterns also change. See Chapter 9 for more information on household structure and its affect on consumers.

**10. A**

You can encourage consumer loyalty and repeat buying by creating an emotional connection with your customers. The emotional connection is what creates committed loyalty from consumers. Chapter 19 explains how to cultivate customer loyalty.

# Chapter 2

# Understanding How Consumers Make Purchase Decisions

*W*hen consumers buy your products or services, they engage in a decision-making process. By taking the time to understand your customer's needs and concerns as they move through that decision-making process, you increase your chances of winning their business. Market research shows that one of the major problems businesses face is that they fail to support the customer in that process.

In this chapter, I help you understand the process of how a customer moves from looking to purchase to the actual purchase itself and thereafter. I also show you how to help customers move through that process and increase your chances of gaining their business.

## Outlining the Decision-Making Process

Research shows that customers go through a five-stage decision-making process in any purchase, whether it's a product or a service. Because the decision-making process is a cognitive one, it's more psychological in nature. So you won't necessarily see the process. Instead, you infer that the decision-making process is in place by careful observation.

Here's a quick look at the five phases that a consumer goes through when making a purchase decision — Figure 2-1 lays them out for you visually:

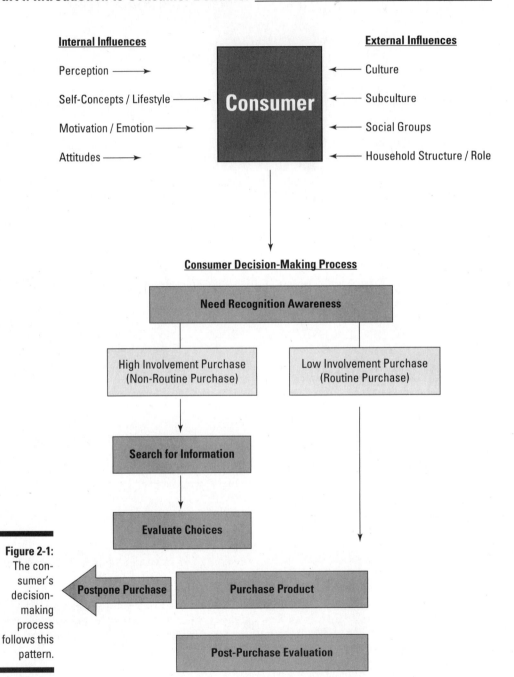

**Figure 2-1:**
The consumer's decision-making process follows this pattern.

**Phase 1: Need recognition and awareness:** In this phase, the consumer recognizes and becomes aware that she has a need.

**Phase 2: Searching for information:** In this phase, the consumer begins to search for information regarding a solution for the need she has identified. The intensity of the search depends on whether the purchase is a big deal to the consumer (or not so big of a deal).

**Phase 3: Evaluating the alternatives:** In this phase, the consumer evaluates each alternative solution to determine which one is best for her.

**Phase 4: Purchase:** In this phase, the consumer evaluates where and when to purchase and makes the purchase. If the need isn't great and the solutions the consumer finds aren't desirable enough to motivate a purchase, the consumer may postpone the purchase until a satisfactory opportunity presents itself.

**Phase 5: Post-purchase evaluation:** In this phase, the consumer evaluates her purchase and decides whether she's happy with the purchase. She may also experience buyer's remorse in this phase.

As a marketer or business owner, it's important that you understand this process. By doing so, you'll not only enhance the customer's experience, but you'll be able to walk her through the process and increase your chances of gaining business. Understanding the decision-making process can help to drive your business goals, your marketing message, and your marketing decisions.

# Phase 1: Recognizing a Need or Desire

During the first phase of the decision-making process, a consumer recognizes that he has a need. The buyer recognizes and senses a gap between his actual state and his desired state. The consumer's *actual state* is his perception of his feelings and situation at the time. His *desired state* is the way he wants to feel or be at that time.

A need can be triggered by *internal stimuli* or *external stimuli*. What are these stimuli? Take a look:

- ✔ **Internal stimuli** are those things from within that get the consumer to do or buy something. For example, an internal stimulus might be feeling sleepy and wanting rest, being hungry and wanting food, or feeling your allergies kick in and wanting your allergy medicine.

- ✔ **External stimuli** are the outside influences that get you to do or buy something. For example, external stimuli include such things as seeing the sign for your favorite restaurant and feeling hunger pangs or seeing an advertisement for new shoes and remembering that your shoes are worn out and need to be replaced with a new pair.

Consumers recognize needs in the following three ways, two of which you can influence:

- ✔ Advertisements or conversation with friends that cause an awareness of a need. (These are external stimuli.)

- ✔ Consultative selling, which is the seller's ability to uncover a need. (This is an external stimulus.)

- ✔ The consumer's evaluation of his current situation, which causes him to detect an area of dissatisfaction. (This is an internal stimulus, so you can't influence it.)

In this phase, you as a marketer can cater your message to a potential need. One way to do this is to identify the need that your potential customer has and speak to that need in your advertising and marketing messages (see Chapter 16, which walks you through the process of positioning). You can't create an internal need, but you can create awareness by triggering a need with external stimuli.

An example of this type of influence would be the pizza shop that advertises by using commercial advertisements at 11 p.m. The shop is targeting its potential consumers with external stimuli (their commercial). This triggers an awareness of a need. The shop's commercial advertisements have made consumers think that they're hungry. Because the consumers are hungry and now know that the pizza shop is open late, the shop has increased its chances that consumers will call and place an order to fulfill their need.

After a consumer realizes he has a need or a problem, he must find a solution. So, in Phase 2, he begins to search for information that will fulfill his need or solve the problem he has identified. However, the need sometimes can rise so high that it becomes a driving force in the individual, and he doesn't spend much or any time searching for a solution. He never reaches Phase 2.

For example, suppose that a guy named John is watching a football game at a friend's house. All the guys have gathered to enjoy the 52-inch plasma television that John's friend has just purchased. John is envious of the television and the attention that the friend is receiving. He decides that he too needs a 52-inch plasma television in order to entertain and be more accepted by his friends. The desire is created, and he's feeling the impulse need to make the purchase. When John leaves his friend's house, he decides to stop off at the electronic store. The salesperson shows him the different models and explains the one-day sale the store is having. John's desire is so strong that instead of going home and evaluating and researching the different models and prices, he makes the purchase without spending money or time to research the solution to fulfill his desire.

# Phase 2: Seeking and Researching Possible Solutions

Consumers begin the information search process by conducting an internal search of what they're looking for and what will fulfill their need and desire on a personal level. Then they follow up with an external search for information from friends, family members, salespeople, and advertisements. This phase provides consumers with criteria for assessing product alternatives and results in a set of potential choices.

It's important to understand that although Phase 2 is represented as the information-gathering phase, it isn't uncommon for anxious buyers not to search for information. If a consumer's need is so severe that her purchasing drive is strong and she sees a product that satisfies her need or solves her problem (and is close at hand), she may skip this information-gathering phase and purchase the product or service on the spot. If the drive isn't significant, the need may be filed in the consumer's memory, and then she will begin searching for information but not act so impulsively.

## How this phase works

As a consumer begins to gather information, the intensity of her search is easily categorized into one of two levels. The level in which the consumer starts depends on the urgency and intensity of the need. The two levels of the search phase are as follows:

- **Heightened attention:** In this phase, the consumer is more open to *receiving* information regarding the item she has determined as a need. She will go online to search for information, look through magazines, and read advertisements to gain the information she's looking for to make a decision — but her search isn't intense; she won't *scour* for the solution just yet.

- **Active information search:** When a consumer's need becomes more intense, she enters the active search phase and really invests in the search process. The consumer will begin to gather information by reading material and asking friends.

The amount of research a consumer does depends on the strength of the need and the drive that it creates. Each consumer has a certain level of basic information stored in memory; the amount of research she does depends on the ease of acquiring new information, the value placed on that information, and the satisfaction she gets from the research.

When you understand the phase that a particular consumer is in, you can better serve her. You can use both of these scenarios to your advantage. For the consumer who's in the heightened attention phase, it's about educating her on why she needs your product. On the other hand, if you're dealing with a consumer who's actively searching, you want to focus on why you're better than your competitors and why she should choose your product over the competition's product.

For example, if you meet a consumer at a trade show and she has happened upon your product and is open to receiving information about your product, you can determine that she's in a heightened attention phase. Even though she hasn't actually sought you out, she's still receptive to the push of your information, and she's probably not aware of your competitors at this time. If another consumer at the same trade show visits your booth and has sought you out because she's been researching the service or product that you have to offer, she's probably educated about what you're offering and has knowledge regarding your competitors.

Consumers often use several sources for information, including the following:

- ✓ **Personal sources:** Family, friends, neighbors, and acquaintances
- ✓ **Commercial sources:** Advertising, salespeople, dealers, product packaging, retail displays, and the Internet
- ✓ **Public sources:** Editorial media coverage and consumer rating organizations
- ✓ **Experiential sources:** Handling, examining, and using the product — perhaps on a trial basis

## How you use this knowledge in your marketing

As consumers gather more information, they increase their awareness and knowledge of available brands and features. So as a marketer or business owner, you must identify the information sources that are most important and influential to your potential buyer — and then you must make sure the information is available there. Refer to Chapter 17 for more on identifying your potential buyer and the marketing options available to you.

For example, you may find that advertising in the Sunday paper is the most influential source that your target market responds to. If so, put an ad there. Or you may find that your target market depends most on the Internet. If that's the case, make your information available there.

# Phase 3: Evaluating the Alternatives

During this phase, the consumer processes information and arrives at his decision. He does so by evaluating, identifying, and assessing the value of the alternatives. The consumer looks at the features that he wants. The depth of evaluation often depends on the individual consumer and the importance attached to the specific buying situation. When it comes to purchasing, situations not only vary from consumer to consumer, but they also can vary from product to product.

For example, a consumer may be making a purchase that he has put a lot of thought into and researched thoroughly; or the purchase may be made on impulse with little or no thought. These situations can determine how much evaluation is put on the alternatives that are available.

## How this phase works

If attractive alternatives are available, a consumer will work to determine which criteria to evaluate and will judge each alternative's relative importance when it comes to making the final decision. Criteria for making that decision can include one or more of the following:

- ✔ Color
- ✔ Durability
- ✔ Options
- ✔ Price
- ✔ Quality
- ✔ Safety
- ✔ Status
- ✔ Style
- ✔ Warranty

In some situations a consumer will use careful calculations and logical thinking. In other situations, however, a consumer may do little or no evaluating; she will rely more on impulse and intuition. Consumers use the following three types of choice processes when deciding between products and services:

- ✔ **Affective choice:** This choice is based on an emotional "it feels right" factor. A consumer will make a decision based not on the fact that it follows decision rules but that it feels right to make that purchase. This may mean that the consumer doesn't go through the research process or that she purchases a product or service even though it doesn't contain all the features she's looking for. The purchase just feels right or makes the consumer feel good.

- ✔ **Attitude-based choice:** This is a systematic, rules-based process. The consumer will go through the entire process from need to research to evaluation, and she will make sure that the product meets each and every need she has identified.

For example, a consumer may decide to purchase a new refrigerator to go with her newly remodeled kitchen. She used to own a Maytag refrigerator. Not only did the refrigerator work well, but she also liked the appearance. Her parents had a Whirlpool model that worked just as well, but she didn't think it had the same sleek appearance that the Maytag did. So, she goes to the appliance store and sees both the Maytag and the Whirlpool models and discovers that they're both the same price, so she purchases the Maytag.

✔ **Attribute choice:** This choice is strictly based on benefit and feature-by-feature comparisons across specific brands or products. You can imagine this consumer sitting down and going through each feature or benefit one by one and crossing a product off when one doesn't fit the bill. The product that's left is the one the consumer purchases.

The choice process that a consumer uses depends on whether she feels the purchase is extremely relevant and personally important. Take a look at the two types of purchases consumers make:

✔ **High-involvement purchases:** This type of purchase includes products or services that involve a high expenditure or a great deal of personal risk. Examples of high-involvement purchases are buying a car or home or making investments.

When a purchase is highly involving, a consumer goes through a more in-depth evaluation process. She puts more time, attention, and energy into the research phase of the buying process. She's making a value decision by weighing several equivalent products and trying to make the best decision she can based on her individual criteria.

✔ **Low-involvement purchases:** This type of purchase includes products or services that involve a lower expenditure and less personal risk. Examples of low-involvement purchases are buying a soda, choosing a hair shampoo, or deciding whether it's beef or chicken for dinner.

Low-involvement purchases are less about value and more often about convenience, which is why they require a simple evaluation process.

If after evaluating options a consumer finds what she wants, she moves on to the next step, where she decides who to buy from and when to buy. If she doesn't find what she wants, she either delays the purchase or resumes her search and returns to Phase 2.

## How you use this knowledge in your marketing

If you know and understand the evaluation process your consumers go through, you can take steps to influence the buyer's decision. For instance, when it comes to high-involvement purchases, it's important to provide your consumer with information that reaffirms the positive consequences of buying. As a marketer you want to stress the important features of your product and the advantages compared to your competitors. This emphasis is extremely important to the consumer in a high-involvement purchase, because it allows him to see value in the purchase.

On the other hand, when it comes to low-involvement purchases, you can generally provide less information and still move the consumer past the evaluation process. He spends less time and attention on research because he's making a decision that's more than likely based on impulse. This is why you often see low-involvement purchase items in checkout lines of major retail chains or on the counters at the local gas stations.

In situations where the consumer can't find acceptable alternatives, a decision to delay or not make a purchase is often made. The best way to avoid this situation is by providing the consumer with all the information he needs, including a list of features that compare your product or service with that of your competitors. This information can make the consumer feel more at ease about the purchase decision, and it often helps him to move forward in the purchase.

 Purchase stalls are most common when the consumer is lacking the information that he needs to make a decision. If you find that providing additional information doesn't help, you may try asking the consumer what information he needs from you in order to make a decision today.

# Phase 4: Assessing the Value of the Chosen Product or Service

After a consumer evaluates and selects the best alternative, she's ready to purchase. However, the consumer isn't done flowing through the process just yet. She must now determine whether she feels that she's buying a product or service that has value. *Buying value* is the perception of the worth the customer is getting by purchasing your product. Buying value isn't just about price; it's also about service, quality, and experience. A consumer wants the most bang for her buck.

## How this phase works

 The two factors that come into play when determining buying value is the quality and the customer service the consumer receives. Two questions receive the most attention during Phase 4: "Who will I buy from?" and "When will I buy?" These questions help the consumer determine what your actual buying value is.

### Who will I buy from?

The consumer considers the following three things when determining who to buy from:

- ✔ **Terms of the sale:** The consumer will evaluate not only the purchase price, but the terms of the sale. For instance, if payments are involved, he has to determine whether he can afford those payments. He also has to decide whether he agrees with the length of those payments. Terms of the sale include delivery and warranties as well. All these terms can affect whether the consumer purchases a product or service from you.

- ✔ **Past experience from the seller:** If the consumer has purchased from you before, he will evaluate the service you provided in the past. If the consumer was satisfied with the past experience, your chances are high that he will be a repeat buyer because that experience built trust. However, if the consumer wasn't happy with the past service, it's easier for him to continue searching for someone else to buy from — unless, of course, you can convince him that you have improved your service level or product quality and now have the ability to meet (or exceed) expectations.

- ✔ **Return policy:** A return policy should be clear to your consumer. A concise and clear return policy gives a consumer a sense of security. It can make him feel that what he's buying is guaranteed to be what you have represented it to be. When you don't give the consumer a return policy, he has a reason to be suspicious and may avoid purchasing your product.

### When will I buy?

The following factors help a consumer determine when to buy a product or service from you:

- ✔ **Store atmosphere:** Does your store provide the consumer with a "feel good" atmosphere? You better hope so, because the atmosphere that you create can move the consumer into a comfort zone that encourages her to move through the steps of purchasing. The atmosphere includes the design of your building, interior space, layout of aisles, texture of carpet and walls, scents, colors, and the shapes and sounds experienced by the consumer.

- ✔ **Presence of time pressure:** Is the consumer being pressured regarding the timing of the purchase? A consumer's availability when it comes to timing is crucial for how she forms her life and how she acts when choosing, buying, and using products in the marketplace. Your consumer is either time-rich, meaning she isn't in a time crunch; or she's time-poor, meaning she needed your product yesterday.

✔ **Specials or sales on products or services:** Are you running a special or a sale on the item the consumer wants to purchase? Specials and sales create a strong consumer demand and increase the consumer's urgency to purchase (so they get the item before the sale is over).

✔ **Pleasantness of the overall shopping experience:** How does the consumer rate the overall shopping experience? It's important to realize that the shopping experience plays a core part in the decision-making process. It's similar to the element of store atmosphere. You must always make the shopping experience rewarding to the consumer; doing so not only moves the consumer to make a purchase, but it also brings her back to your store.

## How you use this knowledge in your marketing

As you can see from the previous sections, the "who" and "when" become vital in the purchasing decision. The more you can help the consumer, the better off you will be. If the consumer is satisfied with your service, experience, and shopping atmosphere, the purchase is made. If he's dissatisfied, however, he may delay the purchase or end up not buying from you at all.

Keep the following tips in mind when working with your customers in this phase:

✔ **Make sure the store atmosphere and experience is what your customer is looking for.** How do you do this? Survey current customers. Some stores already do this. Take, for example, the credit card terminals at the checkout lane that ask you whether your cashier was friendly or whether your shopping experience was pleasant. Retail stores survey customers in order to ensure that the customer is having a positive experience. Other questions you may want to ask include the following:

- If you're the manager of a candle shop, you may want to ask if customers liked the scent of the candle you were burning in the store that day.

- If you own an art gallery, you may want to ask about the lighting. For instance, you may want to find out whether it was suitable for viewing the pieces of art in the gallery.

- If you play music in your store, you may want to ask whether the music is pleasant and whether it enhances the shopping experience.

✔ **Save the customer time.** If the customer is feeling time pressure, he needs to save time. You can help with this by being clear upfront with your terms of sale and return policy. Saving your customer time can increase the chances of him purchasing your product or service.

✔ **Have a sale.** Sales promotions and specials are effective when trying to keep existing consumers or gain new consumers. Having a sale or a special can often increase sales more than any other type of marketing.

✔ **Pay attention to your customer service.** Experience can be created by providing incredible customer service and competitive prices and by making the shopping process easier with consistency in service. Also, be sure to ask the consumer questions throughout the sales process to ensure that anything that may delay or stall the sale is addressed.

If you can equip yourself to ensure that the preceding items are clear to the customer and that he's in agreement with them, you'll save yourself from delaying or losing the sale.

# Phase 5: Evaluating the Purchase after the Deed is Done

After the purchase is complete, your job is done, correct? Wrong. Remember that the end of the sale isn't always the end of the buying process. In fact, it could be the beginning of another sale if you follow the process through to completion and satisfaction.

This phase in the buying process focuses on the psychological response of the buyer to her purchase decision. It's at this phase that your customer will often undergo a degree of reflection about her purchase decision. She may wonder whether she made the right choice. She also may be considering the effort she put into this purchase and the worth of the initial expense. The consumer who has made a high-involvement purchase will spend the most time in this phase. When it comes to low-involvement purchases, this phase is often nonexistent. (See the section on Phase 3 earlier in the chapter for an explanation of high- and low-involvement purchases.)

## How this phase works

You can categorize post-purchase outcomes in one of the following three categories:

✔ **Outcome 1: Purchase is below expectation.** The chances of this customer returning and asking for a refund or exchange are high. He has evaluated his purchase and he isn't happy. The purchase didn't meet his expectations. This unhappy consumer will return and expect you to make the situation right. The chances of him recommending your product to any of his friends, family, or associates are slim to none.

When a consumer doesn't return to your business because he's unsatisfied, this can spur negative word-of-mouth advertising. Here's why: even though you may not be aware of his dissatisfaction, the chances are that his friends, family, and associates *will* be.

✔ **Outcome 2: Purchase matches expectation.** The purchase the customer has made matches the expectation that he had. In the post-purchase phase, you probably won't hear back from this customer. You only hear from him if he begins to doubt the ability to afford the purchase or if he feels that he didn't gain value through pricing or the terms of sale.

✔ **Outcome 3: Purchase exceeds expectation.** If you achieve this outcome, you've reached what all businesses hope to reach: You have exceeded the expectations of your customer. Congratulations! The chances that you will hear from the customer (except for repeat business) are slim to none. Your customer feels that he has received value from the purchase and that you provided top-notch service. This customer will likely be a repeat customer and will send new buyers your way with word-of-mouth marketing. For more on encouraging repeat buying, flip to Chapter 19.

In this phase, the consumer is comparing his level of satisfaction or dissatisfaction by comparing his expectations with his perceptions of what he has received from the purchase. It isn't uncommon for consumers to experience concerns after making a purchase. These concerns arise from the concept known as *cognitive dissonance,* an uncomfortable feeling or stress caused by two contradicting ideas simultaneously. In this case, it's the battle between whether he should have or should not have purchased the product.

All purchase decisions produce some degree of conflict. If the consumer experiences cognitive dissonance, he will begin to search for more information to reinforce his purchase decision. If you haven't provided the customer with information to combat the internal struggle, he can move into a deeper guilt, which is known as *buyer's remorse.* This feeling creates regret for the purchase.

## How you use this knowledge in your marketing

Why do you care how a customer reacts to a purchase? Good question. By understanding post-purchase behavior, you can understand the influence and the likelihood of whether a buyer will repurchase the product (and whether she will keep it or return it). You'll also determine whether the buyer will encourage others to purchase the product from you.

Satisfied customers can become unpaid ambassadors for your business, so customer satisfaction should be on the top of your to-do list. People tend to believe the opinions of people they know. People trust friends over advertisements any day. They know that advertisements are paid to tell the "good side" and that they're used to persuade them to purchase products and services. By continually monitoring your customer's satisfaction after the sale, you have the ability to avoid negative word-of-mouth advertising.

### Avoiding dissatisfaction before and during the sale

You can help your customers remain happy with their purchases by

- **Making sure your products and services deliver on their promises.** Offer quality products and services, and market them in a way that will meet the expectation of the customer. For example, if you know a product isn't meant for children, don't market it as a product for children. If you know the product will only last 60 days, don't market it as if it will last 90 days. And if you know a product has an unfavorable flavor, don't fool folks and say it tastes great.

  Set the expectation in the way you market as well as in your marketing message. Refer to Chapter 15 for more on drafting your marketing message.

- **Mitigating cognitive dissonance.** You mitigate cognitive dissonance by

  - Summarizing the product's benefits after the purchase

  - Repeating to the customer why the product is better than the alternatives

  - Emphasizing how satisfied the customer will be

  - Providing toll-free numbers to encourage communication after the sale

  - Offering liberalized return and refund polices and making your customer aware of them

### Following up after the sale and handling dissatisfaction

After the sale or provision of service, it's important as a businessperson that you help customers deal with post-purchase discomfort. As part of your customer's purchase analysis, she's trying to reassure herself that her choice was the wise one. The more you're able to show her that you're available, the less remorse she'll feel. She'll feel value by your attentiveness after the sale rather than just during it. This decreases the chance for buyer's remorse and increases the chances of her recommending you to others. This situation happens even more when you're in the business of selling high-involvement products (see the section on Phase 3, earlier in this chapter, for a discussion of high- and low-involvement purchases).

To ensure overall satisfaction and a repeat purchase, train your staff on how to deal with customer complaints, and implement a follow-up program that includes a *post-purchase evaluation*. This assessment, which is performed on customers after they've purchased from you, helps to gauge their satisfaction with not only the product, but their overall shopping experience with you. The evaluation can be done electronically, by mail, or by telephone.

By developing post-purchase activities and services, you have the ability to reduce a customer's anxiety, build goodwill, and lay the groundwork for future sales. A post-purchase evaluation reduces any uncertainty or doubt within your customers by assuring them that you're there to make sure they're happy and their needs have been met by their purchases.

You conduct a post-purchase evaluation by

- ✔ Using customer-satisfaction surveys
- ✔ Making follow-up phone calls
- ✔ Mailing cards or letters
- ✔ Sending e-mail follow-ups

Sometimes a customer is dissatisfied with her purchase despite your best efforts to satisfy her, and she may ultimately return the product or demand a refund for the service you provided. What do you do in this situation? The good news is that you can turn the situation around by viewing it as an opportunity to satisfy the consumer's need rather than viewing it as a loss. Then you try to meet that need. Be grateful that the consumer brought the problem to your attention for resolution.

If your customer isn't satisfied, you must evaluate whether the product you sold her was deficient or whether the customer's expectations were too high. To do this, examine the quality of the product and how you marketed the product, and then gauge how often a customer complains about the product. Are you receiving multiple complaints? If so, tally those complaints to determine the root of the problem. If you have only received a few complaints, determine whether the complaints are the same. If they are, the problem could be with the product rather than with the customer's expectations or experience.

# Chapter 3

# Applying Consumer Behavior to Marketing Strategy

*W*hen you understand consumer behavior, you can improve your marketing strategy. This knowledge of consumer behavior helps you understand issues such as how the consumer thinks, feels, reasons, and selects between alternatives. You can use this knowledge to create effective marketing campaigns.

A lot of components go into creating your marketing strategy. If done correctly, your marketing strategy can be used as a detailed road map that combines your consumer behavior knowledge with your marketing initiatives to achieve your business goals.

Consumer behavior allows you to understand your customers and stay close to them, and your marketing strategy helps you to effectively reach out to them. In this chapter, you explore how to apply consumer behavior to your own marketing strategy.

## Knowing Where You're Going: Defining Your Marketing Objectives

*Marketing objectives,* which are goals that you have set to accomplish by using your marketing program, are put into place with the hopes that your marketing leads to sales. Your marketing objectives help you to identify the goals and then create the process and initiatives you put into place to achieve those goals.

It's crucial that your entire marketing strategy supports your marketing objectives, because your strategy is used to guide you step by step to the success of those objectives. Marketing objectives should be in line with your company's growth and sales goals as well. You define the growth that you want to occur and then you determine what goals you will set that correlate with the marketing of your company.

Your marketing strategy is wholly based on your predictions and assessment of your customers' behavior, so before you even start strategizing, you need to get your marketing objectives in place. Your objectives need to be

- ✔ **Clear:** Your objectives must be easy to understand and specific. Can you look at your objective with clarity? Is it clear to you what that objective means to you and your company?

- ✔ **Measurable:** You must be able to measure your objectives by percentage, quantity, or revenue. How much do you want to sell? What percentage do you want to grow?

- ✔ **Time specific:** An objective that isn't time specific will never occur, because it will always be seen as a future objective rather than a goal with a timeline.

Here are a few examples of marketing objectives that meet the previous criteria:

*Increase product awareness by 20 percent in the next six months.*

*Educate my target audience about the benefits, features, and functionality of my product and by doing so increase my sales by 35 percent in the next year.*

*Increase our database by 15,000 names in the next 90 days.*

If you have more than one marketing objective, it's important that they not conflict with one another. They should all be working toward the same goal. For example, you don't want to set a marketing objective to promote a product or service that you plan to phase out. If you have an objective that's in conflict with other objectives, you will likely hinder the success of your marketing strategy and plan.

As you implement your marketing strategy, consistently gauge these objectives over time to ensure that you're moving in the right direction and that your marketing is achieving your goals.

# Understanding How You Get There: The Four Ps of Marketing Strategy

Before I can discuss the components of your marketing strategy and how you can use market research to form each part of your strategic marketing plan, I must first explain the four main areas of interest in marketing (called the *four Ps*) and note why each one is an important part of your overall plan.

The four Ps (product, promotion, price, placement) provide you with the foundation that your marketing plan is built around. You could almost describe them as the skeletal system that supports your plan. Your *products* represent what your target market is looking for. The *price* of the product gauges what your products will sell for in the marketplace based on your selected target market and what that market can afford. *Place* refers to how you distribute your products, and, of course, *promotion* is how you promote products to your target market.

If one of your four Ps isn't defined, it's nearly impossible to create an effective marketing strategy. Say, for example, that you have the perfect place in mind and you have terrific ideas on how to promote, but you really haven't defined the price at which you'll offer your products. In this case, you'll be able to distribute your products and promote them, but how will consumers know what they have to pay to purchase them? I know this is an extreme example, but it shows you why having all four Ps clearly defined can help in creating a successful strategy.

Take a look at this rundown of all the components that make up the four Ps of marketing strategy:

- ✔ **Product:** Your product strategy works to define your products and determine who they're targeted to and what benefits they offer to consumers. It also singles out the differences between your products and those of your competitors. When I speak of *product,* I'm referring to something that's marketed to consumers in exchange for money or another unit of value.

  In the case of consumer packaged goods, retail, and business-to-business companies, the product is a tangible object. When it comes to a service business, however, the product takes the form of an intangible offering, such as a true benefit or future promise. All products are offerings to the consumer, but remember that there's an inherent difference between what's sold by a retailer and what's sold by a service firm, and the way you present that offering depends in part on whether it's a tangible object or an intangible service.

  When selling a product that a consumer can touch and feel, you must focus on the benefits, features, and customer service that you offer surrounding that product. When selling a service, you must sell on the perceived value because a consumer can't touch, see, or feel the product that you're offering. Instead, your strategy must be centered on testimonials or recent work you've completed. It's vital to focus on how your service can help consumers achieve their desired results. You can still find strength in focusing on the benefits of the service you offer, but you must have something to back your claims. After all, the consumers aren't walking out with something tangible, and really their purchase is only as good as your word.

✔ **Promotion:** The *promotion* element of your marketing mix consists of two-way communication that's used to inform, persuade, and remind consumers. Your promotion strategy outlines the promotion tools that you plan to use to accomplish your marketing goals, from advertising to public relations and everything in between.

Promotion strategy is an important part of the overall marketing mix because it defines how you'll promote your products and what methods you'll use for the different products you offer and the different market segments you're trying to reach. You could almost call it your "communication plan" because it really does define how you will communicate your product to your target market.

Many new business owners or inexperienced marketers tend to think that a promotion plan is the only plan needed in your marketing strategy. However, promotion is only one piece to the puzzle. If you haven't defined your products, prices, or placement, how can you promote what you're offering?

✔ **Price:** *Price* always seems to be one area that business owners struggle with. And why not? Price is one of the most important business decisions you make. You must set a price that allows your target market to afford your product and what you have to offer, but at the same time you need to produce a profit for your company.

✔ **Placement:** *Placement* is often known as *distribution* and refers to how you get your products or services from your hands to the hands of your customers — that is, it determines which *distribution channels* you'll use. Distribution channels fall into one of two camps: direct and indirect. *Direct channels* go straight from you to the end consumer. *Indirect channels* go from you to an agent that sells the product or service to the end consumer (or to another agent, who then sells to the end consumer).

When creating your placement market strategy, you have to define the best way for a transaction to transpire and then determine what mediums you'll use to get it done. When you look at product, price, and promotion, it's always important to consider placement, because without it you haven't defined the means in which you pass on the product. So your market strategy wouldn't be complete.

# Product: Developing and Selling a Marketable Product or Service

Your *product strategy* lays the groundwork that your other Ps of marketing will work around. You can't determine price, placement, or promotion without first identifying the details around your products.

The focus of your product strategy is on the goods or services that you offer to your consumers. A thorough product strategy includes information regarding features, benefits, customer service, and warranty details. It also defines the target market for each product that you offer and who that product appeals to.

## Assembling the components of your product strategy

In order to have a clear definition of your products and an understanding of who you're targeting with your products, your product strategy must do the following:

- ✔ Clearly identify and define the offering.
- ✔ Describe the offering.
- ✔ Label the offering with a memorable name.
- ✔ Describe the offering's functionality, features, and benefits.
- ✔ Evaluate the offering's *adaptability* — that is, the measurement of acceptance in the current marketplace, gauging the ease of change if the marketplace is to experience a change in demand or benefits and features

In the following sections, I give you an overview of what each of those tasks entails.

### Product or product line identification and definition

Your product is the item or service you'll be offering to your customers. You need to identify and explain your product from the customer point of view in order to really focus on the benefits and features that your product offers.

You also must determine whether you're offering one product or a line of products. After you've made that decision, create a *product definition,* which explains the purpose of your product and how it serves your consumers. I know what you're thinking: "Why do I need to have a product definition?" Here's why: Most business success or failure is determined by its product definition.

Your product definition serves as the explanation of "why" behind the consumer purchase. Why should consumers choose your product? What benefits and features are you offering that they need? Your product definition should answer these questions. A clear definition also helps you with the other components in your product strategy.

### Product name

Your product name helps consumers recognize your product in the marketplace. Name recognition is important to standing out from among your competitors. Keep in mind that even though your name doesn't have to be flashy, it does need to be memorable. When naming your product, also take into consideration who your consumers are and what will appeal to them.

The name that you choose will follow your product throughout its lifetime and can impact the perception consumers have regarding your product, so this isn't a step you want to rush through. Brainstorm, gather ideas, ask for opinions, and then test the name you've chosen. You want to be happy with your first choice, because it's extremely difficult to go through a product name change and come out successful.

If you're offering your product in foreign countries, make sure that the product name is translated correctly and that the name of your product doesn't carry negative connotations.

### Product description

Your customers obviously need to know what you want to sell them. So that's where the product description comes in. To create a product description, you simply state what your product is in one sentence.

This step should be a little easier than the development of your definition, because your definition actually helps you in this phase. You use your product description to explain the details of why your product works to fulfill the product definition you've created.

For example, if your product is a dish soap, your product definition may look like this:

*DW Dish Soap washes dishes.*

Your product description, on the other hand, may look like this:

*DW Dish Soap washes dishes in $1/3$ of the time when compared to other leading brands, and it leaves hands smooth at the same time.*

While your product definition is the why, your description incorporates the benefits of the product and describes the product in a way that makes consumers want to purchase your product rather than a competitor's.

### Description of functionality and list of features and benefits

In order to begin to understand the product from your consumer's viewpoint, you need to list and identify the functionality, features, and benefits of your product. You want this to be a detailed description of not only current functions, benefits, and features but also of future enhancements that you're considering. The benefit of this consideration is that it helps you keep tabs on the pulse of your industry and your competitors. By the way, a *feature* represents what a product has. A *benefit,* on the other hand, is what a product does. *Functionality* describes how the product works.

When positioning your product, you'll use this list of features, benefits, and functionality extensively, so don't skip this step. You can read more about positioning in Chapter 16.

### Evaluation of product adaptability

The more adaptable your product is to consumers, the easier it will be to sell in a competitive market. The point of this step is to enable you to sit down and not only evaluate the current market that you're selling your product to, but also to evaluate and anticipate change that may happen in the marketplace in the future.

Product adaptability is about forecasting the market for your product in the future and gauging your ability to meet anticipated changes when they happen. Why is this important to your marketing strategy? If you can anticipate change before your competitors and take action first, you're a step ahead of the game. If your competitors do this and you don't, you'll always be one step behind. If you find that your product or service isn't as adaptable as it needs to be, you may want to consider ways you can increase its adaptability in the marketplace.

## Seeing how consumer behavior affects your product strategy

When you have an understanding of consumer behavior — specifically the behavior of your potential consumers — you can accurately determine what products your customers are looking for. You can then use that knowledge to create a product strategy that will enhance the chances of your products being successful in the marketplace. You can do this because you have an understanding of what the consumer is looking for and what benefits and features will move them to purchase from you and not from your competitors.

Companies that have a grasp on consumer behavior more often develop products that contain the features and benefits that the market demands, and they almost always come out ahead of their competition. The following sections show you how to use consumer behavior research as you craft each part of your own product strategy.

### Consumer behavior and your product identification

You want to analyze and define objectively what you're selling, based on why people want to buy it. It's important to remember that consumers purchase because of needs and desires. When you can take a step into their shoes and view your product in the same way they will, you can better entice them to make a purchase.

Consumers go through a series of steps before making a purchase; you can guide them through each one of those steps by not only objectively looking at your product and pointing out features and benefits, but also by counteracting any negative feelings a consumer may have about your product. (Refer to Chapter 2 to gain a better understanding regarding the decision-making process.)

You want your product definition to be:

- ✔ **Specific:** It must be easy to understand and clearly identifiable by the consumer.

- ✔ **Marketable:** It must carry marketing value. In other words, you need to determine why consumers should pay attention to your product.

- ✔ **Profitable:** Obviously the goal of the product definition is to make a consumer want to purchase that product and provide you with a profit.

- ✔ **Achievable:** Your definition must be true and the consumer who purchases your product must be able to see the truth. For example, you don't want to say that your dish soap softens hands when it doesn't actually do so.

- ✔ **Vision matching:** Your product must meet the vision you've created in your product definition.

- ✔ **Easily understood:** Flashy or wordy definitions often only confuse consumers, so make sure yours is easily understood. Would a fifth-grade student understand your product definition? If not, it may be time to reconsider a rewrite.

- ✔ **Easily communicated:** Can your definition be easily communicated or are consumers stumbling over your message and having to review it several times to get your point? The goal is to be able to use your product definition in a way that consumers have an understanding of that product within 30 seconds.

An example of a product definition might be "one-of-a-kind, hand-crafted engagement rings for women." You can see how this example fits each of the previous requirements:

- ✔ **Specific:** It tells the consumer exactly what the product is.
- ✔ **Marketable:** The rings are one-of-a-kind and hand-crafted.

✔ **Profitable:** A consumer would want to make a purchase based on this definition if she were looking for a one-of-a-kind ring.

✔ **Achievable:** If the consumer purchases the ring, it will be one-of-a-kind and no one else will have one like it.

✔ **Vision matching:** If the consumer is looking for a one-of-a-kind, hand-crafted ring (and that's what she visualizes when reading your product description), she can in fact purchase a ring that meets that visualization.

✔ **Easy to understand:** When a consumer reads this description, she will know exactly what she is getting.

✔ **Easily communicated:** You can explain what the product is in 30 seconds or less and the consumer walks away with a clear understanding.

### Consumer behavior and your product name

Creating a product name is the fun phase of product strategy. However, keep in mind that when crafting your product name, it's more important to be descriptive than creative. Often people try to be so creative that their product names hide the messages of what their products do. And make sure that your name is memorable, relevant, and of course, easy to pronounce. It's important to understand that if your product name is difficult to pronounce or spell, consumers will have trouble finding your product or asking for it by name.

Consumers often purchase based on emotion, and studies have shown that product names that focus on emotions tend to sell better than those that simply focus on function. So if you really want to be creative when developing your product name, concentrate more on creating a descriptive product name that focuses on emotion rather than a function. An example of this is the fragrance put out by Clinique called Happy. Consumers have the perception that if they wear this fragrance they will be happy. So clearly this influences their decision to purchase the fragrance.

Your product name is dependent on who your target market is as well. If your target is edgy and more alternative, you need to create a name that attracts them. If you're dealing more with seniors, however, your name will be very different. You know your target market more than anyone else (or at least you should!), so choose a name that appeals to that market.

One of the best ways to determine a name for a product is to spend a few moments brainstorming. However, you need to follow these rules:

✔ You can't reject or criticize any idea.

✔ Consider this free-form brain dump. In other words, write down anything that comes to mind. Write down a few adjectives, and then grab a thesaurus and let your mind wander.

✔ Keep a written record of everything. Keeping your thoughts locked up in your brain isn't enough — you're human, so you'll forget things.

✔ When you have a list of ideas, rank them one by one.

✔ Evaluate pros and cons for each idea.

✔ Get the opinion of trusted external sources.

If your product is an extension of a product line, be sure the name fits in with brand structure of that product line and offers you the possibility for product add-ons.

### Consumer behavior and your product description

When crafting a product or service description, your goal is to address your chosen consumers specifically and tell them in one sentence what the product or service can do for them. To do so, you need to determine whether your offering is a product, a service, a solution, a feature, an accessory, a tool, or some other thing. Come up with a noun that describes your item.

Now use this formula as a guideline when creating your own description, plugging the noun into the (Product) slot:

> (Target Audience), (Product Name) is the type of (Product) that (Performs this Task).

If the formula doesn't fit your product, don't worry. It's just a tool you can use if you choose to.

It's critical that you explain in only one clear sentence why your product is perfect for a specific buyer and what it does best. The reason this is so important is because clarity and the ability to communicate the purpose of the product is crucial. If you're using more than one sentence, the description can become difficult to understand, and worse yet difficult to remember. The more sentences and words used, the less clarity in the description. I know it seems like a mouthful, but you can do it.

Here are a few examples of what a good product description looks like:

> *Kids, Icy Milk is the type of beverage that quenches your thirst in an instant.*
>
> *Moms, Quicky Detergent is the type of simple laundry detergent that gets all stains out in the first wash.*

As you can see, these examples aren't long. They're to the point, but they address your audience and get right to the benefits of the product.

### Consumer behavior and your description of functionality, features, and benefits

The idea of consumer behavior is that you can take the knowledge of why your consumers behave the way they do and use that information to increase the chances of them purchasing from you. In order to do this, you must define the target market that you're aiming toward and single out the benefits and features that matter to that specific target market.

The following steps help you identify functionality, features, and benefits of your product:

1. **Evaluate each feature, benefit, and function to determine how your consumer will see that the product has value.**

   List each one by one on a piece of paper. Doing so will help you recognize the consumer's need or want that you're satisfying. And remember that purchases are made based on a need or want that a consumer feels.

2. **Investigate the product by asking current customers how they use it and what they like about it.**

   This investigation can help you identify whether you need to make any product changes to enhance the experience your consumer is having with your product. Seeing how consumers are using your product can make you aware of any unusual usages, thereby inspiring you with new product ideas.

3. **Evaluate whether your product delivers true benefits, features, and functionality.**

   The more a product brings to the table, the more the importance of price diminishes. Consumers don't purchase based on price; they purchase based on benefits. So by evaluating the benefits, you can analyze whether your product is delivering in the way that you intended it to. It also allows you to see changes or enhancements that you need to make in order to create customer loyalty.

Keep in mind that all products and services have obvious benefits to your consumers, such as price and convenience of distribution, but there are also hidden benefits like customer service and guarantees. Don't forget these. By finding these hidden benefits and bringing them to the forefront, you have the ability to make your product more valuable in the mind of your consumers. For example, a consumer may walk into your place of business to purchase your product because of the convenience and price that you offer, but when you share with him the exceptional customer service that he will receive or the guarantee surrounding your product, he will have a higher perceived value of purchasing from you.

After you've identified each feature, function, or benefit, prioritize them according to your market segments and the target markets within that segment that you want to reach. This prioritization can help you determine development of the product going forward.

### Consumer behavior and your product's adaptability

When evaluating product adaptability, you're assessing the flexibility that your product has to adjust to market demands and changes. When consumers purchase a product, they often evaluate the value of that product and whether it's adaptable to their lifestyle. Lack of adaptability can detour a consumer from the purchase.

For example, consider the VCR. This dinosaur of the electronic world is an item that few consumers purchase. That's because they can now purchase a DVD player, which provides a much better picture. Companies that manufactured VCRs began to evaluate the adaptability and realized that soon there wouldn't be a market for these electronics. Many of them moved right into manufacturing DVD players so they wouldn't lose the market share they had gained with the VCRs.

The following five factors help you measure the adaptability of your product:

- **Attractiveness:** It's important that you can entice consumers to try your product and allow them to experience it before purchasing. Samples and trials are great for this, because they allow consumers to begin the adaptation process of changing products without financial risk. It also shows that you believe so much in your product that you're willing to let consumers "try before they buy."

- **Compatibility:** You want your product to fit the usage of consumers today. If it doesn't, consumers simply won't purchase from you.

- **Complexity:** You must offer a product that consumers understand. Even though you may feel that your product is innovative and presents a new way of doing things, your consumers may not necessarily see it the same way. And then they won't make the purchase. It's vital that consumers understand not only the benefits, but the purpose behind your product.

- **Product advantage:** You want to be able to stand against your competitors and be the product that consumers choose. If you can't identify an advantage, consumers won't be able to either.

- **Visibility:** It's easier for consumers to adapt to a new product when they see others using the product successfully. You want your product to be visible to consumers, because the visibility diminishes the fear of the unknown.

By evaluating the adaptability of your product, you can see how flexible your product is and how flexible your consumers believe it to be. Consumers don't particularly embrace change, so if they can view a product as easy to use, you will decrease their anxiety about making the purchase. Evaluating adaptability helps when creating your marketing plan, because if your product proves to be adaptable in the marketplace, you can use that as a benefit to your product. If you find that your product isn't as adaptable as it needs to be, you can begin to make the necessary changes to appeal to consumers. When you attain an appropriate level of adaptability, you create a stability that allows you to adapt without shaking the core of what your product represents.

# Promotion: Deciding How You'll Spread the Word

Your *promotion strategy* is the part of your marketing strategy that explains how you'll bridge the gap between the places where you're selling your product or service and the places and ways your customers gather and absorb information. A complete promotion strategy contains a description of the promotion methods you'll use in your marketing plan. The following sections highlight those methods and explain how consumer behavior knowledge affects their presence in your marketing mix.

## Perusing the possibilities

You can promote your products in a variety of ways. In fact, it's always good to use a mixture of methods that can help you reach your target market. In this section, I show you the different methods of promotion. To give you an overview, here are the methods I cover:

- Advertising
- Marketing collateral
- Media relations campaigns

- Promotional activities
- Publications
- Public speaking and conferences

### Advertising

*Advertising* is the impersonal form of promotion. It's considered impersonal because it deals with general messages that aren't directed at one specific person. Instead, it's delivered to a variety of media outlets and is directed at an entire target market. The objective of advertising is to saturate your target market with your name. You typically use advertising to reach mass amounts of people at one time.

Examples of advertising include the following:

- ✔ **Print advertising:** Programs for events, trade journals, magazines, and newspapers
- ✔ **Direct mail:** Postcards, special offer letters, and coupons
- ✔ **Outdoor advertising:** Billboards and bus boards
- ✔ **Broadcast advertising:** Radio, television, and podcast

### Marketing collateral

*Marketing collateral* is promotional material such as a brochure, newsletter, flyer, or poster. It's a great tool for informing consumers of your products and services — even when you aren't around. Marketing collateral is that memorable piece that consumers take with them in order to remember to contact you. You can create your marketing piece in a way that answers the questions of consumers and speaks directly to them. It lasts longer than a 30-second advertisement and can be designed to explain your product or service in detail.

### Media relations campaign

A *media relations campaign* is about contacting and staying in touch with targeted members of the media. This type of promotional activity is great if you think your company would benefit from being mentioned in a newspaper, magazine, or a television broadcast. A great way to get started in a media campaign is by writing press releases and developing a press kit that you can send to media outlets.

Your story must be newsworthy if you're going to be picked up by the media. They received hundreds of submissions daily, so make your pitch interesting and unique.

### Promotional activities

*Promotional activities* generate awareness and recognition in the market. In other words, they're great for letting people know that your company exists. With these activities, consumers gain a deeper understanding of who you are and what you do. You can participate in a variety of promotional activities. Here are a few examples:

- ✔ Community projects
- ✔ Contests or sweepstakes
- ✔ Coupons and product samples
- ✔ Fairs or festivals
- ✔ Giveaways
- ✔ Sponsorships for special events
- ✔ Trade shows

You can find promotional activities to participate in no matter what your marketing budget is. The best way to find these activities is to find companies that serve the same target market as you, and then research where they're speaking, what trade shows they're attending, and which community projects they're involved in. (Refer to Chapter 12 for more information regarding market research.)

### Publications

*Publications* are similar to public speaking and conferences, because by being published in trade publications you're projecting yourself as a credible source and expert in your industry. A publication can be anything from a newsletter or magazine to a trade journal or book.

Don't confuse publications with media relations campaigns, however. Being published in publications is about providing education without the idea of promotion behind it.

### Public speaking and conferences

Making speeches at conferences, professional association meetings, and other events position you and your company as experts in the field. This form of promotion is also a fantastic way to make new contacts that can eventually lead to sales. You'll find that this activity increases your credibility within your target market, and in return, the credibility will drive your sales up. As with publications, this method is less about advertising and more about educating.

## Developing a consumer-centric promotion strategy

Consumer behavior explains the "why" behind a consumer's purchase. When you understand the "why," you can create a promotion strategy that speaks directly to that consumer. In other words, understanding your consumers enables you to recognize their needs, motivations, attitudes, and intentions to buy. Then you can create a promotion strategy that supports those behaviors and moves consumers to purchase directly from you.

Knowledge of your customers' behavior affects the various components of your promotion strategy in many ways. I explain in the following list:

- ✔ **Advertising:** Advertising doesn't drive an immediate purchase. That's because customers can't quickly purchase a product when they see it advertised. Think about it this way: You post a billboard and your targeted consumer is driving 75 mph down the freeway to get to work on time (or to get home for the night). The chances of that person being able to immediately purchase your product are slim to none. However, with that mind, remember that the billboard may trigger a need or serve as a reminder to consumers that they need to make a purchase. This reminder may then entice them to contact you when they're ready to make the purchase.

Some methods of advertising are easing the ability for consumers to quickly react to an advertisement. An example is online advertisements. Say that a consumer is browsing her favorite news portal and your ad is displayed. She can quickly (and simply) click on that ad and be immediately driven to a Web site where she can purchase your product.

✔ **Marketing collateral:** You normally won't see an immediate purchase from these promotional tools. They're created to serve as a reminder to your consumer, because typically the consumer takes the marketing collateral home to evaluate and contemplate the purchase. Your collateral can be used to identify, recognize, and speak directly to the needs of your consumers. In doing so, it also presents to them the benefits they receive when they purchase your product. If your collateral is created in an effective way, it's like sending a member of your sales team home with your consumer.

✔ **Media relations campaign:** Media relations campaigns don't carry as much credibility as public speaking, conferences, and publications, but there's something to be said for creating media campaigns that are informative and educational. Most consumers must see a message approximately seven times before making a purchase, so media relations campaigns are one way to achieve that goal.

The important thing to remember with media relations campaigns is not to make them sales oriented. Instead, give the consumers something of value — something that educates them so they walk away with a perceived value that makes you memorable to them.

✔ **Promotional activities:** Promotional activities create not only awareness about your company and products, but they also create a trust around your company. This trust eases the mind of your consumer when she's making a purchase. In other words, she won't have to fear that you're here today and gone tomorrow.

✔ **Publications:** Publications are similar to public speaking and conferences; the difference is that with publications, you can often reach a broader audience to share your knowledge with. When you have been published in a trade magazine or a journal that your target reads, you have created almost instant credibility and trust with potential consumers.

✔ **Public speaking and conferences:** Public speaking and conferences tend to carry the most weight in light of consumer behavior. That's because you're presenting to an audience that contains your target market. You're sharing with them a topic that they're interested in, and they can see your knowledge firsthand. These activities also create a level of trust and enhance your credibility as the expert in the market. This type of promotion is most beneficial if you're a company that offers more service-oriented products.

## Creating a marketing budget

Business owners often ask how much they should spend on their marketing budget. You can choose from different methods to determine your budget; it really comes down to your business and what works for you. You can determine your budget by:

✔ Allocating a percentage of your revenue

✔ Allocating a percentage of your net sales

✔ Allocating all profits back into your business for marketing

Allocating a percentage of your revenue is one of the most popular ways to determine your budget. The formula is easy. You simply take a fixed percentage of everything that your company brings in and allocate that amount for marketing. Common percentages are anywhere from 5 to 10 percent for big businesses, approximately 20 percent for smaller businesses, and 2 to 5 percent for larger businesses that are pulling in millions of dollars worth of revenue.

Allocating a percentage of your net sales is a method that's similar to the previous one. The difference is that you're only allocating a fixed percentage of your net sales. This method isn't as aggressive as the previous method, because you'll be excluding expenses from your revenue.

Allocating all profits back into your business for marketing is a more aggressive approach, especially for small businesses. You'll find that there's a little more risk involved with this method. You take the revenue that you make, subtract the expenses that keep the business alive, and put the remainder right back into marketing. The trick to this method is having a backup source of revenue.

It's important to remember that a marketing budget is only a projection or an estimate of what you will spend in marketing. Sometimes your spending will be more or less than your estimated budget. By having a budget, you have something to work from. With no budget, you're simply setting yourself up for marketing failure.

# Pricing: Offering Deals That Goldilocks Would Find Enticing

Your *price strategy* helps you determine and set the prices for your product or service. It's important to your marketing strategy because it can often mean the difference between success and failure. Your price depends a lot on who your target market is and the prices that your competitors set.

For instance, you can't succeed when you offer a product that your target market can't afford. Similarly, you won't survive if your competitors are underpricing you and your consumers can't see the value of spending more to buy your product.

An effective price strategy takes into account the cost of production, the demand, the target market, and the necessary revenue needed to keep your businesses alive and thriving.

# Evaluating the factors of pricing strategy

Your pricing strategy offers a lot of flexibility. It isn't just about the price tag of your product; the perks and payment options that you offer to your consumers are also important. Here's a rundown of these factors, which I explain in more detail in the following sections:

- ✔ Your *price* is what you sell your product for. You could call this the *product price*. It's the price that your market can pay for a specific product.

- ✔ *Perks* include discounts, rebates, or incentives that you offer when a consumer purchases your product.

- ✔ *Payment options* represent the different ways a consumer can pay for your product. Those options may include cash, check, credit card, financing deferred payments, or payment plans.

## Pricing (cost-based and value-based)

When deciding on pricing for your product, you have to compare the two different methods before making any solid decisions: cost-based pricing and value-based pricing. *Cost-based pricing* is a method of pricing in which you determine a fixed sum or percentage that's added to the cost of the product. This sum or percentage represents the profit your company makes when the product is purchased by a consumer. *Value-based pricing,* on the other hand, is a method of pricing that's determined by the price you believe that your consumers will pay for the product.

Which method is best for you? It depends on the type of business you run, the market influence you carry, and the competition that surrounds you. Cost-based pricing works well for companies that deal with the sale of large quantities and whose markets are saturated with competitive pricing. Value-based pricing works well for companies that have strong benefits and can prove their advantage over competitors because they carry a higher perceived value that consumers can see and are willing to pay. By understanding what your customers perceive as value, you can begin to understand the maximum price they will pay for your product or service.

Some examples of cost-based pricing strategies are as follows:

- ✔ **Initial profit strategy:** With this strategy, you establish a higher price to make a profit initially. Typically you would use this strategy to cover costs of research and development time. You may also use this method to maximize your profits before competitors hit your market.

- ✔ **Quick sales strategy:** To apply this strategy, set a low price on one or more of your products. This helps to drive in revenue by using a quick-sale method. You can then use this revenue to support other products and developments in progress.

> ✔ **Profit goal strategy:** For this strategy, you create a profit goal and then set your prices to meet that goal. For example, say you have a goal to reach a 35 percent profit per unit and you're selling your units for $10. You can increase that unit price to $13.50 to achieve the goal.

Here are a few strategies you can use to determine what your consumer views as value pricing:

✔ **Same price strategy:** When applying this strategy, you price your product the same as your competitors. However, with this strategy, you need to spend some time evaluating how you can lower your production cost in order to increase your profit margin.

✔ **Go low strategy:** With this strategy, you set a low price initially to capture a large number of customers in the marketplace. You can use this strategy to increase product awareness or to create an image of being the low-cost option. In order to use this strategy effectively, however, you have to maintain profitability at a lower price.

✔ **Prestige pricing strategy:** That's right. This strategy has you marking that price up. You can get away with this method if your product carries a certain uniqueness or if you're catering to an affluent market. By pricing your product on the high end, you create a certain "prestige" with its purchase.

This is a risky strategy, so you must stay aware and be willing to lower your price if your consumers start thinking that you're making too much of a profit.

## Perks

Consumers like to know they got a deal. In fact, sometimes they'll even pay more money if they can walk away feeling like they were the ones who benefited. To give your consumers that feeling, try using the following perks:

✔ **Discounts:** A *discount* represents a reduction in the regular price of a product. If you aren't rewarding your customers with discounts, you're missing out. They tend to give customers a sense of loyalty and a desire to be a returning customer.

✔ **Bundling:** *Bundling* is a marketing strategy that combines several products as one combined product at a discounted price. Bundling enhances your offering, and it takes the thinking out of ordering. Bundling is beneficial because you can increase the initial price tag and get consumers trying more of your products — while at the same time providing them with the feeling that they're gaining value. It's often seen as the win-win from both the company's and the consumers' perspectives.

Bundling works. If you don't believe me, ask the cable companies who now provide cable, Internet, and telephone at a bundled price. I guarantee you that by bundling, companies have increased their add-on sales. And what about those fast-food restaurants that now offer you the combo or meal deal? These are other bundling techniques.

### Payment options

In order for your business to be successful, you need to offer your customers convenient and easy ways to pay for your products and services. In fact, did you know that by offering several payment options, you can increase your sales?

Consider, for example, these recent statistics put out by the Federal Reserve: 34 percent of consumers use credit or debit cards and 55 percent use cash or checks. So, if you don't offer both credit and cash options, you could lose a significant amount of business. By offering several different payment options, you're showing your customers that you're flexible and willing to cater to their needs.

You can choose from many different payment options, including cash, check, credit cards, financing, deferred payment, and in-store payment plans. Choose the options that work best not only for your consumer but also for your business.

## Linking consumer behavior to pricing strategy

Consumers don't base their decisions solely on price, but price obviously does play a role. If the price is too high, consumers may not even take the time to learn more about the benefits that drive the price up. If a price is too low, they may not perceive any value in the product and will go for the competitor's product instead.

Pricing is always about value. If consumers see a higher value, paying the extra few dollars may not be an issue. But if they don't see value in a product, it's easier for them to walk away. It's important to price within the value zone of consumers. In other words, if your price is higher than your competitor's price, you must be able to explain why in order for a consumer to be willing to pay the extra money. If it's less than your competition, you need to be able to explain why you're able to sell the product for less while still providing a highly valuable product.

Before you can even begin to think about how to price your product, you need to know how much it costs you to produce and sell. Your *break-even point* is the point at which you're neither making money nor losing it. Your *break-even unit* is how many units you must produce or sell to break even. The break-even point and break-even unit are important to consumer behavior, because they allow you to see the room that you have to move in order to offer discounts or free trials to potential new consumers. Check out the nearby sidebar, "Calculating your break-even point and unit," for more information.

The following sections provide information showing how consumer behavior can affect each component of your pricing strategy.

# Calculating your break-even point and unit

To determine your break-even point, you need to know what your fixed costs and variable costs are. Then you can simply plug these numbers into a formula. I start off by explaining both of these costs:

- **Fixed costs:** These costs make up your overhead. They're expenses that don't vary according to production rates. Examples of fixed costs are rent, office equipment, insurance, and utilities.

- **Variable costs:** These are the expenses that do vary with the amount of service provided or goods produced. Your variable costs include costs such as hourly pay and raw materials. Other variable costs include promotion and advertising expenses.

Here's what the break-even formula looks like: (Fixed Costs) / (1 − (Variable cost per unit / Selling Price Per Unit)). To see how this formula works, suppose you're running a service business. Your fixed costs total $60,000. Your variable costs total $50 (you pay your consultant $50 per hour). You sell consulting services at $125 per hour. So your formula to determine your break-even point looks like this:

$$\$60,000 / (1 - (50/125)) = \$100,000$$

If you aren't making $100,000, you can't cover your costs. If you make more than $100,000, you're making a profit.

After you figure out what you need when it comes to revenue for your business to survive, you need to determine how many units you must produce and sell to break even. In the previous example, your consultant makes $50 per hour. Your company bills out $125 per hour, so how many hours do you need to spend consulting in order to break even?

Your formula looks like this: (Fixed Costs) / (Unit Contribution Margin) = Number of Units Needed to Break Even. The Unit Contribution Margin is your selling price per unit minus your variable cost per unit. So here's how it looks when you plug in the numbers:

$$\$60,000 / (125 - 50) = 800 \text{ units (hours per year)}$$

## Choosing your pricing method

Pricing can be considered one of the most difficult of the four Ps of marketing strategy. The reason for this is because there's no single "right" method to pricing your product. You have to consider many things when pricing your product, including your position in the marketplace, the demand for your product, and the cost to produce your product.

You also have to determine the goal you're trying to achieve in pricing. It isn't always just to sell a product. For example, your goals may be any of the following:

- You may be looking for short-term revenue.

- You may want to price in order to sell in large quantities.

- You may want to maximize your profit margin.

- You may be looking to differentiate yourself in the marketplace.

After you've considered the components of pricing and have determined the goal you're trying to achieve, you have to align your findings with the behavior of your consumers. Will they see value in the price you've chosen? How does your price compare to the prices of your competitors? Can you quantify the benefits of your product in order to show value to consumers? These questions are important to consider, because consumers don't base their purchases on price alone; they base them on the value that the products bring to their needs or wants.

### Dealing with discounts

Discounts work well when enticing consumers to try your product or to gain repeat business from consumers who have already purchased your product in the past but haven't returned in a while. They're also great when you're looking for quick ways to achieve sales targets or short-term market gain.

Be careful not to overuse discounts, because overuse can diminish perceived value over time with consumers.

Say that you're a business owner who's running on a thin margin. You just don't have a lot of profit margin to spare. How can you afford to offer discounts to your consumers? Here are a few strategies that won't make you dig too deep in your profit pocket:

- **Prompt pay discount strategy:** Offer cash discounts for customers who pay promptly. This strategy helps you maintain a steady cash flow and reduce what you may end up spending in collection costs.

- **Quantity discount strategy:** Offer a discount for customers who order a large number of products at a time. Typically the cost-per-unit declines as the quantity increases.

- **'Tis the season strategy:** Offer seasonal discounts to customers who purchase items in the slow season, such as a lawn mower when it's snowing. This type of discount helps you balance your cash flow and meet your production demands.

Evaluate the previous strategies and decide which ones work best for you. Keep in mind that value is important to consumers. So no matter what discount strategy you choose, you must ensure that consumers see value in your offer.

### Bundling products or services as a package deal

How can you create your own bundle? Think about the products that you offer that complement one another. Then take a look at your past sales reports, keeping consumer behavior in mind. What have your customers purchased from you in the past? What items do they typically purchase together? For example, if you're selling toothpaste, how about adding a toothbrush to it — now you have a bundle.

If you still aren't sure what bundles your customers would be interested in, ask them. You'd be surprised at what customers will tell you when you ask.

### Offering various payment options

You not only want to offer the different payment options, but you also want to make sure that your customers are aware that you offer them. You can inform customers of payment options by mentioning the options in your marketing collateral or by using signage where customers make their purchases.

You can offer payment plans if you sell high-priced items. These plans allow your consumers to pay over time rather than right away. The flexibility of payment plans often increases the sales of high-ticket items that consumers have trouble paying cash for upfront.

Payment options are often seen as positive by consumers, because you're giving them options to obtain a product they need or want. Just make sure that consumers understand the terms of the payment options you offer. You don't want to them to be disgruntled and feel that you talked them into terms that they didn't agree to.

# Placement: Getting Your Goods from Point A to Point Z

Your *placement strategy* defines how you distribute your product and what vehicles you use to do so. It also defines the locations where you'll make your products available. When developing your placement strategy, it's important to keep in mind that not all consumers shop the same way, so product placement is your key to getting your products in front of the right consumers at the right time.

You have several options to choose from when it comes to placements and distribution channels of your products. By *placement,* I mean how you get your products or services to your customers. You can select many methods, not just one. It simply depends on what works best for you and your placement objectives.

Methods of distribution take three different forms — direct sales, indirect sales, or both. Here's a rundown of these forms:

- ✔ **Direct sales:** When using the *direct sales method,* you're selling directly to the customer or end-user. No one facilitates the sale between you and the customer. Examples of direct sales include catalog or Internet sales.

✔ **Indirect sales:** With the *indirect sales method,* you're selling to someone who then sells your product or service to the end-user or distributes it to others who sell to the end-user. Indirect sales occur in two different outlets:

- **Retail:** When using the *retail method,* you're selling to a retailer, which turns around and sells to the customer. An example of the retail method would include a farmer who sells his vegetables to the local grocery.

- **Wholesale:** When you use the *wholesale method,* you sell to a wholesaler or an agent, who in turn sells to a retailer. Typically the wholesaler or agent represents several companies, not just one. An example of this method would include a jewelry dealer who resells your product to several jewelry stores.

✔ **Multilevel marketing:** With *multilevel marketing,* you sell both directly to the customer or end-user and to other people who distribute and sell your product. An example of this method would include vitamins that are sold directly to consumers and to distributing partners that sell the vitamins to their consumers.

You can use many channels to sell your product, but you want to select channels that appeal to your target market. For example, if you're selling software to teenagers, you may want to focus on the marketing channel that uses the Internet. This method would clearly target those who are interested in purchasing your product. In other words, use your placement strategy to break down the distribution channels in accordance to where your consumers shop and where they're most likely to look for your specific product offering.

## Evaluating your options: Distribution channels

Most businesses find that by selecting multiple distribution channels they can make more sales and attract more consumers than when they select only one. Having multiple distribution channels allows you the opportunity to gauge what channels work best for your specific product. Here's a rundown of the different channels you can choose from:

✔ **Retail:** Using retail stores that sell to the final consumer. This is a direct channel because you're in touch directly with the consumer.

✔ **Wholesale:** Working with wholesale dealers that act as the go-between for you and retail stores. This would be considered an indirect channel, because you aren't in direct contact with your consumer; you're more than likely selling to the middleman.

✔ **Direct mail:** Selling directly to consumers through catalog merchants at retail prices (plus shipping). This would be considered a direct sales channel, because you're reaching out directly to the consumer with no go-between.

✔ **Telemarketing:** Selling directly to consumers via the telephone. This can be considered either direct or indirect marketing, depending on whether you did the telemarketing within your company or you outsourced it to another company.

✔ **Internet marketing:** Selling directly to consumers at retail prices or wholesales prices (plus shipping) via the Internet. This channel can be considered direct, indirect, or multilevel marketing, depending on what sources you use to sell your products online.

✔ **Outside sales force:** Using salaried employees or independent commission contractors who sell your products to either the consumer or to wholesale dealers. This can be considered a direct channel or an indirect channel, depending on whether your sales force was employed by you or outsourced to contractors.

Distribution channels can have significant implications on the following:

✔ **Product margins and profits:** The channel you use to sell your products will determine the amount of profit you make. If you choose an indirect sales method, you have to pay the middleman for selling your product.

✔ **Your marketing budget:** Outsourcing sales often can save on your marketing budget, because the middleman does the product marketing for you in order to meet their own sales goals.

✔ **Final retail pricing:** Direct and indirect sales channels will determine your final product pricing differently. If you use indirect sales channels, they're allowed to price the product at the price they choose. Otherwise, you may need to increase the price in order to cover their commission or fee.

✔ **Your sales management practices:** The control you have over your sales management practices is solely dependent on whether you outsource or sell directly. When outsourcing, you'll often use some percentage of that control.

## *Observing how consumer behavior affects your placement strategy*

To determine your placement objectives, you need to get a handle on your placement strategy. By answering the following questions, you can identify the objectives in your strategy and determine the best methods to use to fulfill your placement goals:

✔ **What are the characteristics of your target market and how large is your market for this product?** If you carry a high-priced item that typically has a small number of buyers, you may want to focus on the direct sales approach, which provides plenty of customer service. If you're selling a lower-priced item that appeals to a large market, such as paper clips, you could apply an indirect distribution approach by using advertising and placement in retail stores so customers could easily find that item.

✔ **Where are your customers located?** Location is important when it comes to placement. If you have a large number of customers in your local area, you could sell through local retail outlets. If your customers are located in multiple geographic locations, you may want to consider distribution through agents, wholesalers, or Internet methods.

✔ **How large are the orders?** You can use the size of your average order to segment your customers according to their order size. You could sell directly to customers purchasing large orders and use an indirect method for smaller orders.

You should choose more than one distribution channel in order to evaluate the one that works best for your company and the distribution of your product.

# Part II

# Delving Into the Psychology of the Individual Consumer

The 5th Wave                    By Rich Tennant

# In this part . . .

In this part, I explain why it's important to understand the psychology of your consumers and show how to gain an in-depth grasp of the internal workings that make consumers think and act the way they do. For instance, I look at the motivation of consumers and how it relates to the consumers' desires to achieve certain outcomes. I discuss the emotions that consumers go through and how they work with motivation to move toward a purchase.

I also evaluate the perception process and the interpretations of consumers. I help you find out how you're perceived by your consumer, how you can make use of those perceptions, and how to reshape them if necessary. As if that weren't enough, I also explain how to use consumer attitudes to predict and change intentions.

Consumers are affected internally not only by emotion but also by their self-concepts. Self-concept often translates into a person's lifestyle, or the way that he lives his life, which he creates by spending (or not spending) money. So I delve into this topic as well.

You'll walk away from this part of the book with a solid feel for how the internal psychology of individuals impacts them as consumers. Having a better understanding helps you communicate with consumers and move them toward a purchase.

# Chapter 4

# Recognizing Need and Desire: Motivation and Emotion

- - - - - - - - - - - - - - - - - - - - - - - - - - - - - - - - - - - - - - - - -

### In This Chapter

▶ Uncovering the motivations behind consumer action

▶ Tapping into your customers' emotions

▶ Using marketing to appeal to consumers' emotions and motivations

- - - - - - - - - - - - - - - - - - - - - - - - - - - - - - - - - - - - - - - - -

*W*hen you understand how specific situations influence certain motives and emotions in your consumers, you enter the sales situation with the upper hand. Motivation and emotion are energizing forces within the consumer that invoke certain behaviors and can make those behaviors purposeful and directed. Understanding the desire components of consumer behavior can help you in product positioning, sales, and advertising.

When you understand motivation and emotions, it's easier to speak directly to consumers in a way that moves them to action. This chapter draws you into the depths of consumer psychology, helping you understand why consumers make purchases in the first place as well as what prompts them to do so. Throughout the chapter, I also help you to identify with your customers on an emotional level and appeal to the emotions that spark motivation and spawn action. The following chapters show you how to get your customers to act by purchasing your product or service; this chapter helps you awaken their needs or desires.

# What Moves Consumers to Action: Factors of Motivation

*Motivation* is the persistent need that stirs up and energizes long-term goals within a consumer, and it plays a serious role in consumer behavior. In order to understand the motivation of your consumers, you must understand what it is that motivates them in general. That task can seem complex, so my goal in this section is to simplify it for you.

## Exploring the major motivators

Motivation can be hunger, sex, curiosity, security, power, and so on, and it begins with the presence of a stimulus that triggers the recognition of a need. Motivators for consumption include status, social acceptance, security, or individuality. These and other motivations are subconscious and can be triggered or reinforced by your marketing message.

When thinking about what motivates your customer, consider the five main motivators that consumers experience and react to:

- ✔ **Basic needs:** Basic needs are easy motivators to understand because they're the things that everybody needs to survive; examples are food, shelter, and water. Consumers don't want to pay extra for basic needs. If your customer is motivated by a basic need, price will be a major factor in the purchase.

- ✔ **Convenience:** As a motivator, convenience is all about saving time, effort, and money. For example, someone looking for a housekeeper may be motivated by convenience, because the act of hiring a housekeeper indicates that the person is interested in saving time and easing day-to-day life. Paying for convenience is common in today's society. Convenience provides people with the opportunity to spend less time on the things they dislike doing and to spend time, money, and effort on the things they enjoy.

- ✔ **Security/safety:** This powerful motivator is about peace of mind; it's triggered by fear of the unknown and the uncontrollable things in life. Everyone's looking to feel safe and secure. This motivator is what drives consumers to purchase insurance, fire sprinklers, smoke detectors, or security alarms.

- ✔ **Self-image/ego:** Although no one likes to admit it, everyone has an ego. People love to look good, feel good, and be envied by others. This motivator is strongly driven by emotions, and purchase decisions triggered by this motivator aren't logical decisions — they're based on emotion. The self-image motivator always brings with it a feeling; it makes the consumer look good, which in return makes him or her feel good. For example, you may purchase a car that you know will gain the attention of other drivers, or you may purchase a house in a specific neighborhood because it shows that you're doing well for yourself. This motivator can be very strong.

- ✔ **Fun:** Ahhhh . . . fun! What more is there to say? The multimillion dollar entertainment industry should be proof enough that fun can be a strong motivator. Fun is about leisure, relaxation, and enjoyment. This motivator pushes someone to buy the pool table, the big-screen television, and that Jacuzzi for the deck out back. These purchases contain no real practical purpose, but they're a source of guaranteed fun and enjoyment.

Motivation affects both the level of importance the product has to the consumer as well as how much interest the consumer has in the product. Having this understanding enables you to focus more on the desired emotional state that the consumer is trying to achieve.

In addition to the various types of motivators, motivation can be either positive or negative. Here are examples of each type:

- ✔ **Positive motivation:** This type of motivation leads to the purchase of a sports car. The consumer is motivated by the ride and the way it makes him look and feel.

- ✔ **Negative motivation:** This type of motivation leads to the purchase of life insurance. The consumer is motivated to purchase because he's worried and uncertain about how a family member would handle the expense of a funeral and burial if he were to pass away. The consumer purchases this insurance to help handle his affairs after his death. This isn't a pleasant motivation; it's actually rather unpleasant, which is why it's considered a negative motivation.

Motivation consists of drives, urges, wishes, or desires that initiate an uncomfortable tension within the consumer that remains until that need is satisfied. The motivation drives them continually through the consumer buying process, so your goal as a marketer is to identify and awaken your customers' underlying motivation; after you do that, you can implement other facets of marketing strategy to promote your product or service.

## An example of marketing-driven motivation in action

Consider the following example from Hair-For-Hunks, which clarifies the effect your marketing messages can have on consumers.

Hair-For-Hunks is a fictitious hair replacement manufacturer that boasts the highest sales in its industry. Entering the marketplace with a bang, the company's newest product, Coverage, is a hair product that targets men in their mid- to late-40s who are experiencing hair loss. In marketing its product, Hair-For-Hunks accepts the significance of consumer motivation and uses popular motivation theories of a respected psychologist when creating its marketing campaigns. The company used a combination of both unconscious and functional marketing tactics to motivate men to buy Coverage.

Hair-For-Hunks acknowledges that men in the target segment want to be viewed as athletic and attractive; they struggle with the fact that they're losing their hair at such an early age. In light of this information, the company decides not to use a traditional male model in advertisements, instead opting to make the potential customer the model and capture his response to the product. Hair-For-Hunks puts the potential consumer in the starring role as the attention getter, not some 20-something model with a full head of hair. This advertising allows men who are potential consumers of Coverage to experience what using the product may be like from a purely egotistical point of view. While starring in the advertisement, these men experience glances from attractive women in their 20s to mid-30s and even enjoyed smiles and envious looks from other men.

Hair-For-Hunks is able to create the illusion that the unconscious desire of its target segment — a full head of hair and attention from others — is fulfilled by using the new Coverage product. The company realizes that its customer base has an unspoken fear of becoming old and bald, and Coverage promises to conquer that fear and rid them of the uncomfortable tension. Pledging to turn back the clock and create the illusion of youth and a full head of hair attracts the attention of other consumers. Hair-For-Hunks has developed a marketing concept that motivates its customers to not only purchase the Coverage product but also to become loyal customers.

In essence, the consumers who purchase Coverage aren't really purchasing the hair product but rather the concept of youth and masculinity produced by the product marketing campaign. By not using a traditional model, the potential consumer becomes the model and therefore the *face* of the product.

Motivation isn't the only factor at work in this example, though. As you see in this chapter, human needs motivate consumers to buy, and as a marketer, you can bring out specific emotions to sell your products and services.

# Energizing Motivation: The Role of Emotion

Emotions influence every decision your consumers make. They shape memories and influence perceptions, dreams, thoughts, and judgments. Emotion drives motivation and triggers the motivation to do something in response to a feeling. Emotions include the gain of power, loss of power, anticipated gain, and anticipated loss. Emotions aren't easy to define, and they don't operate alone.

Think of emotions as first impressions: They're important because they influence a response and behavior. In truth, a consumer's emotions may determine whether any action follows at all.

Emotions move consumers to purchase, revisit a place of business, and decide whether the price for a product or service is worth it. The bottom line is that specific emotions trigger a consumer to purchase. And emotional experiences with products and services can often lead to building consumer loyalty. So emotions are important in understanding why consumers buy what they do. Engaging your customer in your advertising and marketing and gaining a favorable emotional response is the beginning of the motivational process.

## Understanding how emotions affect purchasing behavior

Consumers purchase products and services to experience certain emotional states or to achieve emotional goals in a process called *emotional arousal.* Emotions can create a feeling of pleasure or satisfaction, but they also can give the consumer the perception that their purchase will help them avoid a feeling of displeasure or pain. Emotions are the commonality behind decision making.

No matter what the purchase is, consumers must somehow associate a positive emotional connection between your product and themselves. Positive emotions can include the fulfillment of a desire, the support of values, or the feelings of safety and protection. Can you identify which role your product fits into?

Similar to motivations, consumers can have both positive and negative emotions that affect their purchasing decisions. They also have both nonexpressed (insecurity and depression) and expressed emotions (excitement, joy, and happiness). It's important to understand the difference between expressed and nonexpressed emotions because if a consumer is purchasing but isn't expressing any emotions toward the product, you may be required to ask more questions in order to understand the end state she's trying to achieve.

Consumers can struggle with conflicts in the decision-making process, because oftentimes they're trying to rationalize their emotions. You often see this as *double talk* from consumers. They'll express one thing and a few minutes later express something contradictory to their initial statement. This double talk is caused by a conflict when choosing between a product that's rational and a product that's pleasurable.

For example, say that a successful businesswoman walks into a car dealership. She explains that she wants a car that gets attention and goes fast. She selects the car that she wants. It's a flashy sports car that seats two. The longer she sits in the dealership, the more she tries to rationalize the purchase. She's feeling unsure; even though her purchase is pleasurable, she wonders whether it's rational. The double talk begins. How does the salesperson handle this? In order to complete the sale, it's his job to remind her of what she asked for when she came in and the reasoning she gave him for the car she was looking for.

In the following list, I show you the emotional cycle associated with consumption, and to illustrate my points, I use examples that go back to the earlier Hair-for-Hunks scenario:

1. **Dissatisfaction:** The consumer feels a need that isn't satisfied.

   For example, Joey, a 36-year-old, is unhappy that he has experienced hair loss at such an early age.

2. **Discomfort and tension:** The need causes the consumer to feel tension that makes him uncomfortable.

   Joey wants to be viewed as athletic and attractive, but he doesn't feel that way because of his hair loss.

3. **Drive to satisfy the uncomfortable tension:** The consumer is driven to satisfy the tension making him feel uncomfortable.

   Joey begins looking for a solution for his hair loss in hopes that he may be viewed as athletic and attractive.

4. **Satisfaction and reduction of tension:** The consumer satisfies his need by making a purchase.

   Joey discovers Hair-For-Hunks and purchases the company's Coverage product.

5. **Reduction of tension:** With the need satisfied, the consumer's tension dissipates and he once again feels comfortable.

   Joey uses the Coverage product and once again feels confident that he's reflecting a younger, athletic, and more attractive appearance.

## Linking marketing efforts to consumers' emotions

As a marketer, you can use knowledge of motivation and emotions to move beyond basic advertising into the realm of the unconscious and conscious desires, fears, and needs in order to successfully market your products and services to consumers. It's simply not enough to promote your products as just filling a functional need; you must touch customers on a deeper level. Doing so helps the consumer feel that she's somehow linked to your product and that it produces the favorable image of her and who she wants to be. This reaction evokes consumer identification with your product and motivates her to buy — and keep buying — your product.

You can use marketing activities as a way to stimulate emotions and satisfy motivation. If you accept that emotions influence consumers' desires, motivations, and behaviors, it makes sense to consider the role of emotions in your marketing and advertising. After all, the purpose of most advertising and marketing is to persuade, motivate, and sell. Creating the appropriate emotions in advertising increases the chances that the advertising will have a positive effect on persuading consumers to purchase your product. By creating marketing materials and advertisements that trigger or reinforce the emotions your consumers are feeling, you see an increased number of consumers interested in buying your product. Figure 4-1 shows a flowchart of the emotional and motivational factors leading up to a purchase.

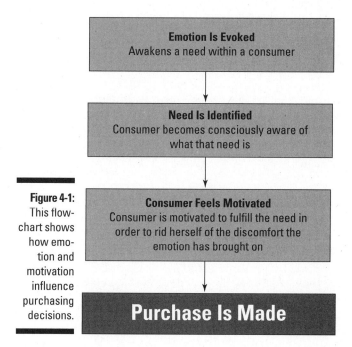

**Figure 4-1:** This flowchart shows how emotion and motivation influence purchasing decisions.

As I mention earlier in this chapter, emotion jump-starts a consumer's motivation to purchase, but how can you use that information in your own marketing strategy? You can use emotion in two ways:

- ✔ **You can use emotional arousal as a benefit of your product.** For example, does your product enhance a consumer's life by giving her more energy, more joy, or overall happiness? If so, use that as a benefit in your product positioning, sales presentations, and advertising.

- ✔ **You can also use the reduction of an emotion as a benefit.** For example, does your product relieve stress, save time, or reduce anxiety? If so, you can use that relief as a benefit.

The idea is to look at the emotional benefits that your product carries for consumers so that when marketing you can use those benefits to trigger the motivation for them to buy your product.

Consider the Hair-for-Hunks example from earlier in the chapter. In this example, the men that Hair-For-Hunks was targeting felt unattractive and less youthful looking than they once did when they had full heads of hair. In order to awaken consumers' motivations, the marketers in this example appealed to the negative emotions that the men were feeling. Then the company bundled its emotional benefits in its marketing message in order to entice the men to purchase the Coverage product.

A real-life example of how consumer motivation and emotions can produce action is the bottled water industry. This industry has become extremely profitable over the past ten years, but when bottled water was first produced, consumers laughed at the concept. Why would they want to buy water in a bottle when they could drink it from the kitchen tap? That's when the marketing message changed: People weren't buying bottled water for convenience but rather for their health. By drinking bottled water, they felt they were protecting themselves from the impurities of tap water. A wariness of drinking tap water developed during this time. Impurities? What would they do to people? Could they be harmful? Now people are sold on the idea of bottled water.

Here's the breakdown of this bottled water example in terms of motivations and emotions:

- ✔ The motivators were personal safety and security of one's health.
- ✔ The emotion of fear moved consumers into action. They began to drink bottled water that they had to pay for in order to avoid drinking tap water.

The marketing message changed consumer behavior by touching consumers and making the issue personal. In return, consumers wanted to feel safe, so they opened their wallets and spent (and continue to spend) money on bottled water.

# Evoking Emotion and Spurring Motivation through Marketing

When consumers are motivated by an emotion, they're looking to either satisfy an emotion or get rid of it, so you have to figure out how to influence their response. To spur the emotions that trigger consumers' motivations to purchase your product, make sure they see the emotional benefits of the purchase. You can then use that information in your marketing strategy and speak directly to the emotions of your consumers.

# Identifying your customers' underlying motivations

The best way to use emotion in your marketing strategy is to start out by looking at the major motivators that consumers experience and then determine which motivators your products address. Do you add convenience to their lives? Do you provide them with a basic need? Do you provide them with fun? What about providing them with peace of mind or security? Keep in mind that it's possible to fit into more than one of the motivator categories.

After you identify what motivators your products address, you can use this information as you draft your marketing messages and advertisements. Your objective is to use the motivators that you've identified to speak directly to consumers. The emotional benefits that you offer to your consumers should be in your marketing and advertising message, and they also must be used to enhance the positioning of your product. (Refer to Chapter 16 for more information on positioning.)

It's important to take time to evaluate your consumers and determine what motivates them to buy from you. How do you know what they're motivated by? Evaluate the problem that your product solves. If you sell security systems, for example, your product offers security. By taking the time to identify the motivators that your consumers experience and by speaking directly to them and providing a way to get rid of any uncomfortable tension, your consumers will quickly see that you offer them a satisfying solution that puts them back into the comfortable zone they desire.

# Motivating action by tapping into emotions

Think back to the last election — national or local. It's quite clear that political marketers have mastered the art of tapping into emotions to sway voters. Believe it or not, you can apply the same principles to tap into the emotions of your customers to sway their purchase decisions. I show you how in the following sections.

## Identifying which emotions to stimulate

The key to tapping into the emotions of your consumers is to help them feel what your product or service offers. What emotion does it serve — happiness, fear, humor, warmth, or maybe even the resolution of anger? Get in touch with the emotions that consumers feel when they come looking for your product.

If your company sells security systems, for example, you know that your consumers are fearful that someone may try to break into their homes. They're looking for a product that offers peace of mind and security. Fear is the emotion that triggers the motivation to purchase the security system, so that's the one you want to address.

Fear can move a consumer to purchase for the feeling of security and peace of mind, but if you abuse this emotion, you risk running yourself out of business. You can use fear as a selling point, but you have to be careful to do so ethically. If your product or service can rid consumers of a fear, move forward. Educate them of the consequences if they don't purchase your product. For example, if they don't purchase your security system, you can tell them that they run the risk of having their homes broken into and of not feeling safe because they're unprotected. Otherwise, don't try to fake it; consumers will see through your ploy and head for your competitor.

### Stimulating the intended emotion with marketing tactics

In order to be successful, your marketing tactics must stimulate an emotional need for your product or service. How do you do this? Use the following three methods for tapping into the emotions of your consumer:

- **Get personal.** Share personal stories of customers or people in your company. No fictional brochure or advertisement can create real-life excitement; you can only gain real consumer excitement and stimulate emotional buying by sharing personal stories. By getting personal, you create credibility for your product or service and give customers something to relate to. Refer to Chapter 5 to find out more on influencing a consumer's perception.

- **Bust out those benefits.** Customers want to know what their purchases will do for them. Stop being wordy in your marketing message and give it to them straight. Point directly to the benefits of the product or service; features are meaningless to your consumer unless they're benefits. If you're having trouble identifying your benefits, fill in the blanks: "What that means to you is _____?" See Chapter 16 for more information about educating consumers about your product.

- **Prove it.** In order to create emotions of excitement and trust, you must prove the benefits of your product. You can do so by using testimonials, providing demonstrations, or offering free trials and samples. At this point, you're no longer actively selling your product or service because your customers are already willing to buy! Refer to Chapter 3 to find more about applying consumer behavior to your marketing strategy.

Suppose a family purchases a new home and has the desire to make sure that it's protected and safe in that new home. The family has had an emotion of fear since moving into the new area, so it's motivated to purchase a security system for protection. A company that sells security systems knows that the motivators behind their consumers are peace of mind and safety. These motivators enable the company to create marketing messages and advertisements specially geared to this family.

As the family began to shop around for information regarding the different alarm systems available, many of the advertisements and marketing messages contained technical jargon that the family didn't understand. However, when browsing the newspaper ads one morning, the family came across the security company I just mentioned. The advertisement spoke to the family and the fear that was motivating it to purchase. The family related to the company and felt understood, so one of the members made the call. The security company was able to provide the family with a solution to satisfy its need and provide peace of mind.

The company that used the high-tech words and technical jargon didn't touch the family personally and didn't relate to what was motivating it to purchase, so that company lost out on a sale and the pleasure of bringing peace of mind to a new customer.

## Recognizing and reconciling internal conflicts

When a consumer decides to make a purchase decision, she may have more than one source of motivation and be faced with a conflict. Consumers often find themselves in situations where different motives, both positive and negative, conflict with one another, and they must deal with the internal conflict. This section discusses each of the three types of motivation conflicts and tells you how you can recognize and help to reconcile them in your customers.

### When the customer equally desires two options

In the *approach-approach conflict,* the consumer is struggling with two desirable alternatives. This conflict generates the least amount of anxiety of the three types of customer conflicts. Although the consumer must make a decision, each option is equally desirable and has attractive options.

For example, say a man is at an auto dealership and has decided that he likes two cars, but he only has enough money to buy one of them. Ultimately, the man will walk away from the dealership happy, but his initial need to choose creates an internal conflict and some anxiety about making the choice. Obviously, a consumer caught in an approach-approach conflict eventually will choose the most desirable option.

You can help your customers deal with the approach-approach conflict by informing them of the benefits and features of each product option and how they compare to each other. If a competitor offers the alternative option to your product or service, it's important to offer a thorough comparison of purchasing from you versus purchasing from your competitor. Emphasize product features and benefits. If your item is identical to your competitor's, focus on the strengths of your company; if the item is different, focus on the item you offer and how it compares to your competitor's alternative.

The consumer's path to the final decision involves thinking and rethinking the benefits of each option. As the consumer analyzes each option, the desire for one over the others becomes stronger. The closer the consumer gets to that one option, the stronger the drive becomes for that particular option. In other words, the benefits of that specific product become more desirable, leaving the other option less desirable.

Here's an example to illustrate what I mean: Suppose a man walks into an auto dealership looking to purchase a minivan for his family. Two used minivans are available. One has all the options, but the price tag is higher. The other is less expensive, but lacks many of the options that the first van does. The man debates with his family because either vehicle would work. After debating with one another and visiting with the salesperson, the man and his family decided that the more expensive option is the better choice. The less expensive minivan no longer captures their interest.

Even though the approach-approach conflict generates a minimal level of anxiety, the outcome is always positive. This is the easiest conflict to recognize and resolve. After all, the consumer gets to choose between two good options. It's just a matter of which one they think and feel is best for them.

### When the customer feels a positive and negative response simultaneously

In the *approach-avoidance conflict,* the consumer is both attracted and repelled at the same time because the desired product may carry with it negative consequences. For instance, the consumer may experience guilt when buying a high-status or pleasurable product or service.

As an example, suppose that in order to purchase a sports car, a consumer must pay a large down payment in order to keep her monthly payments manageable. She feels some resistance to purchasing the car unless the stress of the purchase is lessened.

How can you resolve this conflict through marketing and advertising? Focus on the pleasure of the purchase, namely the features of the selected car and the importance of those features to the consumer. If that doesn't work, offer a model with fewer options (and therefore a lower price), or get creative in financing the purchase.

Your objective when faced with an approach-avoidance conflict is to draw attention to the pleasure of the product and take the attention away from the stress that's halting the purchase by offering options that alleviate or lighten the consequences that are holding back the consumer.

### When the customer faces two undesirable options

In the *avoidance-avoidance conflict,* the consumer is faced with two undesirable alternatives. Neither choice is pleasing, but he must select one. The options in this scenario don't matter; what's important is the fact that the consumer wasn't looking to purchase a product. Instead he finds himself in the situation that it's *necessary* to purchase, not pleasurable.

For example, say a consumer needs to repair a 20-year-old refrigerator or buy a new one. Both choices are undesirable because both involve spending a large sum of money. Consumers facing this type of conflict generally do an in-depth search for information and seek out ways to possibly avoid at least one option. How can you assist in resolving this conflict? Point out how purchasing your product or service may save the customer money, or offer up payment option plans that can ease the burden of spending a large amount of money at one time.

The quicker you can ease the conflict, the easier it is to move the customer past the conflict and into the purchase. Your objective when your customer is in an avoidance-avoidance conflict is to turn a negative alternative into a positive one.

# Chapter 5

# Supplying Information and Influencing Perception

**In This Chapter**

▶ Understanding the value of perception and how it works

▶ Knowing how consumers form perceptions

▶ Influencing consumers' perceptions so they do what you want

Consumers are faced with a wide variety of stimuli every day. They analyze and interpret each stimulus with their built-in screening systems. These systems help consumers select and recognize what information is relevant to them and ignore what isn't. Ultimately, this recognition leads to their purchasing decisions.

In this chapter, I explain what perception is and how a person's perception forms. I also explain how perception influences purchasing behavior and how you can influence consumers' perceptions of your products or services with your marketing efforts.

## In the Eye of the Beholder: A Primer on Perception and Consumers

Ever wonder why people buy certain products? It's all about perception. *Perception* is how consumers understand the world around them based on information received through their senses. In response to the stimuli, consumers subconsciously evaluate their needs, values, and expectations, and then they use that evaluation to select, organize, and interpret the stimuli. This process of receiving and interpreting information is an internal one.

For example, suppose you're throwing a dinner party and have two unlabeled bottles of wine available to your guests. One bottle carries a price tag of $75 per bottle. The other you picked up at $12 per bottle. Your guests love the $12 bottle of wine and can't rave enough about it. All evening you're collecting compliments for your wine selection. At the next gathering that you hold, you offer the same selection of wine to the same guests from the previous party, but just for experiment's sake you left the labels and price tags on the wine. You notice through your experiment that the guests are drawn to and more impressed by the $75 bottle of wine. Because it tastes better? Nope. It's because subconsciously your guests perceive the $75 bottle of wine as a higher quality wine that *should* taste better than the $12 bottle. That's how the subconscious mind works with consumers.

Consumers make decisions based on what they perceive instead of on the basis of objective reality, so accounting for consumers' perceptions of your business and product or service is a crucial part of devising your marketing strategy. Even though you can't force a perception on a consumer, you can work hard to understand it. You can determine the factors that influence it and find out how that perception is processed. By knowing the general perceptions that your consumers may carry, you can tailor your marketing and advertising messages specifically to them.

# Understanding How Perception Forms

By understanding how consumers construct their perceptions, you can better influence consumers to do what you want: buy your product or service.

Perception takes place in three stages:

- ✔ **Stage 1 — Selection:** The selection stage of perception takes place when a person encounters a particular stimulus.

- ✔ **Stage 2 — Cognitive organization:** In this stage, the consumer organizes his thoughts about the stimulus. This is when the consumer shapes his response to the stimulus.

- ✔ **Stage 3 — Interpretation:** This is the stage in which the consumer solidifies his perception and then executes a response. This response can be expressed physically or verbally.

Figure 5-1 shows a flowchart of the process and the influences that affect consumers. The following sections expand on these three stages.

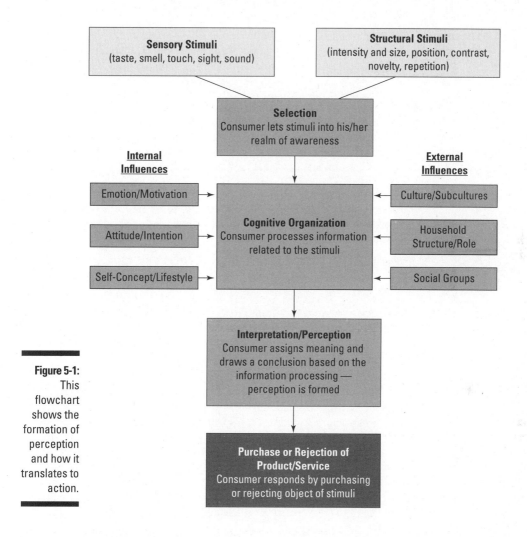

**Figure 5-1:**
This
flowchart
shows the
formation of
perception
and how it
translates to
action.

# Selection: Letting in stimuli

Two categories of stimuli affect a person's perception: *sensory characteristics,* which involve the senses, and *structural characteristics,* which are external elements.

It's important to realize that consumers don't select the stimuli that affect them. Stimuli response is automatic, because it provides them with an internal trigger. It acts as the red light or green light and then guides them in their response. For example, when I smell vanilla, the scent triggers my subconscious and reminds me of the candles my mother used to light at dinnertime when I was a child. I have the green light to anything that smells like vanilla, because I like the memory it recalls for me.

### Sensory stimuli

Sensory characteristics affect a consumer's senses. As a marketer, you can use your knowledge of the characteristics to stimulate the consumer's perception. Sensory characteristics include vision, taste, smell, sound, and feel. Here's a rundown of these stimuli:

✔ **Vision:** Vision is the most dominant of the senses, so you're probably more familiar with using it in marketing than with using any of the other senses. Vision is known to stimulate physiological changes. You can affect the perception of consumers by using color, shape, and size. For example:

   • **Warm colors, such as red and orange, increase blood pressure and heart rate.** Orange is also often used in fast-food restaurants to stimulate diners' appetites.

   • **Cool colors, such as blue and green, decrease blood pressure and heart rate.** Blues and greens are often used in hospitals for their calming effect and to reduce patient anxiety.

   • **Unique size and/or shape:** The size and shape of your packaging has the ability to attract new consumers to your products. For example, consider the last time you walked into a retail store and saw a uniquely shaped shampoo bottle. You more than likely were intrigued and picked up the bottle to have a second look.

✔ **Taste:** Culture plays a powerful role in perception, especially when determining taste. Taste affects the success of food and beverages. For example, European food tastes very different from Korean food. The two types carry different flavors, different appearances, and different textures. The difficulty of taste as a stimulus is that everyone likes something different, so what may taste good to one consumer may not taste good to another.

If you depend on taste to sell consumers on your product, your best course of action to ensure success is to conduct taste tests with them. You won't be able to please everyone, but try to provide items that appeal to the mass of your target market.

✔ **Smell:** Smell is the most direct of the senses for consumers. No other sense evokes memory more than smell. It's proven that smelling scents remembered from childhood can result in moods like those experienced in the person's younger years. Marketers have begun to understand this, so some are using smells to build mood effects into products. Marketers also know that using certain pleasant scents in a store increases the time consumers spend browsing. An example of the impact that smell carries is to think of the cinnamon roll shops located in malls or airports. The aroma of fresh-baked cinnamon rolls draws consumers in to purchase.

While some smells work to your benefit, others that are too overpowering can repel consumers. Consider the consumers who avoid the fragrance section of department stores because of the overpowering odor.

✔ **Sound:** Sound, in the form of music and speech, can capture consumers' attention quickly. Research has shown a positive connection between the use of popular songs in ads and consumers' ability to recall those ads. It's also proven that consumers react to what they hear in stores. Pleasant music results in increased store sales, and unpleasant noise results in lower store sales.

In order to use sound to enhance consumers' perceptions, consider your target market and what sounds appeal to them. If your business is a book store, classical music may encourage concentration. On the other hand, if your business is a clothing store for teenagers, you'll likely want to focus on popular music that appeals to them.

✔ **Feel:** When a consumer can touch and feel a product, she obtains vital information that can have a positive or negative effect. Consider a pillow, for example. As the consumer touches and feels the pillow, its softness may remind her of the way her grandmother's pillows used to feel. This creates a pleasant perception and moves the consumer to purchase the pillow. However, the reverse also can happen. I may touch the pillow and be reminded of the itchy sweater my mother use to make me wear. This creates a negative perception that results in me not wanting to purchase the pillow.

You don't have control over negative perceptions for any of the previous stimuli. You just can't please everyone. What you can do, however, is ask the consumers what they don't like about the product you have shown them, and then point them in the direction of different products that will hopefully produce a positive perception. In other words, try to find out why the product triggers a red light for them. That way you can move them on to something that will trigger a green light.

### Structural (external) stimuli

Structural characteristics that affect a consumer's perceptions are external, not internal. They deal less with the consumer's senses, and yet they rely on visual elements to gain the consumer's attention. (A lot of what follows relates to advertising; if you'd like more info on using advertising effectively, flip to Chapter 3.) Here are the structural stimuli that you might use:

✔ **Intensity and size:** These characteristics often are the first things to attract the consumer's attention. *Intensity* refers to the number of times consumers see your product or advertisement. You can gain consumers' attention by creating an advertisement that's brighter and larger in size than average advertisements. An example would be a full-page newspaper ad.

If you have a retail location and want to use intensity and size to your benefit in that location, consider the number of places you put your product and the sizes of the displays that house your products. If you place one display at the entrance of your store and then another one where a customer might check out, you have not only increased the

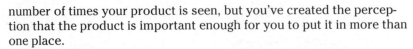

number of times your product is seen, but you've created the perception that the product is important enough for you to put it in more than one place.

✔ **Position:** Whether a consumer sees an advertisement or product depends largely on where it's positioned. This includes where an ad is placed on a newspaper page or where a product sits on the shelf.

✔ **Contrast:** When you employ contrast, you set off one thing against another. Consider grabbing a consumer's attention by placing a black-and-white advertisement in a colorful publication or creating a commercial that plays softly during a television rock show.

Placing an element where consumers don't expect to see it attracts attention. You don't always have to be the most colorful or the loudest; sometimes the contrast alone attracts more attention than the norm.

In a retail setting, consider the colors you use in the displays that house your products. Also use lighting to really enhance and draw attention to your product. The objective is to make it stand out from among the other products available.

✔ **Novelty:** Most people love novelty, whether the uniqueness is a new look, sound, taste, smell, or feel. Your child may choose a particular candy because of the novelty packaging; he's not especially concerned with what's inside. Consumers don't necessarily buy items because they're the least expensive either — most of the time they aren't. They buy the items because they're different and stand out.

✔ **Repetition:** Repetition works. Advertisements often are repeated to help consumers recall a product and create a strong interest in that product. You hope that the desire created by the ad translates into a sale. Repetition works extremely well with *low-involvement purchases,* which are purchases that are less involved and carry a lower expenditure and less personal risk. Examples of these products are shampoo, toothpaste, or laundry detergent.

Because consumers use these products every day and they typically don't cost much, consumers are more willing to take a risk in trying them out. When they see an advertisement that interests them or that sticks in their minds due to the repetition, they will often take mental note so that when they're standing in the aisle to purchase the product, they recall your advertisement and choose to try it.

Knowing which stimulus is right for you depends on your target market. Market research and testing of the different structural stimuli for your specific product allows you to see which one works for your product. You also can watch competitors to see what they're doing and then glean ideas from the information.

# Cognitive organization: Processing information

When it comes to developing a perception, the consumer must process the stimuli to interpret it and conclude the steps of perception development. The processing phase is extremely subjective and is based on the following things:

- ✔ What the consumer expects to see in light of her previous experience
- ✔ The number of explanations she can envision
- ✔ The motives and interests at the time of perception
- ✔ The clarity of the stimulus itself

In this stage, consumers compare the stimuli to their own beliefs, attitudes, and involvement. This is a mental process that's affected by things such as race, color, religion, gender, or other past cultural experiences. In response to stimuli, consumers usually perceive things they need or want, and block unnecessary, unfavorable, or painful stimuli.

Consumer response to stimuli isn't a proactive thought-out process. A stimulus triggers the beliefs and attitudes that are stored in the memory of the consumer. For instance, consider the fact that I like the smell of vanilla. I don't sit down to process why — I just know that I do. I like it because it reminds me of dinner with my family when I was a child; vanilla was the scent of the candle my mother lit during our meals. Now, obviously, if I take time to analyze why I like the scent of vanilla I would remember, but the truth is that subconsciously I already remember.

The same is true for stimuli that trigger painful memories. For instance, when I walk down the grocery store aisle, the thought of peanut butter makes me sick. I know it's because I choked on a peanut when I was younger, but I don't stand there and ponder why I don't like peanut butter. I just automatically know that I don't.

The response to stimuli for each consumer is built in. If it isn't, the opportunity to create a positive experience to the stimuli is available, but the internal trigger won't already be present.

How do you as a marketer handle a stimulus that creates either a positive or negative response? You do it by observing consumers and asking questions. Why do they like or dislike that smell? What is it that attracted them to that specific product? Was it the feeling it gave them when they touched it? Why was that consumer turned off by the spice in that entrée?

The truth is that there are some responses you can't change no matter how you modify your marketing. But what you can do is get to know your consumers, ask questions, and help them find what it is they need. Then find what product will give them the green light to purchase.

## Interpretation: Giving meaning to the stimuli

*Comprehension* is the process in which consumers understand what a message is saying. Factors in comprehension of advertising and marketing messages include product development, existing expertise in the product area, expectations consumers already have of what they will learn, and individual differences across consumers.

The consumer's interpretation gives meaning to the stimulation that the consumer has received. This meaning is based on internal and external factors. Interpretation then leads to action. After the consumer has received the stimuli and organized it, he interprets the information by using the following:

- ✔ **Physical appearances:** Consumers draw conclusions based on physical appearances. For example, when consumers see people they know, those who resemble them, or those whom they'd like to imitate, they recall the positive attributes of these people and make a positive interpretation.

  This is why attractive models are more persuasive for luxury products (think jewelry, expensive cars, high-end clothing). Consumers see these beautiful people and think that they'll be beautiful too if they own that ring, SUV, or tux. But when marketers want to promote common products (cleaning supplies, computers, cellphones, and so on), they turn to the everyday man or woman — people "just like me" in the consumer's mind.

- ✔ **Stereotypes:** Our own ideas, thoughts, and preconceived notions of how people should be influence how stimuli are perceived. Take for example the face you put with your customer service claim. Is it friendly? Is the person smiling? Does he look eager to help?

- ✔ **First impressions:** A consumer's first impression determines which stimuli is relevant, important, or worthy of acting on. Your customer's first impression is gauged on your eagerness to help him, the clarity in your offering, and whether you took the time to listen to his needs.

- ✔ **Early information:** People usually don't listen to all the information that's available before making a conclusion. So make sure you put the persuasive arguments first in your advertising and marketing message.

> ✔ **Halo effect:** Consumers perceive and evaluate multiple objects based on just one factor. An example of this is a brand name or a company's spokesperson of choice. Say a company that makes a popular athletic shoe breaks into the antiperspirant/deodorant market. If the consumers' perception of the shoe is positive, they're likely to have a positive perception of the antiperspirant as well.

# Cultivating and Shaping Consumer Perception

A common mistake that businesses make is in assuming that perception is built on the features and benefits of their product or service. The truth is that perception is built on the *value* that the consumer believes the product or service carries.

You must create value for your consumers to shape and cultivate their perceptions. You create value by focusing on what your consumers believe is essential. Consumer perception depends on

> ✔ The stimuli to which consumers are exposed
>
> ✔ How that stimuli is presented to the consumer
>
> ✔ The quality of products and services that you offer
>
> ✔ Customer service and the support that you provide
>
> ✔ The deliverability of what you promise

Essentially, all consumers want a compelling return on their investment with you. That doesn't just mean money; it means time too.

## Identifying what's important to your customers

Consumers' perceptions of value are based on their individual sets of criteria. However, consumers typically see value in some common ways, which I explain in the following sections.

### Recognizing common factors in value assessment

Quality, service and support, and delivery contribute to the consumer's perception of value. Every point of contact with your customers is a potential moment of truth regarding your company's value. If your customers experience a moment that isn't positive, their perception of your value won't be positive either.

When you constitute a good value with customers, I guarantee they'll tell everyone they know. This is how potential customers begin to form a perception about your product or service, which of course means more business. When considering how to shape and cultivate perception, realize that nothing is a stronger influence than the endorsement of a satisfied customer.

Here's how you can ensure that consumers place great value on your service or product:

- ✔ **Quality of the product or service:** Quality is the first and most important component of value, and it encompasses quality in service and quality in product. Consumers see value when they see quality. As a business, do you work to improve your products consistently? Consumers judge quality by the improvement a company makes to its offerings.

   Quality boils down to the moment that your customer experiences a positive or a negative impression when interacting with a given product or service. You create value by providing quality.

- ✔ **Service and support:** The service and support that you provide must be top-notch in every way that you communicate with your customer. In other words, you need to uphold promises, take the time to listen to your customer, and stand behind your product. Service and support come from everyone that's employed by your company, from the production line to the receptionist that answers the phone. Every element within your business that supports the promise to service what you sell impacts the value that consumers perceive.

   It's important to ensure that your customers receive exactly what your company has committed to deliver. If they don't, their perception of your value will fall. Service and support includes everything from meeting customer expectations to accurately filling orders. It's the extension of your commitment to your consumer beyond the quality of your product.

Every person and every department within your company must understand the importance and contribute to the value that your customer buys — including service and support. Look for opportunities to delight your consumers, not only at the point of sale, but at the point in which a problem occurs. If you ignore service and support, you could risk losing the customer forever.

Your customers will make it clear when they enjoy doing business with you. Not only will they tell you that they're pleased, but they'll tell everyone they know. People with professional and likeable personalities should have direct customer contact; they're the front line to creating the perception of value.

- ✔ **Delivery:** When it comes to satisfying consumers or exceeding their expectation as it relates to delivery, it depends entirely on the right time, right price, right destination, right condition, right quantity, right product, and right packaging.

I like to call delivery the last mile of cultivating and shaping the perception that your consumers hold. Use this last mile to not only improve, but also to differentiate yourself from your competitors.

### Accounting for individuality

Consumers see what they expect to see, and what they expect to see usually depends on their general beliefs and stereotypes. Because different groups of people have different beliefs and stereotypes, they tend to perceive stimuli in the marketing environment differently.

When crafting your marketing strategy, remember the following facts:

- ✔ **Perception is unique to each consumer; no two people view the world exactly the same.** As a result, you must look at each consumer as an individual and realize that not all consumer response will be the same.

- ✔ **Perception is not necessarily as the world is in reality, but more often it is as we think of the world.** Perception is the way a consumer "takes in" your message. As a result, individual consumers often behave differently to the same stimulus presented under the same conditions. Evaluate your marketing message, but realize that it may not always have the same effect on everyone. Just because a consumer doesn't respond well to your product doesn't mean that your message doesn't work. Instead, it could just mean that the consumer wasn't the right one for you.

As a marketer or business owner, you must be aware of this so you can tailor your marketing stimuli, such as ads, packaging, and pricing, for each segment you're trying to attract.

You can target a positive perception within a specific group. With most purchasing decisions, consumers usually can come up with one reason why they shouldn't purchase a product or service. This is the misperception you need to control.

You must identify the single most important decision-making factor that is critical in bringing about the desired behavior from your consumers. This factor will vary from business to business. Why do consumers pick you? Are they most interested in the quality of your products, the service and support that you provide, or the delivery method you use? When you isolate that factor, you can focus on sales, product development, and creating a positive influence on the consumers' perceptions of your product or service.

# Gaining attention with the use of stimuli

As a business owner, how do you ensure that the stimuli you're placing in front of consumers aren't ignored, but rather recognized, interpreted, and stored in their memories? Know how to recognize the three *concepts of perception,* or processes that consumers go through. And depending on the process at hand, use specific stimuli to gain consumers' attention so they can complete the purchase. The concepts of perception include the following:

- ✓ **Selective exposure:** Consumers are more likely to notice stimuli that relate to their immediate needs. Consumers in this phase seek out messages that are pleasant, that they can empathize with, and that reassure them of good purchases.

- ✓ **Selective distortion:** After the consumer has decided to purchase a product, he tends to only seek out information that reinforces that decision. At times this information can distort what's true.

- ✓ **Selective retention:** Consumers remember more accurately messages that are favorable to their self-image than messages that are unfavorable. In other words, consumers tend to remember the good and forget the bad.

By understanding these concepts of perception, you have a better chance of ensuring that your marketing message isn't ignored by your potential consumers. When you understand which types of perception are associated with each stimulus, you can focus on a particular stimulus or combinations of stimuli that evoke the most favorable perception in your potential consumers. You can use the process that the consumer uses to direct your marketing message to them and trigger the stimuli that they need to get the green light for the purchase.

For example, if you're finding that the majority of your consumers are in a selective retention process of perception, you want to draft your marketing message in a way that's favorable to their self-image. Think of the cosmetic dentist down the street. He knows that his patients are mostly interested in teeth whitening, because it enhances their self-image, increases their confidence, and makes them feel beautiful. He creates a marketing message that caters to potential patients and places the message in a magazine that's distributed to 38- to 45-year-old successful women. Why? He knows they're looking for ways to enhance their self-image, they know that beauty is important to success, and his marketing message will reinforce their values and their decision to have their teeth whitened. They'll then perceive him to be the dentist they contact for this service, because he understands them.

# Avoiding sensory overload

The *sensory threshold* of a consumer represents their sensitivity level to specific stimuli and how many stimuli they can take before they must respond. Consumers are exposed to different types of stimuli every day. The truth is, however, that consumers can't process large quantities of stimuli at one time. They have been equipped with the natural ability to limit their sensory processing; because of this limitation, some stimuli never enter the conscious awareness of consumers. So, because consumers have multiple encounters with stimuli on a daily basis, an individual stimulus must be adequately intense in order for a consumer to perceive it.

Understanding sensory thresholds enables you to analyze the stimuli that you're using and determine how they affect customers and the purchase of your product. In other words, you have to find out whether you're reaching consumers at the correct sensory threshold.

## Identifying the sensory thresholds

Consumers have different levels of sensory threshold, but they generally fit into one of the following categories:

- **Absolute threshold:** This is the lowest level at which you can experience a sensation. The point at which a consumer can detect a difference between something and nothing is that person's absolute threshold for that stimulus. As exposure to the stimulus increases, you notice it less.

  For example, the point at which a driver can see a billboard is her absolute threshold. After an hour of passing billboards on the highway, the person develops an internal blindness to the billboards, and it's doubtful that any of them will make an impression.

- **Differential threshold:** The minimal difference that can be detected between two stimuli is the differential threshold. A professional wine taster demonstrates differential threshold. The wine taster frequently perceives a difference between two bottles of wine, yet an amateur may find the wine identical.

- **Subliminal threshold:** This threshold is only recognized subconsciously by the consumer because of the shortness in duration and differences in messages. Suppose, for example, a teenager is watching a music video during which the word "fast" appears on the television for 5 seconds and then disappears; then 20 seconds later an image of a specific energy drink appears. Even though the teenager doesn't consciously remember the message, in the subliminal threshold she has stored the word "fast" along with the image of the energy drink. The idea is that when she enters a store, she will associate "fast" with the energy drink and purchase the drink when she needs a pick-me-up.

Research suggests that subliminal perception has a limited effect on consumers, although evidence does show that the stimuli presented at the subliminal threshold can reach your sensory register. However, some believe that if the message is exposed to the consumer above the subliminal threshold, it should have the same impact. This makes the use of subliminal stimuli unnecessary.

This threshold has generated a lot of controversy in the marketing industry. Some claim subliminal advertising is an act of marketers brainwashing consumers, but marketers deny it. Consumers believe they're being marketed to without their permission, which has raised concern regarding marketing ethics.

### Using thresholds in your favor

The key is to understand the different sensory thresholds in order to use them in your favor. When it comes to consumers' absolute threshold, you must create advertisements above this threshold. For example, say you're advertising in an area that houses multiple advertisements or billboards. Because of these advertisements, your consumers are experiencing sensory overload and are unable to process the advertising messages. You may want to choose to advertise in another venue that isn't so saturated. This way you can more easily gain the attention of consumers.

You often use the differential threshold when you don't want your consumers to sense a change, as when you need to raise your product's price. In order to use the threshold in this way, you must focus on the benefits of the product to outweigh the differences. If a consumer is presented with both the positive and the negative, he can outweigh the negative perception with the positive. For example, suppose you raised the price but your lotion is the best on the market. In that case, you might advertise as being rated the #1 lotion without focusing on the price increase.

At other times, though, you want your consumers to recognize the differential threshold, perhaps when you increase the size of your product. For example, consider the shampoo bottle that reads "25 percent more," but yet remains the same price. In this situation, you want consumers to notice the difference, so you focus on both benefits, 25 percent more but for the same price.

The subliminal threshold is broken when a person is exposed to two different messages, which are only shown for a short time. The messages are so short in time that the consumer isn't consciously aware of them. Here's an example of when you might use the subliminal threshold: You may advertise a 30-second spot that talks about the new sandwich that you have just introduced, and then shortly thereafter you play a 30-second spot about being hungry. The consumer subconsciously stores both of these messages and perceives that he's hungry and should purchase the new sandwich.

# Chapter 6

# Uncovering Attitudes: General and Lasting Evaluations

Attitudes can tell you a lot about your consumers as long as you're paying attention. The consumer's *attitude* is a general evaluation of something — it encompasses the consumer's knowledge of that something, her liking or disliking of it, and the strength of her feelings regarding it.

*Intent* can be looked at as the result of the attitude. It's the state of mind at the time the consumer carries out an action. You must work to change attitude in order to produce change in the intention. Intention is usually one or two steps away from the actual purchase.

All the strategies used to change consumer attitudes take the traditional view that attitude precedes consumer behavior. So, in the marketing world, we use the relationship between attitude and behavior in order to create the change of intention if needed.

In this chapter, I give you an overview on attitude. I show you how attitudes are formed and how you can gauge the attitude and work to change it if necessary.

## Nailing Down the Basics of Consumer Attitude

The attitude of a consumer refers to what that consumer feels or believes about a product or service. An attitude is a learned predisposition to behave in a consistently favorable or unfavorable way with respect to an object. In the realm of marketing, attitudes are the enduring feelings, evaluation, and tendency consumers have toward your product, service, or company.

## Dissecting an attitude: The sum of its parts

An attitude can be defined as a relatively lasting cluster of feelings, beliefs, and behavioral tendencies that are directed toward a specific product, person, idea, object, or group. The three components of attitude come from this definition.

By understanding the components of the attitude, you can gain a better understanding of the consumer. The three components of attitude are *beliefs* (what a consumer thinks about a product), *feelings* (how a consumer feels about a product), and *intentions* (how a consumer is likely to act as a result of those beliefs and feelings). The following sections discuss these components in detail, and Figure 6-1 shows how they influence attitude formation and the purchase decision.

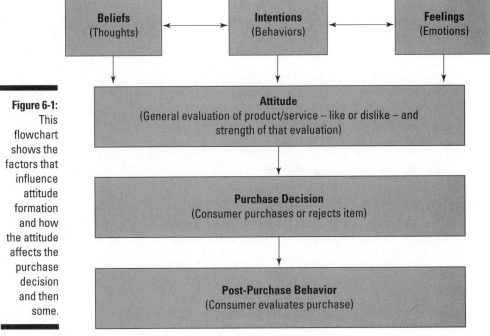

**Figure 6-1:**
This flowchart shows the factors that influence attitude formation and how the attitude affects the purchase decision and then some.

## Beliefs

This component is the cognitive component of consumer attitudes. It's related to the general know-how of a person. To really grasp this component, you need to understand the difference between a belief and a feeling and how they both construct the attitude of the consumer. A belief is an opinion; an attitude is a point of view. So, in other words, belief represents the opinion or the way someone "thinks," which helps that person form the point of view that's reflected in his attitude toward a product.

Clear as mud, right? Well, here's an example to help you along: Consider a person who says that smoking is bad for your health. This statement is the belief component of his attitude; it's what he "thinks" about smoking. This belief works to create his attitude (or point of view), which states that he "doesn't like" smoking and doesn't think people should smoke.

## Feelings

The feeling component is the emotive component of consumer attitudes, and it's derived from emotions a consumer feels toward a product or service. This component of attitude is developed by past emotional association with a product and by emotional effect of belief.

Consumer purchases are influenced by feeling. How does your product make the consumer feel? How does she feel about the marketing messages you send out? The feeling component is comprised not only of the consumer's knowledge of the product, but also of her internal emotional evaluation of the product — how she "feels" about the product.

The feeling component is the one that helps consumers reach purchase decisions by evaluating the functions of their attitudes. When consumers evaluate their feelings toward a product or service, they tend to evaluate the adjustment, ego, value, or knowledge function that it provides. (I discuss these functions later in the chapter.)

## Intentions

This component is the behavior (intentions) component of consumer attitudes. As with the feeling component, the intentions component is sometimes a logical consequence representing action. However, it can sometimes reflect other circumstances as well. For example, even though a consumer may not like a department store and believes that it isn't good for the community, he may go there with a friend and end up purchasing a product.

In other words, intention is the component that creates the readiness to respond and the intent to either purchase or not purchase the product or service. The intentions component is a much stronger indicator of behavior than either beliefs or feelings, because it represents action.

## Seeing how attitude affects purchase decisions

Market research and behavioral science studies have shown that consumers' attitudes toward a product influence their overall evaluation of whether to purchase that product. It also influences whether they relate positively or negatively toward that product.

Attitudes can help you gauge your acceptance into the marketplace. They tell you how well you're meeting the needs of your consumer and show you how the consumer perceives your logo, endorsers, products, or marketing messages. As predictors of behavior, attitudes create the intentions of consumers.

Consumers screen information that conflicts with their attitudes. In their minds they change information to make it consistent with their beliefs and attitudes. They also selectively remember bits of information that reinforce their attitudes (and forget the rest). This is why working to change negative attitudes about your products is important; otherwise you'll never reach the buying intention that you're striving for.

Because attitudes are difficult to define, measure, and observe, you may need to do some research to fully understand the attitudes of your consumers. (Refer to Chapter 12 for more information on conducting market research.)

The interaction between beliefs and feelings and underlying values can make it difficult to understand the role of attitudes and how they affect consumers. Because they're internal, it's often not easy to gain a visual perspective of how the consumer is being affected by beliefs and feelings.

Attitudes have a level of consistency, but they can and do change. Changing them, however, isn't always easy. Find out more in the later section "Marketing to Create Positive Attitudes and Influence Negative Ones."

# Understanding How Consumers Form Attitudes

Consumer attitudes develop over time from childhood. Consumers are continually subjected to new knowledge, input, experiences, and influences. The formation of an attitude is helped along by direct personal experience and is influenced by the ideas, personality, and experiences of friends, family members, and the media.

Attitudes can change in response to the following:

✔ The introduction of new or improved products by you or your competition

✔ The addition of new consumer experiences

✔ The marketing efforts of your competition

✔ The performance of the product after purchase

All these things can affect a consumer's current attitude and her likelihood of attitude change. Attitudes that are relative to purchase behavior are often formed as a result of

✔ Direct experience with the product

✔ Word-of-mouth marketing

✔ Exposure to media advertising, the Internet, and direct marketing efforts

In the following sections, I discuss two important components that cause consumers to have the attitudes that they have. Attitudes are created by a consumer's own internal power of reasoning, which I refer to in this section as *internal assessment,* but they're also affected by outside pressures, which I refer to as *external influences.* When you can comprehend the cause of attitude, you can gain a better understanding of the attitudes consumers possess and why those attitudes may exist. Understanding also enhances your chances of changing negative attitudes.

## A preview of attitude models

Five categories of attitude models have received attention in the study of consumer attitudes:

✔ The *tricomponent attitude model,* which focuses on the cognitive (belief), affective (feeling), and conative (behavior) components of attitude

✔ The *multiattribute attitude models,* which include the attitude-toward-object model and the attitude-toward-behavior model

✔ The *trying-to-consume attitude model,* which focuses on what consumers are trying to achieve by purchasing a product or service

✔ The *attitude-toward-ad model,* which focuses on how consumers respond to advertisements

✔ The *theory of reasoned action,* which looks at both internal and external influencing factors that affect purchasing behavior

You can use these models to gain a better understanding of the role that attitudes play in consumer behavior. The models deal with the structure and composition of a developing attitude. Throughout this chapter, I cover the concepts you need to know; you can use the preceding list as a starting point if you're interested in doing more research on these commonly used models.

# Perceiving a customer's internal assessment

Because attitudes are difficult to measure, it's useful to understand and measure the influence of product-purchase attitudes in terms that relate to the way a product functions in supporting the attitude that it causes. After becoming familiar with these functions, their roles, and how they affect consumers, you can use them to further understand the attitudes of your consumers. The four primary functions are adjustment, value, ego, and knowledge; I expand on each one in the following sections.

## Adjustment function

The *adjustment function* gives a product the ability to help a consumer achieve a desired goal or avoid an undesired goal. An example of the adjustment function would be a consumer who finds a fantastic pizza shop; he repeatedly orders pizza from this restaurant in order to avoid the risk or dissatisfaction of another pizza shop.

How can this function work in your favor as a business owner? If you were the owner of another pizza shop, you could offer a money-back guarantee if the consumer wasn't satisfied.

## Value function

The *value function* gives a product consistency with the consumer's central values or self-image. After all, value, which is an expressive function of attitude, serves as a means of making a concrete expression about certain consumer values. An example of this function would include a consumer who only chooses to purchase American-made automobiles. This decision would be an expression of her value not to purchase foreign-made vehicles. In this case, the consumer feels that she's portraying her values in the vehicle that she drives.

The value function is the most difficult one to deal with because it relates to personal values, and values tend to be something that most consumers hold onto as being important to who they are.

## Ego function

The *ego function* gives a product the capability to defend the consumer's self-image against internal or external threats. For example, consider the purchase of designer-label clothing over nondesigner–label clothing. Some consumers believe that their clothing is an extension and an expression of their self. The clothing conveys the consumer's self-image.

Attitudes that are caused by the ego function often are used as a protection mechanism for consumers. The ego function is a function of internal assessment that you must be careful of, because it's working to protect consumers from feeling inferior. If you work to change the consumer's attitude, he may do the opposite of what you want, which is reinforce his defenses. Instead, when you come across the ego function, your course of action must focus on what rewards the consumer. You want to avoid a potential backfire that pushes the consumer to cling to the attitude rather than change it.

As an example, consider designer clothes again. If you're a company that sells knockoffs, you may find it difficult to counteract the consumer who feels that he's less inferior because of the designer labels he wears. You must find a way to reward the consumer, perhaps explaining that you can't tell the difference between the two lines of clothing. Or you might remind the consumer that because of the decreased price he can purchase more items of clothing, which gives him a broader wardrobe without depleting his budget. Whatever you do, you must not criticize the consumer for his previous purchases of designer labels. Doing so will only make him cling to the previous attitude that he must have designer labels in order to not feel inferior.

### Knowledge function

The *knowledge function* gives a product the ability to provide meaning to the consumer's beliefs and experiences. In other words, it recognizes that people are driven by the need to gain information to organize and understand their environments. It fulfills the need for order, meaning, and structure.

An example of the knowledge function would be the consumer gaining information about a new medical procedure through advertisements. Marketers often use the knowledge function by applying "need-to-know" strategies in their advertisements and marketing materials.

You can use the cognitive needs of a consumer to approach this function when trying to change an attitude. Provide the consumer with as much knowledge and advice as possible. In this function, the consumer's desire is to learn. She wants to feel like an expert and like she's making an educated decision.

## Accounting for external influences

External influences are the inputs from the outside world that consumers use to bring cause to their attitudes. These influences can be friends, family members, or peers. Because consumers are interested in what others have to say, they listen and use the information they receive as a cause for the attitudes they have. External influences have the ability to affect attitudes in both negative and positive ways. Following are the three general categories of influence on attitudes:

- ✔ **Ideas:** Ideas can be influenced by friends, family members, peers, and the media. For example, a consumer may gain the idea from some external influence that in order to give off the impression of success, he must wear only tailor-made suits. This influences him to purchase only tailor-made suits and causes a particular attitude that tailor-made suits connote success.

✔ **Personality traits:** A consumer's personality traits represent how he responds to things around him. It isn't uncommon for consumers to also be influenced by the personality traits of those closest to them. For example, suppose that a consumer has surrounded himself with people who stay on top of technology. They always purchase the newest gadget, and so because of the consumer's association with this group, he also purchases the newest gadgets when they're introduced.

✔ **Experiences:** The experiences of others affect consumers in their attitudes toward products. For example, if your mother visits a new restaurant and tells you that the food was horrible, the chances of you visiting that restaurant are slim. However, if she purchases a product and can't say enough good things about it, the chances of you purchasing that product are much higher.

You could almost look at external influences as being equivalent to peer pressure. Consumers don't always agree with those around them, but they do often listen to them to gain their point of view. In fact, after a span of time, they begin to understand or even accept those attitudes as correct, especially in specific situations.

However, do remember that the effect of attitudes on the behavior of consumers depends on the situation in which the behavior occurs. A specific situation may cause consumers to behave in ways that aren't consistent with their own attitudes. Consider the situation in which the behavior takes place; otherwise you may misinterpret the relationship between attitude and behavior. (I discuss the consistency of attitudes in more detail in the later section "Understanding the roots of attitude inconsistencies.")

Also keep in mind that the influences of family and friends have major impacts on a consumer's values, beliefs, and attitudes. For this reason, most people carry over many of their attitudes from childhood into their adult lives. As you can imagine, these long-time attitudes can be difficult to directly influence; however, if the attitude is positive, you may be in luck. This source can be a great word-of-mouth referral for you. But, if the attitude is negative, it can have a detrimental effect on potential or current customers.

## Understanding the roots of attitude inconsistencies

Consumers often behave inconsistently when it comes to the components of attitude. They are human, after all. Inconsistency happens for several reasons:

✔ **The lack of ability:** A consumer may want a new vehicle, but she may not be able to afford it. She lacks the ability to purchase the vehicle.

- ✔ **Competing demands for resources:** A consumer may want a new vehicle *and* a new house. She can only afford one, so she has to make a decision about which item to purchase.

- ✔ **Social influence:** A consumer may enjoy gambling, but because she's with friends who don't agree with gambling, she chooses not to gamble. This type of influence can come from family, friends, co-workers, and any other social acquaintances.

- ✔ **Attitude measurement problems:** Consumers sometimes have difficulty measuring their own attitudes. In many situations, consumers don't consciously set out to specify how positively or negatively they feel about a certain product.

  For example, consider a hybrid car. A consumer doesn't always give reliable answers when a market researcher asks her how she feels about hybrid cars, how important her beliefs are about the car, and what her overall evaluation is of the hybrid car. Consumers may not answer honestly because they're confused by the question or fear that the research may not agree with their point of view. Inaccurate answers often cause erroneous measurements, because the consumer may go on to act on her true attitudes.

# Marketing to Create Positive Attitudes and Influence Negative Ones

It's important to realize that you have the ability to shape and direct the attitudes of prospective consumers. You also can reshape consumers' attitudes. Obviously it's easier to work to create a positive attitude or to confirm existing positive attitudes than it is to change an attitude. After an attitude has been formed, it's difficult (but not impossible) to change. It simply takes a considerable amount of effort to change what a consumer believes to be true.

You can position your product or service by using messages that focus on certain beliefs and feelings of consumers. What belief do you want the consumer to have about your product? How do you want to make the consumer feel? These two things must drive the intent.

For example, a grocery store by the name of Food-4-Cheap, which is locally owned and interested in positioning itself by using a belief message that triggers both a belief and feeling and drives intent, may run an advertisement that says, "Food-4-Cheap. Always Open. Always Less." The grocery store in this example triggers all three components of attitude. The store gave consumers the belief that its products are cheap and its hours make shopping convenient. These two triggered the intent of the consumer to go to that grocery store.

In the following sections, I show you how you can influence consumers' beliefs and feelings about your offering with your marketing mix.

# Inducing positive attitudes

Creating a positive attitude in prospective consumers can be done by using your marketing efforts. You can use the following approaches to do so:

- ✔ **Create a positive emotional connection.** Focus your marketing message so that you gain the consumer's attention. After you have the consumer's attention, you want your message to create a positive emotional connection between him and your product.

- ✔ **Create curiosity.** Using your marketing message, arouse the curiosity of potential consumers. This curiosity will motivate them to contact you. When they do, you can help construct their positive attitude by giving them top-notch customer service.

- ✔ **Consider a two-sided message.** Consumers tend to have a natural level of skepticism when it comes to marketing messages, so using a two-sided message often leads to them feeling as if you have more credibility. For example, consider the marketing of prescription drugs. They're required by the Federal Food and Drug Administration (FDA) to present both the positive effects of the drug as well as the side effects and dangers of using it.

- ✔ **Take advantage of comparative marketing.** Don't be afraid to compare your products to those of your competitors. Doing so creates credibility from the consumers' point of view and can lead to a positive attitude toward your products. Just keep in mind that you must be able to back your comparison claims.

- ✔ **Use credible sources.** You have to focus not only on the message of your marketing, but also on where you advertise and put your message. Consumers pay attention to the source of the message; in fact, the source is often used in the development of their perceptions of a product.

# Reshaping negative attitudes

Attitude changes are learned. They're influenced by personal experiences and information gained from various personal and impersonal sources. Consumers also are affected by their own personalities. Personality affects both the consumers' acceptance and the speed at which their attitudes can be changed.

If a consumer has a negative attitude toward a product, your challenge is to identify the key issues that are affecting the consumer's attitude toward that product. Then you can adjust your marketing to make your consumer's attitude a more positive one. You can only ask people what their attitudes are or infer them, because it's impossible to directly observe them.

Even though attitudes can be changed, keep in mind that the task isn't easy. In general, weak attitudes are easier to change than those that are strongly held. Consumers tend to develop strong attitudes when it comes to areas that they consider to be of great personal importance. Strong attitudes can be either negative or positive, however. In areas of limited importance, consumers tend to be ambivalent or neutral, so their attitudes are weaker and more vulnerable to change. It's also easier to change attitudes that deal with low-involvement purchases (versus high-involvement purchases).

In this section, I help you recognize areas where negative attitudes are likely to be strong or weak, and I offer strategies to help you turn those frowns upside down, so to speak.

### Assessing the strength of the attitude

When a consumer is highly involved in her purchase, she's committed to the brand or the product. In this scenario, it's often easier to change her beliefs about the product than it is to change her attitude. For example, consider a consumer who's in the process of purchasing a car. She knows that a particular brand of a car shows people that she's successful and has achieved a level of financial status. It would be difficult to persuade her that the specific brand she's looking at doesn't reflect that type of message. However, you could change her belief that perhaps the brand of vehicle you're selling makes that same statement. You would do this by providing her with advertising reports or statistics of sales that reflect the wealthy image.

When it comes to low-involvement purchases, such as toothpaste, deodorant, or laundry soap, it's easier to change a consumer's attitude. Why? Because in low-involvement purchases, consumers are less likely to be committed to the brand. They're less self-identified with these products and services than they are when it comes to high-involvement purchases. They're also more likely to accept messages that don't conform to their beliefs.

### Selecting your strategies

When you're faced with stagnant or slipping market share or active competitors, you need to develop strategies that attempt to change or intensify your consumers' attitudes. Attitude change strategies can focus on one of the attitude components — beliefs, feelings, intentions — or a combination of all three. (Refer to the earlier section "Dissecting an attitude: The sum of its parts" for more on these components.)

The struggle that consumers face with the belief and feeling components of attitude is that they're learned and sometimes consumers are unaware of where they were learned from. Similarly, you as a marketer may not know where consumers' attitudes are generated. Their attitudes may have nothing at all to do with your product or service, so be sure to consider the following:

✔ **A consumer may hold beliefs or feelings that aren't accurate.** Here's an example of a consumer's inaccurate belief: "If I let a doctor X-ray me, I will get cancer from the radiation." In a case like this, you want to provide the individual with more information and show him how you can protect him from the radiation.

✔ **A consumer can have multiple feelings and beliefs.** In fact, some may even conflict with other beliefs and feelings. For example, a consumer might say, "I believe that going to the gym is important, but it takes away from my family time after work and that makes me feel guilty." In this case, you want to relate to the consumer's conflicting attitude. After summarizing the conflict, advise him that if he does go to the gym, he will lead a healthier lifestyle and live longer and in turn will actually be able to spend more time with his family.

✔ **A consumer may have both positive and negative beliefs and feelings about a single product or service.** Here's an example: "I like red wine, but it stains my teeth." When facing this scenario, both beliefs are true, so you want to focus on the attributes of your product. This way you get him to focus more on the positive rather than the negative.

When you face these struggles, you can only work to change consumers' attitudes. You can choose from any of the following six strategies:

✔ **Change the basic motivational function.** This strategy takes into account that attitudes serve four functions: adjustment, value, ego, and knowledge (see the earlier section "Perceiving a customer's internal assessment" for more on these functions). By changing the basic motivational function of your product, the attitude toward your product can be changed. For example, you can offer free trials, money-back guarantees, and coupon promotions. Market in a way that drives consumers to try your product. The end result — with any luck — is that they develop a positive attitude toward it.

✔ **Associate your product with a special group, event, or cause.** Attitudes can be altered by indicating your product's relationship to a particular group, event, or cause. Concern for the environment is a cause that has been used frequently. For example, an environmentally conscious consumer may change his mind about a company when he finds out that it's going green.

✔ **Relate to conflicting attitudes.** Consumers like harmony and shy away from conflict. If you can show that their attitudes toward your product are in conflict with other attitudes, they may be persuaded to change one of the attitudes. (Just hope they change the one that pertains to you!)

✔ **Alter components in product attributes.** You can use this strategy to change the evaluation of the features your product offers. You can do so by upgrading or downgrading significant features, changing consumer beliefs by introducing new information, adding features, or changing the overall product rating.

✔ **Change beliefs about competing brands.** You can directly compare your product to competing brands in an attempt to change consumer beliefs about both products.

✔ **Provide information at the right times.** Consumer attitudes can be changed by either central or peripheral routes to persuasion. In other words, you need to give the consumer more information when he's most receptive to that information. Sounds complicated doesn't it? Here's what I mean: In the central route, attitude changes occur because the consumer seeks and evaluates additional information about your product. Motivation levels are high and the consumer is willing to invest the time and effort to gather and evaluate the information.

# Chapter 7

# Defining the Role of Identity: Self-Concepts and Lifestyle

## In This Chapter

▶ Exploring the impact of identity on consumers

▶ Understanding and marketing to consumer self-concepts

▶ Evaluating lifestyle characteristics that affect consumer behavior

*T*he self-concepts and lifestyles of consumers set up their identities. These two components show not only how consumers see themselves, but also how they portray themselves to others. They also affect consumer behavior and consumption patterns. When consumers identify a product as relating to their self-concepts and lifestyle, they often form an emotional identification with that product. This makes them feel as if the product was created just for them.

In this chapter, I explain the many different self-concepts and lifestyles and show how you can use your understanding of them to help consumers feel as if your product was created just for them.

# Understanding the Dynamic Effect of Identity (Self-Concepts + Lifestyles)

*Self-concept* is a consumer's perception of himself. It's a collaboration of subjective thoughts and perceptions that he holds. In other words, it isn't an objective evaluation. A self-concept is composed of multidimensional characteristics, and it includes not only physical attributes, but psychological ones as well. Some attributes that are included are: personality attributes; knowledge of skills, abilities, and talents; and occupation. A consumer's perception is also intertwined with the various roles that he takes on, including family roles, personal roles, and professional roles.

Self-concept refers to how consumers see and feel about themselves; it's the image of themselves that they have shaped and created. How does self-concept affect consumer behavior? Well, in order to reflect the image they have of themselves, consumers buy and use products that support that image.

At times, lifestyle is reflective of self-concepts. *Lifestyle* refers to the way a consumer lives. It represents the external characteristics that pertain to how a consumer lives: the activities he engages in, his habits and possessions, and the interests he expresses. In other words, lifestyle represents what he sees as value in his life. This value is reflected in the way that he spends his time and money. Lifestyle is the result of a consumer's motivations, education, attitudes, behaviors, beliefs and opinions, demographic factors, and personality. At the same time, lifestyle also represents a consumer's income level, marital status, culture, social class, and buying power. These different roles all combine to reflect the consumer's lifestyle.

## Studying how identity affects purchasing behavior

Self-concept is an important determinant of consumer behavior, because it describes how consumers see themselves and how they think other people see them. Consumers define their sense of self at least partially from the products and services they consume. They attempt to support their self-concepts by using those products that communicate particular personal characteristics to themselves and those around them. For example, self-concept is the basis for why a consumer wears certain fashions, purchases particular products, and drives specific cars.

Products and brands are an important part of how an individual defines herself. In other words, products and brands help a consumer stay in line with the self-concept she has developed. The subjective meaning of a product ties in closely with one's self-concept or image. A consumer will buy products that she feels reflect her established image.

Like self-concept, lifestyle determines what products consumers buy, how they use them, and how they feel about them. Consumers purchase products and services to support their lifestyles.

In essence, a person's self-concepts influence her attitudes, interests, and opinions, which in turn influence her lifestyle; together these factors determine her *identity*. Figure 7-1 shows you how the concepts relate to one another.

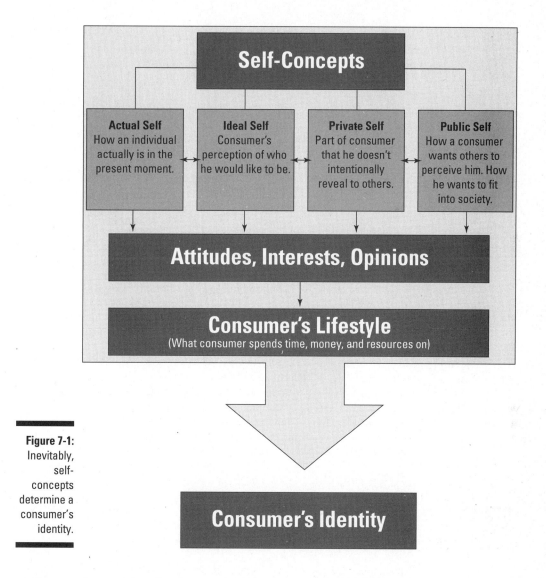

A person's self-concept can change over a period of time. This change most often happens during an identity crisis or traumatic experience. During this time an individual will often go through a reassessment and develop a new self-concept. When a person's self-concept changes, her lifestyle may also change as a result of both internal and external factors. That's because a consumer's lifestyle is reflective of her self-concepts; the corresponding consumption patterns change as well.

## *Seeing how identity factors into successful marketing plans*

Advertising and marketing can influence consumers to buy products that symbolically represent the self-concept they're attempting to achieve. When your advertisements and marketing messages are passed on to consumers by using reinforcement of their self-concepts, consumers are more inclined to purchase your products. On the other hand, if consumers feel that your advertisement doesn't fit with their self-concepts, they're less likely to accept the advertisement and purchase your product.

If you know the specifics of your consumers' lifestyles, you can profile their patterns of acting and interacting with the world around them. And even better is the fact that you can develop marketing strategies targeted to common market segments based on similarities in lifestyle. You can then use this information to not only get the right message about your product in the right places for your intended consumers, but you also can develop your products to meet the lifestyle interests of your target markets.

For example, suppose I'm a home builder who's looking to develop a new housing addition in a specific zip code. I decide to do a lifestyle assessment of people located in that zip code. The lifestyle assessment shows me that the median income is $450,000 annually and that most of the homeowners in the area are married and have two kids. The average home purchase price is $800,000. Because of this assessment, I now know that if I build my housing development in this area, the houses can range from $750,000 to $950,000 and should sell with no problem. After I've selected my area and finalized the plan, I can then begin marketing to this zip code.

# *Identifying Consumer Self-Concepts and Then Marketing to Them*

In the past, people believed that humans only had one self, but it has been proven that we actually have multiple selves. No, I don't mean you're schizophrenic. I simply mean that individuals act differently with different people in different situations. Here are the four basic dimensions of self-concept:

✔ **Actual self:** The *actual self* reflects how an individual actually is at the present moment. A consumer's actual self-concept can include social status, age, gender, occupation, and so on. For example, I'm a marketing consultant. This is a real perception of me, and it's what I portray to others.

- ✔ **Ideal self:** The *ideal self* is a consumer's perception of who he would like to be (but isn't). As consumers, many people are in constant pursuit of bettering themselves, whether it's through education, income, health, or occupation. Because they aspire to have the ideal life, they often purchase products that make them feel closer to that ideal self-concept.

- ✔ **Private self:** The *private self* is one that isn't intentionally revealed to others. The private self represents who a person is or would like to be to himself (versus who he wants to be to others). Private self-concept can represent how you believe that you act, such as friendly, creative, loving, or adventurous.

- ✔ **Public self:** The *public self* is revealed to others. The public (or social) self-concept is how a consumer wants to be seen by others — how he wants to fit into society. For example, consumers may want to feel attractive, intelligent, and successful.

Self-concepts work in two ways: They're both dynamic and organized. Because self-concepts are dynamic, they provide consumers with direction in their lives. They view their actual self and take direction to achieve their ideal self. Self-concepts are also organized, and because of this, they provide consumers with a feeling of stability. This stability makes the consumer want to protect and support his concepts in order to maintain a feeling of stability, which comes from the consistency that is provided by self-concepts. Consumers maintain stability by purchasing products that are in line with their self-concepts.

## *Tracing the formation of self-concepts*

Research shows that humans aren't born with self-concepts. Instead, they begin to emerge in the early months of a person's life. They're shaped and reshaped through repeated experiences. Specifically, self-concepts are a product of interacting with others. Through these interactions, people develop perceptions of themselves, which become their self-concepts.

The following are the three distinctive ways that self-concepts are developed in individuals:

- ✔ **Received messages:** Self-concepts are a reflection of a person's interaction with others. As the person takes in messages (both positive and negative) that are received throughout his life, he begins to construct the image he has of himself. These messages are not just verbal; they can be nonverbal as well. Here's a verbal example: If an individual's mother tells him every day that he will be successful, that message becomes a part of his self-concept (as his ideal self). He will work every day to better himself and reach toward that success.

- ✔ **Social comparisons:** When a person evaluates himself and compares that evaluation to someone else, he forms a self-concept (his actual self). An important factor to take into consideration when it comes to social comparison is who the individual is comparing himself to. For example, a 37-year-old man would likely compare himself regularly to other 37-year-old men.

- ✔ **Culture:** The culture an individual was raised in contributes to self-concepts as well. (Refer to Chapter 8 to read more about how culture affects consumers.) For example, an individual who was raised in a very loving home would have a private self-concept that causes him to act loving to everyone he meets.

An individual arrives at a self-concept by taking all three of these things into account. It's important to realize that because self-concepts are a part of a person's identity, they're fairly stable and difficult to change, especially as the individual gets older. Often the only way for a self-concept to be changed is through a new life experience or drastic life change.

Because self-concept isn't instinctive (but rather a product of interaction with others), it has limitless potential for development and achievement. In other words, consumers are always in the development phase of their self-concepts. And you can help them achieve those concepts by providing products that work to support and protect the self-concepts that are important to them.

## Understanding how self-concepts affect the individual

By understanding self-concepts and how they affect consumers, you can use the knowledge to position your products in a way that's attractive to consumers, thereby causing them the desire to purchase. The following list provides you with information on how self-concepts affect consumer behavior:

- ✔ **Individuals perceive themselves differently than others because of previous experiences and present perceptions.** You must understand how your consumers see themselves, which is often based on the messages they have received throughout life. Do they perceive themselves as successful? If so, position your product in a way that makes them feel successful.

- ✔ **Individuals perceive different aspects of themselves at different times with varying degrees of clarity.** Understand the perception of your consumers. Are they focused on their families or careers? For example, if your consumers are focused on family, it probably isn't a good idea to try and sell them a sports car that only has two seats.

- ✔ **Any experience that an individual perceives as inconsistent with her self-concept can be perceived as a threat.** Consumers purchase products that support their self-concepts, so if your consumer feels that your product is in conflict with her self-concept she may not purchase it in fear that it will threaten her feeling of stability.

✓ **Consumers tend to resist change to their self-concepts.** When you understand the purpose of self-concepts to consumers (to provide stability and consistency), it's easier to support those concepts rather than to try and change them. So make sure your product supports your consumer's self-concept.

✓ **The more central a particular belief is regarding an individual's self-concept, the more resistant she will be to changing that belief.** Drastic life changes or experiences are usually the only times that consumers change their self-concepts. This is particularly true in older consumers. If you have a consumer who believes that buying your product is frivolous and a waste of money, you'll find it nearly impossible to sell her that product — unless, of course, you can find a way to relate it to another self-concept that the consumer holds.

For example, if I'm an elderly woman and you're trying to sell me a security system, I may see it as frivolous and a waste of money — until you explain to me how it will keep me safe and protect me from intruders. The consumer's belief that it is a waste of money is in line with her actual self, but safety is in line with her ideal self, which is being safe and secure in her own home.

✓ **Perceived success and failure impact self-concept.** Failure in a highly regarded area lowers evaluations in all other areas. Success in a prized area raises evaluations. Understand where your consumer is. Is she in a place of feeling success or failure? For example, if you ask her about her job and she tells you she was just laid off, it probably isn't the time to show her your most expensive item. However, if she tells you she just opened up her third business, you can probably bring up that big-ticket item and close the deal.

✓ **The world and the things in it aren't simply perceived; they're perceived in relation to an individual's self-concept.** You must realize that consumers see things differently. The unfortunate thing is that self-concepts aren't visible to the eye. So you have to ask questions and really listen to your consumers in order to understand their perceptions of your product.

✓ **The development of self-concept is an ongoing and continuous process.** The self-concepts of consumers are always developing and consumers are always working to achieve them. So the positioning question that you must ask yourself to reach out to consumers is "How does my product help consumers achieve their self-concepts?"

✓ **Individuals strive to behave in ways that are in line with their self-concepts.** It's difficult for consumers to step outside of their self-concepts, because they're sort of like comfort zones. So if your product pushes them outside of their self-concepts, you'll find it difficult to get their attention. You must put your product in line with consumers' self-concepts.

✔ **Self-concept usually takes precedence over the physical body.** In other words, individuals often sacrifice physical comfort and safety to achieve emotional satisfaction. When consumers are outside of their self-concepts, they experience discomfort, and so this is why they work hard to stay inside of them. If a consumer has the ideal self-concept that she wants to be in a beauty pageant and win, she'll go out of her way to achieve that goal — even if it means getting to the gym by 4 a.m. As a marketer, show the benefit of what you offer and how you'll help that consumer reach her ideal self.

✔ **Self-concept continuously guards itself against self-esteem loss.** Self-concepts work to protect consumers. They evaluate the self-concept support that they gain from a product in order to make a decision on purchasing that product. If it's in conflict with their self-concepts, including self-esteem, it's easy for the consumer to walk away. So be sure you know how your product supports the self-concepts of your consumer.

Self-concept affects more than just the here-and-now, one-time purchase. It also affects the following:

✔ **Memory:** When your marketing message or advertisement relates to a consumer's self-concept, she has a greater level of recall than she does with advertisements that don't relate to the self-concept she strives to achieve. This is because of the dynamic component of self-concepts. A consumer is always developing and trying to achieve her ideal self-concept, and memory often serves as a reminder of how to do that.

✔ **Attitude and intention:** A consumer's self-concept affects product preference through the attitudes she forms when she sees your advertisement. Advertisements or marketing messages that are congruent with the consumer's self-concept can create a positive attitude toward your product. Similarly, when your advertisement is in line with the consumer's self-concept, her desire (intention) to purchase the product is strengthened. (Refer to Chapter 6 for more on attitudes and intentions.)

## *Directing your marketing strategy to engage consumer self-concepts*

You can use your understanding of the four different dimensions of self-concept — actual self, ideal self, private self, and public self — to target your products to consumers. (I explain these dimensions earlier in the chapter.) Here's how you can effectively target consumers with each of the different selves:

✔ **Reinforce the actual self:** Many products on the market attempt to reinforce one's actual self-concept (who a consumer is at the present time).

So marketers target consumer segments based on that concept. Where do consumers live at the moment? What are their lifestyles like right now? How does your product work in those lifestyles? The idea is to find out where your consumers are right now, and then you can present your product in a way that supports the actual self-concept.

For example, consider how minivans are marketed. They're marketed as a product that's intended to be driven by busy parents who constantly transport their children from place to place. Those who market minivans know that parents see themselves as busy people who care about the safety of their children. Parents relate to this self-concept, so they have a desire to purchase a minivan.

✔ **Convince consumers to make their ideal selves a reality:** Consumers use their ideal self to compare the value of their actual self. They want their actual self to have similar characteristics to their ideal self. If these two concepts aren't similar enough, they'll attempt to achieve their ideal self by purchasing products that reinforce that self. So determine how your products help them get there. How do your products help support the ideal self of the consumer?

Take for example a person who desires to be wealthy. He may not make enough money to be considered wealthy or upper class, but he aspires to be. This consumer may purchase certain things that make him feel like he belongs to the upper class. By purchasing an item that's known to be affordable to the upper class, this consumer may feel closer to achieving his ideal self. He may lean toward buying a home in a specific neighborhood or a specific type of car.

✔ **Evoke the behavior of the private self:** You can use a consumer's awareness of his private self to market your product. You can evoke private self-concepts by using images in your marketing that portray internal self-concepts, such as happiness, joy, or health consciousness.

A health food, for instance, may represent an image of living well and eating healthily. This image taps into the private self-concept of someone who feels that he's health conscious. Consumers who see themselves as health conscious will buy products that reinforce their desire to be healthy.

✔ **Encourage leadership of the public self:** Physical attractiveness can be a public self-concept. In fact, it has become extremely important to many individuals in today's society. Advertisements and the media enforce this importance by glamorizing popular role models, such as news anchors and celebrities. Consumers feel that physical attractiveness is a sign of social power, self-esteem, and wealth. So both males and females who value good looks feel they should emulate this attractiveness. Because consumers want to purchase products that make them feel attractive, they focus on specific clothing brands, fine jewelry, and sometimes even cosmetic surgery. As a marketer you want your marketing message to use images that are attractive and that portray the idea that by using your product or service the consumer is attractive as well.

Public self can also represent the desire to feel neighborly, friendly, successful, tasteful, and so on. So, for example, a consumer may buy a finer wine to serve at a dinner party in order to create the perception of having good taste.

It's important to really evaluate your consumers and their lifestyles, because lifestyle is the reflection of self-concepts, and while self-concepts aren't visible to the eye, you can gain a better understanding of them by viewing the lifestyles of your consumers. Do they enjoy fine wines and restaurants? What are their cars like? And how big are their houses? When you have found the lifestyle that your consumer represents, you'll have a greater understanding of what marketing messages you should use to market your product.

You can effectively target your marketing message by including slogans, celebrities, and product images that give consumers the idea that if they purchase something, it can help them create or maintain a certain dimension of self.

# Reflecting on and Targeting Consumer Lifestyles

Lifestyle is reflective of the self-concepts that consumers hold. It's what consumers put their time, money, and other resources into. It represents their values as well as their interests. So you can gain a wealth of information about your consumers by taking a deeper look into their lifestyles.

Lifestyle is technically measured by a technique known as *psychographics,* which involves measuring consumer responses to activities, interest, and opinions. This measurement process is known as an *AIO.* After gathering the responses, you combine them with demographic information and other factors. Next you analyze them to find distinctive lifestyle characteristics, and then put them into groups according to these characteristics. Finally, you segment the groups so the products can be positioned and the marketing campaigns can be created.

It's difficult to perform an AIO without consumer data, so in this section, I spend some time explaining the different key lifestyle characteristics and help you increase your knowledge of how you can specifically use that information to market to consumers with those characteristics.

Lifestyle characteristics and understanding how people live provides you with more usable information than personality assessments do. You can use these characteristics to develop and create marketing strategies that are positioned in a way that appeals to your consumers. That way your message relates to your consumer's lifestyle. You also can use lifestyle characteristics to help select the right venues to display your advertising and marketing messages.

# Recognizing lifestyle-determining factors

Consumers are affected by many factors pertaining to their lifestyles. These factors include income, marital status, culture, social class, and buying power, among others. All these factors determine the way of life for a consumer. Some factors may be more important than others to some consumers, so you want to target those first. Targeting correctly really comes down to market research and what your consumers are looking for from you. (Refer to Chapter 12 for more information on market research.)

## Income

A person's disposable income is extremely important when it comes to consumer patterns and consumption behavior. A consumer may aspire to buy certain goods and services, but her income may become a restriction. On the other hand, a consumer may have an unlimited amount of income, and so she may be able to buy whatever she wants. So, as you can see, income often determines what consumers purchase and when.

A consumer's lifestyle can change if income increases or decreases. Market studies show that as a consumer's spendable income increases, she's more apt to spend money on her wants rather than her needs. She feels a sense of spending freedom. Consider, for example, lottery winners. Is a winner's first purchase a loaf of bread? Typically not. It's a new home, a luxury car, or an extravagant vacation. Specifically, when income increases, the following behaviors takes place:

- ✔ The percentage of money spent on basic necessities, such as food and clothing, increases. The reason for this is that consumers are now no longer worried about running out of money. Instead, they feel free to spend more.

- ✔ The percentage spent on housing remains constant, but utilities like gas and electricity decrease, because they're now spending more money traveling and vacationing in the tropical islands and less time at home.

- ✔ The percentage spent on other items — such as recreation, education, self-help, and luxury items — increases.

Change of income for consumers often creates either freedom in spending or restraint in spending, depending on whether the income increases or decreases. What typically happens is that in the initial phase of an income increase, consumers spend money rapidly, because their income boundary feels lifted by more discretionary income. If a consumer's income decreases, she will begin to look for ways to save money. In both of these scenarios, the consumer's lifestyle is affected by the amount of income.

### Marital status

As you can imagine, consumer spending patterns change in direct proportion with marital status. For instance, when a couple marries, they have more disposable income to spend. When a couple divorces, however, each party has less disposable income. The same is true for consumers who find themselves widowed. In each of these scenarios, incomes change and consumption patterns are also affected.

Here's an example: If you're single, you're more likely to purchase frozen dinners or eat out more often, because it's difficult to cook for one. By doing so you save money as well. If you're married, your grocery bill will likely increase, and your family will dine at home more often, because spending time at home is important and eating out is too expensive for a family.

The bottom line is that if your product is of benefit to singles, married couples, and divorcees or widows/widowers, you have to create three types of messages. You want to cater your message specifically to each of those groups and their lifestyles so you don't turn off one group.

### Culture

A *culture* is a segment of society that shares the same beliefs, learned values, and attitudes. It isn't uncommon for a culture to share similar history, religion, language, thoughts, knowledge, and morals as well. All these factors affect consumer lifestyle and consumer beliefs. (Refer to Chapter 8 for more information on how culture affects consumers.)

Culture is part of the external impact that influences the consumer. It represents the pressure that's put on him by others within his culture. Here are some of the ways that culture affects consumers and purchasing:

- ✔ It affects prepurchase and purchase activities as well as consumption patterns.
- ✔ It affects consumers' buying habits by impacting how they perceive a specific product.
- ✔ It can determine which purchases consumers view as frivolous.
- ✔ It affects the way consumers search for information.
- ✔ It determines the importance placed on specific features of a product and product alternatives.
- ✔ It impacts the amount negotiated during the purchasing process.
- ✔ It impacts consumption — how consumers use and consume products.
- ✔ It can influence how individuals dispose of products. They may resell them after use, give them away to others, or recycle them.

Culture influences the following lifestyle characteristics as well:

- ✔ **Communication and language:** The way consumers communicate and the language they use often affect their lifestyle by who they associate with, what neighborhoods they live in, and at times what social classes they participate in. Keep in mind that this doesn't just include verbal communication. Nonverbal communication, such as hand gestures and facial expressions, also affect lifestyle. As a marketer, you must respect the way your consumers communicate and the language they use — not only for clarity, but so you don't offend.

- ✔ **Dress and appearance:** In many cultures, consumers dress differently. In some cultures, consumers wear more clothes and in others they wear less. This affects consumers' behavior because it dictates what clothing they wear as well as what they deem appropriate or offensive.

- ✔ **Food and eating habits:** Cultures often determine how, what, and when consumers eat. Eating habits affect consumers because they influence the food that they buy as well as what restaurants they go to.

- ✔ **Time and time consciousness:** Culture affects time because in some cultures time is more flexible. The lifestyles of some consumers may be more lax when it comes to timing and appointments; others will be more prompt. You want to be sure that you understand this so you don't offend (or become offended) when dealing with certain consumers.

- ✔ **Relationships:** Different cultures look at relationships with different importance levels. Some hold them with great respect and others see relationships as less formal. When working with consumers, you want to have an understanding of the relationships in their lifestyles so you can appeal to their needs.

- ✔ **Values and norms:** This is the most common factor of lifestyle when it comes to culture. Cultures carry different values and norms, so if you're serving a specific culture, you need to be familiar with these values and norms in order to avoid being offensive.

- ✔ **Beliefs and attitudes:** Cultures carry different beliefs and attitudes toward lifestyle. Some think it's okay to have an abundance of money, while others find it a blessing to live in poverty. So, obviously, these types of beliefs affect consumers' lifestyles and buying habits.

- ✔ **Mental process and learning:** Each consumer learns and processes things differently, so this often has an effect on lifestyle. For example, it may determine where consumers send their children to school or what language they speak.

- ✔ **Work habits and practices:** Work habits and practices are affected by culture and they also affect lifestyle. A consumer may work 15 hours a day because it's what he was taught from his culture. Or a consumer may only work three hours a day and then take a nap. It's important to understand how this differs from culture to culture in order to understand the lifestyle of the consumer you're trying to reach out to. Here's another issue to consider: Is it okay to call your consumers on Sunday to discuss business? Some consumers would see that practice as disrespectful and therefore wouldn't do business with you.

As a marketer or business owner, it's your responsibility to know the culture of your target market. If you aren't familiar with the culture that you're marketing to, you may make a huge marketing blunder that could be to the detriment of your business. In fact, if an advertisement is offensive or puts off a consumer and his culture, you'll have a tough time gaining traction within the market of that culture. After all, certain acts in different cultures are considered disrespectful, and after you've disrespected them they may no longer do business with you. Even worse, they could share with everyone your disrespectful act, which would influence whether other people in that culture do business with you.

For example, in the French culture, people don't smile when meeting strangers. In fact, they don't trust folks who smile at them before establishing a connection or relationship. So, if a company runs an advertisement in France where two strangers meet and smile, the consumers probably wouldn't be receptive to that advertisement.

### Social class

All societies possess a hierarchical structure that stratifies residents into classes of people called *social classes*. Groups and individuals are classified into this hierarchy on the basis of esteem and prestige. The groups differ in status, wealth, education, possession, values, occupation, lifestyles, friendships, and manners of speaking. Consumers of the same social class tend to share the same values, beliefs, and behaviors that unite them. A person's social class is relatively permanent. Members of social classes tend to socialize with each other rather than with members of other classes.

Here are the six social class divisions within the United States:

- **Upper upper class,** which represents those who have old money (money that has been passed up through the family). Consumer purchases in this class often focus more on economic status and behavioral standards in order to uphold their social status.

- **Lower upper class,** which represents the new rich. Consumer purchases in this class often focus more on upholding economic status, educational credentials, and behavioral standards in order to reach their desired social status.

- **Upper middle class,** which represents professionals or business owners. Consumer purchases in this class often focus more on educational credentials, increasing economic status, and behavioral standards in order to reach their desired social status.

- **Lower middle class,** which represents lower-paid white-collar workers and higher-paid blue-collar workers. Consumer purchases in this class are geared more toward behavioral standards; economic status is less important to them.

- ✔ **Upper lower class,** which represents the blue-collar worker. Consumer purchases in this class are geared more toward behavioral standards, but economic status isn't important to them.

- ✔ **Lower lower class,** which represents the underemployed or unemployed. Consumer purchases are geared more toward behavioral standards; economic status and educational credentials aren't important to them.

The interesting thing about social classes is that both actual and perceptual factors distinguish the groups. Social class is the only lifestyle factor that deals with both the actual and the perceptual. In perceptual terms, individuals perceive that the many classes have different amounts of prestige, power, and privilege.

Social class tends to be a predictor of resources owned. Consumers often buy products and services to demonstrate their membership within a specific social class. Consumers also have been known to purchase goods and services to help advance their social standing within a specific class, because a membership in a higher social class leads to greater influence within the workplace, organization, and society as a whole.

It's common for social class to be erroneously confused with income. But the fact is that social class captures those lifestyle differences that income ignores. For example, different social classes

- ✔ **Value education differently.** Consumers who value education will spend more on higher education, self-improvement, and workshops. Those who value it less will conversely spend less.

- ✔ **Have different attitudes toward family life, raising children, the role of the women, and so on.** Consumer attitudes regarding family life affect consumers because they have a great effect on consumption patterns. If a consumer believes that the role of women is to stay home, this situation often creates less discretionary income for the family. If she works outside of the home, however, the family will be more apt to purchase convenience products, such as day care, dinners out, housekeepers, and so on.

- ✔ **Exhibit different lifestyles.** The importance that consumers put on their public lifestyle affects their consumption patterns. If perception of others doesn't matter, they'll pay less than those who find the exhibition of their lifestyle a definition of their social class.

- ✔ **Have different activities outside the home.** A consumer who participates in multiple activities outside of the home will spend more on convenience items in order to accommodate that lifestyle of activities. On the other hand, the consumer who stays at home will have fewer outside expenditures.

### Buying power

*Buying power* is often referred to as a consumer's purchasing power — the consumer's ability to use the cash she has to purchase products to meet her current wants and needs. Buying power, which is based on the consumer's income level and credit, allows her to change her lifestyle characteristics.

Buying power gives the consumer the power of choice, meaning that when consumers have unlimited buying power, there are no limits to what they can purchase to meet their needs. However, if a consumer has limited buying power, her purchasing decisions may not be as uninhibited.

Manufacturers often analyze the buying power of specific market segments, which allows them to design products and services that are a good match with the average amount of disposable income that a consumer within a specific income bracket is expected to use. As a marketer, it's important to understand the buying power of your consumers, because if you have something to sell, you must have people who have money to buy.

It isn't uncommon for consumer groups that share some of the same lifestyle factors to gather and create buying power by purchasing in quantities. How can you use this to your benefit? Consider tapping into groups that have the buying power to purchase in quantities. You can often find this by evaluating lifestyle. An example would be a group of attorneys who purchase legal journals at a discounted price because they purchase them in a quantity. This isn't to say that you can't target individual consumers who have a large capacity of buying power; they're just typically a little harder to reach than groups. Keep in mind that this also can be true for services that are purchased. Consider, for example, the corporation that offers a discounted rate at a local gym to its employees. The gym offers the discount because it's reaching consumers in masses rather than individually.

In order to determine buying power for consumers within your market, you must gather the spending data of targeted consumers, which can be obtained from third-party market research companies. (Refer to Chapter 12 for more information.) You can take this information to target specific consumer groups with your offer. (Chapter 10 discusses group influences of consumers.)

## Working lifestyle factors into your marketing mix

When it comes to focusing your marketing on lifestyle factors, you must first understand what lifestyle factors are common within your target market. Are the majority of your consumers married? Are they professionals? Do they belong to specific social classes or cultures? You gain this information from market research, and then use the information to segment your market and identify the lifestyle commonalities. Use these commonalities to draft a marketing message that appeals to your target market. (Visit Chapter 13 for more information on identifying your target market.) In the following sections, I show you how to successfully market with each of the lifestyle factors in mind.

### Income

Products that are considered to be luxury items are more income sensitive than products that consumers consider necessities. So if your product is considered more of a luxury, you want to go after consumers who have more disposable income or buying power — or at least be able to show consumers who have a limited amount of disposable income why your product is important to them and why they should purchase it.

If your product is a luxury item, you need to keep a close eye on income and saving trends to avoid a decrease in sales due to a weak economy or recession. Research has shown that during slow economic times consumers tend to hold on tighter to their pocket books, especially when it means buying items of luxury. If your product is a necessity, however, you need to focus on the value of your product compared to your competitor's. You need to prove why consumers should spend their hard-earned money to purchase your product rather than your competitor's.

### Marital status

In order to market your product or service to individuals based on marital status, ask yourself how your product or service enhances the lifestyle of that group, whether single, married, or divorced. Then craft your message directly to those consumers so it attracts and appeals to them.

For example, travel agents, homebuilders, and health clubs have recently recognized the purchasing power of single individuals, so they have begun to market to this important segment of the population.

### Culture

When marketing to consumers in specific cultures, it's important to adhere to their values and beliefs. When you do so, you have a better chance of causing those consumers to be receptive to your marketing. If you fail to adhere to their values, you take the risk of offending them to the point that they never purchase your product. (Check out Chapter 8 for more information on the influence of culture on marketing.)

### Social class

You can use social class distinctions to separate marketing programs and strategies in terms of product and service development as well as in terms of advertising and communication. To be positioned in the best possible way, manufacturers and retailers need to familiarize themselves with the class membership of their target markets and the members' needs, wants, purchasing motives, and requirements in terms of product features and benefits.

As a marketer or business owner, you can use social class to increase product influences by:

- ✔ **Creating different products, services, and product/service lines intended for different social classes:** For example, try offering your top-of-the-line product to those in the upper class (who can afford it and view it as a product that sets them apart in social status), but then also take the time to create products that are specific to young professionals in the middle class. Even though they can't afford the top-of-the-line products, they'll still have an option of purchasing a product from you. For example, consider the BMW 1 series that was created for the middle class individual who couldn't afford to purchase the BMW 7 series.

- ✔ **Marketing the types of products you offer to the social class whose members typically buy them:** For instance, upper class is a good market for real estate, prestigious cars, designer clothes, foreign wines, expensive hobbies, posh restaurants, and so on.

- ✔ **Selling items of status, or *conspicuous items,* which are products that social classes are likely to talk about and compare among themselves:** Fashion, jewelry, or flashy automobiles are all visible items that create status for consumers. They're items that others will talk about. These items often make consumers feel important and be perceived as being in a higher social class than their peers (which is often the reason behind purchasing these products).

- ✔ **Aiming your promotional messages to appeal to a specific social class:** For example, the promotional messages directed to the upper class consumers have to stress status, style, taste, and sophistication. These messages must also show these high-end consumers what they can do with the product to express themselves.

Different products and stores are perceived by consumers to be appropriate to certain social classes. For instance, working classes tend to evaluate products in more utilitarian terms and more affluent consumers tend to evaluate products based on appearance and body image. So when you evaluate social classes, you can evaluate the opportunities to create products and marketing strategies that enable you to go *upmarket,* by appealing to high-income consumers, or *down-market,* by appealing to low-income consumers.

### Buying power

You want to be sure that the market you're targeting has the buying power to purchase your product. If it doesn't, you could very well be wasting your marketing dollars. When evaluating buying power within your target market, consider providing several quality levels of the same types of products that match the buying power and the demand in a given sector of the market.

For example, if you're marketing $1.5 million houses to consumers who can only afford $950,000 houses, you're missing the market. If you want to create diversity in your product, consider creating products in the price range that's within your target market's buying power.

# Part III
# Consumers in Their Social and Cultural Settings

"Take that ridiculous thing off your neck and put on a proper shrunken monkey head!"

# In this part . . .

As if internal influences weren't enough to understand, you also must consider the external influences that have an impact on your consumers and their purchasing patterns. In this part, I help you explore those influences. I examine cultures and subcultures and explain how they affect your marketing strategy.

Also, because families go through stages as well as change household structures, I explore the family life cycle. In this discussion, I include some information on why the roles of men and women have changed over the years. All this information will help you understand how each stage creates different consumer demands. Knowing the phase each of your consumers is in enables you to help them in the decision-making process.

Consumers also identify with social groups. In the discussion regarding social group influences, I show you how to identify social groups and understand their influences. I also provide you with steps that you can take to locate the group leader. Knowing the group leader helps you have an even greater impact when marketing to social groups.

Finally, an interesting segment you'll find in this part of the book is on consumer misbehavior. I explain to you the different categories of misbehavior as well as give you insight on what motivates it and how to detour it from happening in your place of business.

# Chapter 8

# Cultural Influences

## In This Chapter

▶ Harnessing the power of culture on purchasing decisions

▶ Getting to the root of cultural conditioning

▶ Letting consumer culture guide your marketing strategy

**M**any factors leverage consumer behavior, including the disposition of a consumer toward a specific product. Culture is one of the most basic external influences on a consumer's needs, wants, and behavior, because all facets of life are carried out against the background of the society in which a consumer lives. Culture is the all-encompassing force that helps to form an individual's personality, which in turn is the key determinant of consumer behavior. The culture of a consumer affects her everyday behavior, and there's experiential support for the concept that culture determines what a consumer purchases and when she purchases it.

When you understand the culture of your consumers, you have a better concept of how to serve them and guide them toward purchasing your product or service. This chapter looks at the power of culture, how consumers pick it up, and what you can do with your knowledge of culture to better serve your customers.

## Defining Culture

The two basic things to understand about culture are that

> ✔ **Culture is a standard of excellence within its own society.** To partici-
> pate in a given culture, you must hold the standards of that culture in
> high regard. Individuals are held to a standard that's deemed accept-
> able, and they must follow these standards in order to uphold the beliefs
> and values of that culture. This means that when purchasing your prod-
> uct, the consumers must evaluate whether your product supports or
> opposes the beliefs and values of their culture.

✔ **Culture is a way of life.** You must live it as a way of life in which you share common experiences, a common language, and values with others in the culture. Individuals as consumers are very protective of their culture. Their culture is what forms their beliefs and values and is reflected in the way they live their lives, including purchases and consumption patterns. Culture is often as natural to consumers as breathing.

The three major parts of culture — beliefs, values, and norms — have distinct and powerful effects on consumers (see Figure 8-1), and you can tap into these elements in order to market your product in a way that's more effective and appealing to consumers:

✔ **Norms:** These are rules within a culture that designate forms of acceptable and unacceptable behavior. In short, they're the way a culture does things. Norms aren't statistical averages; they're linked with acceptable social standards of appropriate behavior within a culture. They may or may not coincide with laws and policies; for example, it's a common norm to drive 5 miles per hour over the posted speed limit.

Norms have different strengths, and the consequences for violating a norm can vary. Cultural norms often are so strongly ingrained in an individual's life that he is unaware of certain behaviors until they're contrasted with a different culture that has different norms.

✔ **Beliefs:** These are mental and verbal statements that reflect a consumer's particular knowledge and assessment of something and that affect an individual's behavior. The belief system of a culture is created through stories or myths whose interpretations can give consumers insight into how they should look, feel, think, and behave. The most prominent systems of beliefs tend to be associated with formal religion.

✔ **Values:** Values are based on the beliefs of a consumer. What a consumer believes is what he sees as valuable. Consumer values are deep-seated motivations that are instilled into the consumer from culture. The values of a culture differentiate right feelings, thoughts, and behaviors from wrong feelings, thoughts, and behaviors. An individual's set of values plays an important role in consumption activities, because in many cases, people purchase products and services that they believe will help them attain a value-related goal. Every culture has a set of values that it imparts to members.

It's important to understand the following specific characteristics of value, because values are often used to guide consumers in their purchasing behavior as well as in their consumption patterns:

- Values are few in number.

- Values are difficult to change.

- Values aren't linked to specific objects or situations.

- Values are widely accepted by members within a cultural society.

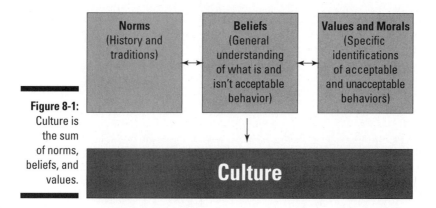

Figure 8-1:
Culture is
the sum
of norms,
beliefs, and
values.

A couple of examples of different cultures and their effects on individuals include the following:

- **American culture:** In America, consumers have a way of life that they try to uphold according to beliefs, values, and norms. What people in this culture may consider acceptable may not be seen as acceptable in other cultures.

- **Generational culture:** Each generation carries its own beliefs, values, and norms. For example, my mother's generation didn't necessarily believe the same things that my generation believes. The things that I see as acceptable probably aren't acceptable for her generation. I will experience the same generation gap as my son grows older. His generation will have different beliefs, values, and norms than my generation does.

# Breaking Culture into Subcultures

Each culture contains *subcultures,* or groups of people who share values. Subcultures can include nationalities, religious sects, racial groups, or groups of people sharing the same geographical location. Hobbies or activities can even create subcultures.

Think of a subculture as a subdivision of a national culture, based on unifying characteristics. Members of a subculture share similar behavioral patterns that are distinct from those within the national culture.

## Ethnicity or nationality

*Ethnicity,* or *nationality,* defines a group bound by similar values, customs, dress, religion, and language. You can use this information to create marketing messages that are specific to the culture you're targeting. For example, when researching an ethnic subculture that you are interested in marketing to, keep in mind that consumers strive to purchase products that support their heritage and appeal directly to the identity they associate with. I would create my marketing message in order to get the consumer's attention and gain her interest in my product.

Here's a look at examples of consumer subcultures based on ethnicity and nationality:

- **Hispanic consumers:** This subculture represents Americans of Cuban, Mexican, Central American, South American, and Puerto Rican descent. They buy approximately $425 billion in goods and services each year and have long been a target of marketing for food, beverage, and household products in the United States.

- **African American consumers:** Although this subculture has proven to be more price conscious than other segments of the American consumer population, members are strongly motivated by quality and selection. They display strong brand loyalty and do less shopping around.

- **Asian American consumers:** This segment is the fastest growing consumer subculture and the most affluent one in the U.S. The group now numbers more than 10 million and has a disposable income of $229 billion per year.

# Religion

Religion is important to people, because it provides them with a set of beliefs. Identifying subcultures based on religion allows you to create messages that identify with the beliefs and values of specific religious groups. Religion and the rules and guidelines it establishes can prevent the consumption of certain products, making it even more important to understand the subcultures you're marketing to. As with most cultures, you must be cautious not to offend or contradict the beliefs and values of those in that culture.

You can segment the market by focusing on religious affiliations, delivery, targeted messages, and promotions using certain media that will reach each segment.

Here are some examples of religious subcultures:

- **Islam:** Followers don't believe in extravagance, and they wear modest clothing. They discourage the use of alcohol, the charging of interest, and the participation in anything that offends the Koran (their holy book).

- **Jehovah's Witnesses:** Followers use conventional foods, including the modest use of alcohol. They're prohibited from celebrating birthdays, Christmas, and Easter.

- ✔ **Mormonism:** Followers participate in mainstream society within reason, but they're discouraged from using alcohol, tobacco, coffee, and caffeine. They're also discouraged from eating excessive amounts of meat. They're prohibited to gamble.

- ✔ **Fundamentalist Christianity:** Followers are encouraged to listen to various religious broadcasts, read religious books, and attend Christian schools. Alcohol is commonly prohibited, and followers are also discouraged from viewing entertainment that's inconsistent with their values.

- ✔ **Buddhism:** Followers are encouraged to fulfill their essential needs in life, but they also are taught to keep life simple and free of attachments to things. It's acceptable for Buddhists to keep replicas of religious objects, and they're discouraged from consuming meat under certain circumstances.

An understanding of these religious subcultures and others should guide you in creating marketing messages. You don't want to make a cultural faux pas in your advertising, for example, by marketing your latest hamburger to a congregation of Buddhists.

## Age or gender

Consumers undergo predictable changes in values, lifestyle, and consumption patterns as they move through their life cycles. You can identify a subculture within a culture by segmenting consumers according to age and/or gender.

When you understand the different age and gender subcultures, you can use that information to cater your marketing message and advertising to draw in their attention and gain their business.

For example, consider the four major age groups in the U.S. and the characteristics of each group:

- ✔ **Baby boomers:** Represent approximately 77 million people born in the U.S. between 1946 and 1964 who share lifestyle similarities. They're the largest and most affluent age group in history, and they have the strongest impact on the housing and car markets.

- ✔ **Generation X:** Represents a younger crowd than the baby boomers that's known for valuing religion, formal rituals, and materialism. They were born between 1965 and 1977. This group is smaller in number than the baby boomers but possesses $125 billion in discretionary income. The members of Generation X have a more negative attitude when it comes to work and getting ahead than baby boomers had at the same age.

- ✔ **Generation Y:** Represents the 72 million children of the baby boomer generation. This generation is more mixed in racial and socioeconomic terms than the baby boomers.

- ✔ **The elderly:** Represents Americans over age 55 that, by 2020, will outnumber teenagers two to one. This generation tends to process information differently from the other groups. When it comes to comprehending marketing messages and advertisements, members of this group have difficulty with fast talking. They have an easier time with written text, which is the opposite of the other age groups.

When it comes to subcultures based on gender, it's important to realize that traditional sex roles have changed and continue to change (see Chapter 9 for more). However, the specifics of these roles tend to depend on the culture. For example, the majority of women in the U.S. are in the workforce, sometimes at the cost of delaying marriage and children. However, this may not be the norm in other cultures.

# Understanding the Power of Culture

Although every individual is different, the culture that the individual grows up in and lives in shapes the person's values, beliefs, attitudes, and opinions toward people, things, and events in life.

The impact of culture is so natural and automatic that its influence on behavior is usually taken for granted. As a result, consumers often make subconscious decisions when it comes to purchases. With an understanding of the power and history of cultures, you're able to cater your marketing messages and advertisement to specific cultures, enhancing your positive effect on consumers and diminishing negative attitudes that they may carry toward your products.

## How culture affects people and their purchasing behavior

The culture of a consumer not only shapes his attitude toward products and buying decisions, but it also creates many detriments that are behind the buying behavior and consumption patterns of that consumer. Here's what I mean: Culture often causes *uncertainty avoidance* in consumers — the avoidance of products that are unknown to them or that they consider to be uncertain. Culture can also be a detriment if you aren't careful to understand the values and beliefs of the cultures you're marketing to. Some cultures can be easily offended.

The behaviors of different cultures at first may seem somewhat strange to anyone outside of the culture, but obviously they make sense to those within the culture. A consumer's needs and culture are closely linked and can create a consumer need, either directly or indirectly. Culture also can influence the satisfaction of needs and the manner in which the need is met.

Culture serves the following functions:

- ✔ It promotes social system stability and facilitates collective commitment.
- ✔ It provides individuals with a feeling of belonging and positive self-esteem.
- ✔ It helps individuals create their own identities by situating themselves in a historical itinerary shared with others.
- ✔ It helps individuals make sense of their surroundings, particularly in attempting to answer the question, "What is the meaning of life?"

In other words, culture gives individuals a road map and directions to follow during times of uncertainty. It can provide a feeling of psychological security and can contribute to a clearer understanding of why society functions as it does and how it pertains to their futures.

As you can see in the preceding list, culture meets many of the emotional needs of individuals. Because of this, individuals strive to protect the beliefs and values of their cultures, which are in turn reflected in their behavior as consumers. Here's how culture specifically impacts consumer behavior:

- ✔ It serves as the lens through which consumers view products as well as your company.
- ✔ It impacts the consumers' values, attitudes, motives, and goal-directed behavior as well as their personalities.
- ✔ It influences the overall priorities that consumers attach to different activities and products.

Culture is often expressed in material objects such as clothing, jewelry, cars, computers, and music systems. Consumers are always working to uphold the values and beliefs of their culture and not to violate the norms. Consider, for example, the generation of kids who enjoy hip-hop music. This culture influences the clothes they wear, the places they hang out, and the music they listen to. You could also look at religion and the attire that some cultures require. For example, in the Islamic religion, women are required to cover all areas of their bodies, except the front part of their face and their hands. This affects the clothes that they purchase.

Culture has a stronger impact on impulsive purchases than on planned purchases. Marketing experiments show that culture-based differences tend to show up when information is processed in a quick and spontaneous manner.

When consumers have more time to deliberate on a purchase, cultural factors tend to have less effect on the decision.

Culture changes continuously, so as a marketer you should be aware of what's happening all the time. Cultural shifts are important environmental changes that can make your marketing strategy obsolete. So, it's important to always keep your eyes and ears open for cultural shifts that can point to new products that consumers may want or to the possibility of an increase in demand for existing products. When you notice a shift, you need to change your marketing tactics in order to meet the needs of the culture.

For example, a cultural shift toward greater concern about health and fitness has created opportunities and even new industries that service consumers who want to buy

- Low-calorie food
- Health and gym memberships
- Exercise equipment
- Activity or health-related vacation packages

Another fantastic example is the increased desire for leisure time. This has resulted in an increased demand for convenience products and services, such as microwave ovens, oven-ready meals, telephone banking, and online bill pay.

## How cultural understanding increases marketing effectiveness

When you understand the basics of why consumers are affected by culture, you can take a deeper look at the components that make up culture. You then use those components to understand the different cultures. This process enables you to make your marketing more effective and appealing to the culture you've targeted.

Understanding how culture influences consumer purchasing leads you to the issue of how consumers from different cultures can behave in radically different ways and yet be completely convinced that they're right.

For example, when you consider different religious cultures, you may find one that believes you shouldn't work on Sunday while the other believes it's okay to do so. Both groups believe they're right, and the truth is that neither is wrong because the belief is held within the norms of their own culture. By understanding these cultural differences, you would know that marketing to the consumer who doesn't work on Sunday could be a waste of your marketing dollars.

Culture is the broadest of social influences that marketers and business owners have to deal with. Products and services that resonate with the priorities of a culture at any given time have a much better chance of being accepted by consumers. Here's why:

- ✔ **Consumption choices don't make sense without considering and understanding the cultural context in which they're made.** Before a consumer can make a purchase, she must validate the purchase with her culture's values and beliefs to ensure it supports and doesn't violate them.

- ✔ **Culture determines the success or failure of your specific product or service.** If your product or service offends core beliefs and values that a culture supports, your chances of selling within that culture are decreased. However, if your product supports the culture, consumers are more likely to purchase from you. The same can be said of your marketing communications.

Sometimes a subculture creates a substantial and distinctive market segment on its own. For example, in the previous section, I show you two different examples of culture: American culture and generational culture. In each of these cultures, you can segment subcultures in order to create marketing materials that appeal to the different segments. You can use age groups in each of these cultures, or you can use gender or nationality. If I specifically target my marketing message to women in the American culture that are between the ages of 30 and 35, I have the ability to speak directly to their needs based on their beliefs, values, and norms.

Marketing strategies are ineffective when they don't adapt to the specific culture that's predominant in your target market segment. Potential customers will respond to advertising messages that are congruent with their culture, rewarding you — through purchasing — for understanding their culture and tailoring your advertisements and marketing messages to them and their needs.

# Seeing Cultural Conditioning in Action and in Effect

Consumers acquire their culture through cultural conditioning. Cultural conditioning not only produces certain behaviors but also affects the values and beliefs behind those behaviors.

Culture is acquired at a very young age through

- ✔ Playing
- ✔ Schooling
- ✔ Sports participation

- ✔ Family and home life
- ✔ Media

Each of these influences plays a role in how culture is acquired and learned. It's difficult to distinguish whether one is more important than another, because the influence is really dependent on the culture itself. The different parts of culture — including beliefs, values, and norms — are often learned and processed differently as you see in the following sections.

## Conditioned behavior: Norms

Culture is present in three distinct learning forms:

- ✔ **Formal learning:** When parents teach children how to behave
- ✔ **Informal learning:** When a child imitates the behavior of others
- ✔ **Technical learning:** When a child learns from teachers and instructors

Although cultural conditioning occurs mostly in early childhood, adults continue to be conditioned as they acquire new behaviors throughout their lives.

Following are the five phases in the process of cultural conditioning. Pay attention to these phases when you're researching cultures that you want to market to; then you can see specific ways the consumers in that culture have been conditioned by that culture and how you can appeal to them with your marketing message.

1. **Observation/instruction**

   An individual is only beginning to become aware of a particular behavior or activity and hasn't tried to perform it yet. For example, in some cultures it's customary to eat with your hands rather than with utensils. In this phase, you may be observing or being instructed on how to eat with your hands, but you haven't yet tried to do it.

2. **Imitation**

   An individual tries to carry out the behavior or activity being learned. For example, you sit down and begin to imitate those within the culture by eating with your hands, no matter how awkward the activity.

3. **Reinforcement**

   An individual is encouraged by those within the culture to continue the cultural norm. For example, you receive encouragement to continue trying to eat with your hands.

4. **Internalization**

An individual begins to internalize the cultural norm, leading it to feel like a natural behavior or activity. For example, it begins to feel natural to eat with your hands rather than use utensils.

5. **Spontaneous manifestation**

An individual is no longer conscious of performing the behavior or activity and does it without paying attention because it's not strange or unusual. For example, you're no longer conscious of the fact that you're eating with your hands and don't notice the absence of utensils.

## Conditioned beliefs and values

Three basic organizations transmit culture values; if you understand the influence these organizations have and have had on the consumers in your target market, you can use those organizations to assist you in speaking directly to those consumers in a way that they will understand and relate to. The three organizations are

- ✔ **Family:** The family is the first to instill a child's belief system, attitudes, and values. It also teaches the language of the culture, and language is the fundamental facet of culture because it binds members of the culture together through basic communication. The family is the primary agent for teaching consumer-related values and skills that are in line with cultural teachings.

- ✔ **Religious organizations:** Religious organizations are responsible for reinforcing the belief systems that a family instills in a child. A child who grows up within a religious organization is continually taught the values and belief systems of the culture. Religious organizations continue to nurture cultural values throughout the life of an individual, providing religious consciousness, spiritual guidance, and moral training.

- ✔ **Educational institutions:** Within a culture, educational institutions work to instill skills, ideas, attitudes, and training in particular disciplines that fit into the cultural setting. Charged with imparting basic learning skills, history, patriotism, citizenship, and technical training, educational institutions transmit cultural norms and values to each new generation.

# Applying Cultural Perspective to Your Marketing Strategy

It's important to realize the impact that culture has on how you market to consumers in different cultures. Consumers uphold the beliefs, values, and norms of their cultures. This affects what they buy, how they buy it, and often who they buy it from. When consumers go to purchase an item, they take the information about that product or your marketing message and subconsciously compare it to the values and beliefs of their cultures. This comparison happens immediately.

# Identifying common cultural factors among your consumers

When marketing to a specific culture, you want to be sure that you have all aspects of that culture in mind. This means looking at how the culture affects the members' lifestyles, the way they talk, and even the rituals they participate in. As I mention earlier, you can do more damage than good by marketing to a culture that you aren't familiar with. So you must take extra steps to make sure that your message isn't only pertinent to your consumer, but that it supports their beliefs and values as well. You need to take some time to gather more information in order to successfully market to a culture segment.

### Where and how to gather the info needed

A culture's values are the fundamental force that drives markets. Look at indications of how people within a specific culture want to live and how they express that desire in the marketplace.

When evaluating specific cultures and working to market to those cultures, ask yourself the following questions:

- ✔ Why are customers doing what they're doing?
- ✔ Who are the customers?
- ✔ When do customers purchase your products?
- ✔ How and where can the media reach customers?
- ✔ What's new on the product front that you can present to customers?

When you're evaluating the values within a culture, it's important to understand why consumers behave a specific way. The reasons behind behaviors and actions can predict the products consumers will use. They also can predict the marketing channel that will be most effective in reaching that culture.

You can find out these reasons by doing some fieldwork. Chapter 12 instructs you in market research, but here are my top suggestions:

- ✔ Monitor a small sampling of consumers in their natural environments. Focus on their behavior and find the answers to the preceding questions. However, remember that it's important that consumers aren't aware that you're monitoring them.
- ✔ Use focus groups and interviews.

## What to look for

It's important to understand how the culture you're trying to reach communicates through language, symbols, and rituals. This way you can communicate with them in a way that they understand.

- ✔ **Language:** Consumers use language as an expression of culture. The language of a culture creates a shared meaning. As a marketer, you should focus not necessarily on what is said but rather on how it's said. For example, you don't want to use words that have a different meaning in one culture than they do in yours. You also don't want to communicate in a way that's considered offensive to those that you're marketing to.

- ✔ **Symbols:** Cultures use symbols to communicate ideas, emotions, and thoughts. Keep in mind that your brand also can be seen as a symbol. Different types of symbols include numbers, colors, gestures, animate objects, and inanimate objects.

- ✔ **Rituals:** Rituals are symbolic activities that consist of a series of steps occurring in a fixed sequence and repeated over time. Cultures use them to uphold their beliefs and values in ceremonial ways. Rituals can be both public and private and are often formal and scripted. Examples of different types of rituals include

  - Religious rituals, such as baptism, meditation, and religious services

  - Rites of passage, such as graduation and marriage

  - Cultural rituals, such as festivals and holidays

  - Civic rituals, such as parades, elections, and trials

  - Family rituals, such as mealtimes and birthdays

  - Personal rituals, such as personal grooming and housekeeping.

You can use language, symbols, and rituals to gain a better understanding of how specific cultures communicate and behave. This information can then be used to communicate with them and market to them in a way that they will understand and be receptive to.

# Appealing to your target audience's cultural background

Consumers are overloaded with advertising and marketing messages each day, so it takes something personally appealing to get their attention on you and your product. When you can appeal to a consumer's cultural background and support his values and beliefs, he takes an interest in what you have to say. In fact, consumers will go out of their way to support businesses that support them, their culture, and the things that they hold dear. To gain this attention, use messages that consumers can relate to and images that reflect their cultural heritage.

For example, suppose you're trying to appeal to the Hispanic market, but you don't speak the language of that culture or understand what they value and believe in. How do you market to this group in a way that the members understand? You can appeal to this market by constructing a radio spot that broadcasts on a Spanish-speaking radio station or creating television commercials to air on a Spanish-speaking television station. You also could put an ad in a magazine that's specifically geared toward Hispanic culture.

The key is this: Before you do any of these things, it's your job and duty to gain the information necessary to understand a consumer's culture. It's a mistake to think you can enter into any culture and market to them without researching first.

# Chapter 9

# The Influences of Household Structure and Role

. . . . . . . . . . . . . . . . . . . . . . . . . . . . . . . . . . . . . . . . . . . . . . . . . .

## In This Chapter

▶ Examining home life, including household structures and roles

▶ Taking a look at traditional and nontraditional households

▶ Using household information to market successfully

. . . . . . . . . . . . . . . . . . . . . . . . . . . . . . . . . . . . . . . . . . . . . . . . . .

*P*eople grow and develop as individuals and as consumers. Over the course of a lifetime a family will go through many stages of development, and with each stage comes an entirely new set of consumer developments. So you must determine the marketing campaigns that will work best not only in targeting the family, but in specifically targeting the structure that the family has.

## Looking at Home Life

In today's society, we have traditional households as well as nontraditional households, so instead of using the older term *family life cycle,* we now use the more modern term *household structure.* Household structure represents the number of people living in a home, the ages of those occupants, and the household income. Household structure is important because it affects the consumption and purchasing patterns of those living in the home. It also has an effect on the roles that individuals in the household play. These roles are used in the decision-making process.

### A primer on household structures

The term *family* can be defined many different ways. So in order to take full advantage of marketing directly to families, it's important to understand the different structures that they can have. Consider the following terms:

- ✔ **Family:** A group of two or more people related by blood, marriage, or adoption who reside in the same home

- ✔ **Nuclear family:** The immediate group consisting of a father, mother, and a child or children that live together

- ✔ **Extended family:** The nuclear family plus other relatives, such as grandparents, uncles and aunts, cousins, and parents-in-law

- ✔ **Family of orientation:** The family into which a person is born

- ✔ **Family of procreation:** The family that's established by marriage

As you study households, you may also notice that some include pets as important parts of the family. So, when I speak of families, I'm not only talking about a family in a traditional sense. Instead, I'm referring to the representation of families in many walks of a consumer's life.

Different households have different needs, so by understanding the different categories of households, you can create effective marketing messages that appeal to the different categories. Households are grouped into the following two categories:

- ✔ **Family households:** The *family household* represents groups or persons that are related by blood or marriage. The following four types of family households are the most common:

  • Married couple that lives alone

  • Married couple with children

  • Single parent with children

  • Extended family, which may include parents, children's spouses, grandchildren, and occasionally cousins

- ✔ **Nonfamily households:** The *nonfamily household* is a household that consists of nonfamily members. Nonfamily households include the following:

  • A single person living alone in a dwelling unit

  • Roommates living together

  • Persons living in boarding houses

  • Elderly persons living with nonfamily members

  • Persons of the opposite sex sharing living quarters

  • Same-sex couples

Family households are most common, but recently there has been a rapid rise in the number of nonfamily households. This means that it isn't enough to just market to the traditional households. You must also look to see how your products can fill the needs of the nontraditional households by creating marketing messages that they can relate to.

# Defining an individual's household role

Household decision making is much different than individual decision making. That's because you have input from more people. Individual household members often serve different roles in decisions that ultimately draw on shared family resources. Just like you have roles in the household, you also have roles when it comes to the decision-making process for the household. Each role is important in the family decision-making process. These household roles include the following:

- **Influencer:** The person in this role is responsible for influencing the purchase decision. This person doesn't necessarily have the power to make the ultimate decision between alternatives, but he makes his wishes known by asking for specific products or acting out if the demands aren't met. Example: The child who screams throughout the discount store because he wants a particular color bicycle.

- **Gatekeeper:** The person in this role is responsible for controlling the flow of information to the other family members. Example: The mother updates everyone on the purchase information and decision as well as when the purchase will be completed.

- **Decider:** The person in this role is the family member who makes the final decision regarding the purchase. The decider evaluates whether to buy, which product to buy, which brand to buy, where to buy it, and when to buy it. Ultimately this person has the power of decision over each of these issues. Example: The father who decides which bicycle to purchase after reviewing the features and costs of two different bicycles.

- **Buyer:** The person in this role is responsible for engaging in the actual transaction or purchase. Example: The mother who goes to the discount store to purchase the desired bicycle.

- **Preparer:** The person in this role is responsible for preparing the goods for use. Example: The dad who puts the bicycle together so the child can ride it.

- **User:** The person in this role is responsible for using the product that has been purchased. Example: The child who rides the bicycle.

- **Maintainer:** The person in this role is responsible for maintaining the purchased product. Example: The child who puts air in the tires of the bicycle or cleans it after running it through mud puddles.

- **Disposer:** The person in this role chooses when and how to dispose of the product. Example: The dad who's cleaning out the garage and realizes that the child has finally outgrown the bicycle. He may choose to put the bike in the trash, or he may donate it.

It isn't uncommon for family or household members to play multiple roles in the decision-making process. And these roles can also often break tradition. For instance, dad isn't always the decider. Mom and child can also play the role of the decider.

## Recognizing how household structure and role affect purchasing behavior

It's important to realize that consumer purchase patterns can be determined by the household structure. Various stages in family life — that is, the household structure at a given time — result in different buying patterns. At each stage, the person plays a different household role and buys symbols of that particular role at that time. For example, when a couple marries in a traditional household, the man buys the woman a ring. Then when the couple has a baby, they buy furniture to prepare for the new addition.

Household roles also play a part in consumption patterns and buying habits. For example, it's the role of the decision maker to decide to buy, what product to buy, what brand to select, when to buy, and where to buy it from. Figure 9-1 shows how all the factors fit together.

### Factors that affect a household's purchasing behavior

Consumption factors within the family are determined by the following:

- **Number of people within the family:** This factor affects consumption because with more people in the family, the more products you need to care for the family.

- **Ages of the family members:** This factor affects consumption because it determines what types of items you need. If you have infants, you will need diapers, baby formula, and other items. If the family members are older, you may need other types of products to care for the family.

- **Number of employed adults:** The main reason this factor affects consumption is because it affects income. The more income a family makes, the more they're likely to spend.

### Variables that change the household structure

Five structural variables can change the household structure. The five variables include

- Age of head of household or family
- Marital status
- Employment status
- Disposable income
- Discretionary income
- Presence or absence of children

Children dramatically change how the family functions in terms of relationships, employment, and purchases. For example, children often reduce parents' participation in the labor force. This change alone affects how families spend money, and it reduces the amount of time and money available to the family for leisure activities.

You may be shocked to know that children influence approximately $1.88 trillion dollars in purchases globally each year. You may wonder how these little tykes can do this. Here's how: Children exert direct influence over parents when they request specific products and brands. They also can exert indirect influence when parents buy products and brands that they know their children prefer without being asked or told to make a specific purchase.

Parents aren't the only ones making purchases; children also make their own purchases with family money or with their own money. Children like to shop for toys, candy, clothing, school supplies, and other personal items. Retailers spend exorbitant amounts of money to adapt specific departments to these young, but significant consumers.

## Understanding how you can market to the many household influences

Common household structures and roles help explain how families change over time. You can use them to identify core target markets and use that data to modify your marketing message. These influences are great predictors of family and household spending.

When you understand the common household structures a family can have, you can better understand the products that consumers use as the structure changes. You can find information through market research that shows you what interests and motivates them and what kind of financial status the average person has. Doing so helps you create a marketing message that's appealing and enticing to them. You also can use the household variables to monitor, measure, and predict changes in demand for specific product categories.

Household structure serves as a more accurate tool than chronological age because there are significant differences in consumer spending habits. Differences include consumption patterns, the amount of money spent, the products purchased, and the products that are of interest to the consumer.

The decision-making process within families is crucial to your business. When you understand the structure and lifestyle of the household you advertise in, you can cater your message to meet its needs. This increases your chance of drawing the household into your business, purchasing your products, and using your services. If you aren't catering your advertising in this way, you're missing what could potentially be a large market.

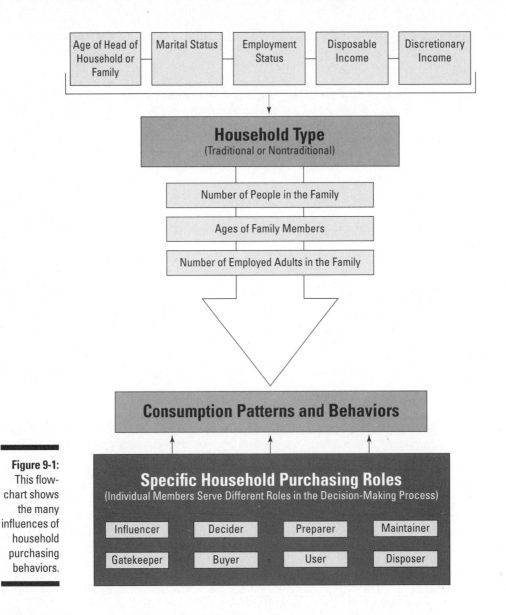

# Examining Traditional Household Stages and Their Buying Influences

Every household goes through stages over time. During these stages, the household's basic structure changes. Nine primary stages have been identified, but not all households go through all the stages. The number of stages that a family goes through depends in part on the family's lifestyle choices. In the following sections, I show you the different stages within the traditional family household structure.

The term *traditional family* has been used since the 1950s when TV shows portrayed the ideal family as a husband who was the breadwinner and the wife who stayed home to take care of the two children who were under the age of 18.

In this section, *traditional* refers to a husband and a wife that have children. The reason it's important to distinguish between traditional and nontraditional families is that it plays a large part in how you market your products.

Market research shows that in today's world of families, less that 6 percent of American families fit into the traditional role. You want to be able to distinguish between the two so that neither the traditional nor nontraditional household takes offense to your marketing message. For example, if you have a commercial that appeals to the wives that do stay home and take care of their children, are you losing the other 74 percent that don't?

It's possible for individuals to repeat family stages if their family situations change, or if they find themselves in stages that are different from most people their own age.

## Young singles

The young singles stage is often referred to as the *bachelor stage.* It's representative of both male and female individuals. In this stage, the consumers don't live at home with their parents; they have branched out on their own.

Young singles are new in their careers and usually have the income level of an entry-level employee. They have few financial burdens. They lead the fashion world with their opinions, and they're recreation oriented. They tend to spend money on basic kitchen equipment, furniture, entertainment, vacations, dating, and clothing.

## Newly married couples

Newly married couples are typically young with no children. They typically have two incomes, and they tend to be better off financially than they are in later stages. They're present and future oriented.

Newly married couples have the highest overall purchase rate and the highest rate of purchasing *durable products,* which are products that are purchased infrequently, such as appliances, furniture, and consumer electronics. They buy automobiles, refrigerators, stoves, and sensible and durable furniture. Like young singles, they still spend money on entertainment, and they like to spend money on vacations.

# Full nest 1

The consumers in the full nest I stage are married, and their youngest child is under the age of 6. They have one to one and half income sources. Home purchases peak in this stage. These consumers have low liquid assets, and they're future oriented.

In this stage, most consumers are dissatisfied with their finances. They're interested in newly advertised products, and they buy washers, dryers, televisions, baby food, vitamins, and children's toys.

# Full nest 11

In the full nest II stage, consumers are married, and their youngest child is 6 years or older but still dependent on them. They're in a better financial position than they were in the previous stage, and they're future oriented.

These consumers have one to two sources of income. One of the spouses is established in a career at this stage. The other spouse may work or may stay home to take care of the children. The consumers in this group are less influenced by advertising. They buy larger automobiles, larger cars, a variety of foods, bicycles, and music lessons. They enjoy luxury and comfort. They tend to put more money in savings than in other stages.

# Full nest 111

The married couple in the full nest III stage is typically older with older dependent children who are typically in their teenage years. These consumers are still in a better financial position and are considering retirement.

More income is available because many times both spouses and even the children have jobs. Advertising has even less of an influence at this stage. Couples in this stage have a high average rate of purchasing durable products, buy more tasteful furniture, travel more by car, and purchase nonessentials like appliances, boats, dental services, and magazines. They enjoy comfort and luxury.

# Empty nest 1

The empty nest I stage represents an older married couple with no children living at home with them. The head of the household is still in the labor force. Home ownership is at its peak. Some of the couples have even purchased the homes they will retire in. These consumers have a good income and are satisfied with their finances. They're considering retirement.

Consumers in this stage have an interest in travel, recreation, and self-education. They make gifts and contributions to charities and organizations that they support. They buy vacations, luxuries, and home improvements.

# Empty nest 11

The consumers who are in the empty nest II stage are usually older married couples with no children at home. The head of the household has retired, and so they've experienced a drastic income cut. They're present oriented.

The consumers in this group tend to keep their homes. They enjoy travel, recreation, and sometimes a new home to better suit their lifestyle. They buy medical appliances and medical-care products that aid their health, sleep, and digestion. Their interest is comfort at a fair price.

# Solitary survivor

In this stage, one spouse is still alive, and the other is deceased. The living spouse is typically employed. That spouse has a good income and is present oriented.

Solitary survivors enjoy their jobs and friends. They like to travel, buy clothing, enjoy recreation, and spend money to take care of their health. They're likely to sell their homes in order to find new homes that better suit their lifestyles.

# Retired solitary survivor

In the retired solitary survivor stage, one spouse is still alive, and that spouse has retired. The spouse has a low source of income due to a drastic income cut.

Retired solitary survivors enjoy traveling, social activity, and recreation. They have special needs for medical products, attentions, affection, and security. They have concern for their security and the economy.

# Familiarizing Yourself with Common Stage Variations

The stages I introduce you to in the previous sections represent the traditional stages. But you have to keep in mind that our society has changed, causing variations within today's families and households. In order to incorporate the variations into your marketing strategy, you have to expand your view of the household stages.

Certain stages don't necessarily fit into the traditional stages. For example, consider single parents, married couples with no children, and older singles. These consumers represent a large percentage of our society today. So when you leave one of them out of your marketing mix, you're missing a selling opportunity. So be sure to create messages that appeal to the market you're specifically targeting. Sometimes this may mean having more than one marketing message.

In the following sections, I give you an in-depth look at the recent trends and how they're affecting household structures and gender roles.

## Exploring the changes and trends

In today's society, households are changing. A larger market share is continually growing outside of the traditional household structure. You have to evaluate the changes in order to understand how they can and do affect your marketing strategy. These changes affect the various stages of the consumer decision-making process and can provide more marketing opportunities if you better understand them. I introduce some of the more recent trends in the following sections.

### Trends in marriage

Many consumers today are delaying the age at which they get married. So you'll see more consumers cohabitating rather than saying "I do." The unfortunate truth is that in today's society more than 50 percent of marriages end in divorce, so it isn't uncommon for consumers to shift between married and single status. These shifts change consumption patterns and spending habits. The changes have been so significant that often divorce is called the "new marriage." These trends are changing the spending habits on household products, homes, therapy, travel, and more.

### Trend in singles

In recent years our society has seen an increase in single households. Singles that are cohabitating with other singles is the fastest-growing segment of the singles market. It isn't just younger singles either. The mature singles population is growing as well. The median age of singles is 66 and most of them are women. These women make up 61 percent of the singles market in the United States. The majority of these women are widowed. The facts are different when it comes to single men. The men are usually divorced or have just never married.

If you haven't tapped into this market share you could be missing out on a large opportunity. This market is most often targeted with travel, financial services, entertainment, and social recreation.

### Trends in the gay and lesbian population

The increased gay and lesbian population is a prime example of why you can no longer depend on the traditional household structures when it comes to your marketing. Many companies are now targeting the gay community, and they're finding that there's money to be made from this consumer group. A recent study by public relations and marketing firm Witeck-Combs reported that by the year 2011, the buying power of this consumer group will be more than $800 billion in the United States alone.

The key is to understand how you can reach this market. You'll have more success reaching this market by creating market activities that build relationships with the members of the group. Marketers have found success in sponsoring gay-oriented events and creating advertising that specifically targets the gay consumer group.

---

## Considering trends in gift giving

It's important to consider rituals within a family structure. Consider, for example, gift giving. Gift giving occurs through family traditions, rituals, and celebrations. When you're familiar with the gift-giving seasons, you can gear up and market your products heavily during that time to increase sales. Take, for example, Christmas. Many people purchase gifts around this time. If your product isn't out there or you aren't marketing during that time, you could lose out on a great deal of market share.

Gift giving and the celebration of holidays within families are increasing in importance. You can tell this by the number of holiday employees that stores hire to accommodate consumers as well as the increased rate of travel during the holidays. In fact, traditional holiday spending and promotions have shifted to other holidays throughout the year, and more retailers are marketing on other holidays throughout the year rather than just during Christmas. Physical movement of large gifts has become difficult, which has lead to an increase of gift certificates, gift cards, and Internet gift purchases.

To take advantage of the gift-giving seasons, create a holiday marketing calendar and use specific holiday marketing techniques to attract consumers to do their holiday shopping with you. You also can market by reminding consumers of holidays coming up that they may forgotten. Think of all the husbands that purchase a Saint Valentine's Day gift because a promotional marketing piece reminded them that the holiday was coming up.

# Identifying new structures that have emerged

Our society is changing. What we used to consider abnormal is now considered normal. We've seen the acceptance of couples that live together but don't marry. We've seen the couples that decide they don't want to have children. We've also witnessed the rise of gay and lesbian couples as well as individuals that decide to live alone by choice. Changes will continue to happen in our society that will reflect in the acceptable and changing lifestyle structure. By continually being aware of the new trends within household structures, you can understand how they're affecting the current marketplace.

Nonfamily households and the trends within the household structure that I explain earlier in the chapter are expected to grow more rapidly than traditional families over the next two decades. However, with that in mind, remember that the highest incomes today are still within the traditional family households.

The following sections explore the newest structures that have emerged as a result of recent trends.

## Single parents

Single parenthood can result from either divorce or from the death of a spouse. Divorce usually entails a significant change in the relative wealth of each spouse. In some cases, the noncustodial parent may not pay the required child support. Even if the child support is paid, however, the custodial parent and children still may not be as well off as they were during the marriage. On the flip side of that situation is the situation where the noncustodial parent is called to pay a large portion of her income as child support. This situation is particularly problematic when the noncustodial parent remarries and has additional children in the subsequent marriage.

Single parenthood generally results in the purchase of low-cost furniture and household items. However, the purchases increase when it comes to time-saving goods and services. If you're marketing to single parents, keep this in mind and make special note of how your products fit into the lives of single parents. Do you have low-cost solutions that you can market directly to them? Do you have a service that can enhance and make their lives a little easier at an affordable price? Really think about how your product benefits single parents, and then market those benefits directly to them.

## Married couple with no children

It's common in today's society for a married couple to decide that they don't want to have children. This decision may be a personal choice or may come as a result of complications in having children.

In this household structure, the couple bypasses the full nest cycles (shown in the earlier section "Examining Traditional Household Stages and Their Buying Influences") and moves forward in the solitary phases. The couple's priorities are different than they would be if they had children. They tend to spend more money on luxury and comfort. They also travel more and enjoy more leisure activities. They're able to save more and spend more on the finer things in life. They're focused on the future, but enjoying the present. This couple is generally supported by two income sources, because they're typically both established in their careers.

### Older singles

A person settles into this structure either because of the death of a spouse or the desire to never marry. This group doesn't fit easily into any of the other household structures, so it's rarely the focus of marketing or advertising messages. And rarely will you find market research on this growing demographic.

This doesn't mean they can't be reached, however. It's actually a market that isn't acknowledged and that is somewhat untapped. So determine how your products fit into the lifestyle of older singles. If you believe your products offer this group a benefit, sit down and clarify those benefits and put your marketing message out there to them. I think you'll be surprised at the results, because they, too, are consumers.

In the past, this group has been known to have low levels of income and not much wealth. However, times are changing and the status of being an older single has become even more common in today's society.

## Seeing how the trends affect gender roles

In today's society, the old stereotypes surrounding the gender roles in a household are no longer one-size-fits-all. The roles that each gender fills are diversified and sometimes even unique. Some would even say their gender roles have become more balanced over time.

Obviously the importance of masculinity and femininity isn't going away any time soon, but as a society we've become comfortable with roles that are less centered on what sex we are and centered more on our lifestyle and household structure.

When you market your products, you need to know who you're marketing to in order to give consumers a message that grabs their attention and entices them to purchase from you. Keep in mind that sometimes focusing more on the lifestyle of your targeted consumers produces better results.

### The changing roles of women

The number of female consumers now outweighs the number of male consumers. This imbalance is mostly due to the fact that women tend to outlive men. Also, over the years, women have improved their purchasing abilities and have established a greater importance within the workplace. In fact, the employment of women has increased and is continuing to increase around the world. It has increased household incomes and family buying power, but it has also increased family expenditures. Families are spending more money on child care, clothing, dining out, and gasoline.

These changes have had an effect on women and the amount of time they have for leisure activities. As their roles outside of the home increase, their leisure time decreases. In turn, their interest and desire for time-saving products, such as eating out, has increased as well. The demands outside of the home have put a greater demand on the women, so they're often unable to perform the tasks women once did when they traditionally worked only within the home. As women find themselves contributing more to the family income, they're expecting in return that other household members pitch in and assist with the household responsibilities.

How do you reach women now that they have gone through this metamorphic change? Well, women are still sensitive to the marketing messages and advertisements that appeal to the "mother" category. However, keep in mind that different segments exist within the demographic of women — even more so than in the past — so you must create your marketing messages and advertisements specifically for the different segments. Each segment looks at advertising, the Internet, products, time, and brands differently. (Refer to Chapter 13 for more information on how to identify key segments within your market.)

As you can see, women face different challenges today than they did in previous years. So depending on the career orientation and responsibilities in and out of the home, time pressure, and society pressures, you need to adapt your ads in order to reach women and grab their attention. For example, a retail shop may advertise special services, such as a personal shopper, or may extend its hours in order to accommodate a woman's work schedule.

Marketing to women isn't a difficult task, but to be successful at it, you must identify the needs that your product provides a solution to and then create that message in a way that will appeal to them directly.

### The changing roles of men

Today the roles of men are changing. They're becoming more involved in family activities, social functions, and household duties. In fact, today men often go to the store to purchase products for the family.

Men are also experiencing a gender role transcendence and are beginning to use products previously seen as feminine and only used by women. This explains the "retro," "uber," and "metro" descriptions recently created for men. For example, companies now frequently use the following terms as marketing tools:

- **Metrosexual:** This term is used to encourage men to take an interest in their personal appearance. This tactic has had great success, and the market of personal-care products is a great example. The increased attention to their personal appearance has had a positive effect on markets such as men's clothing, accessories, and toiletries.

- **Ubersexual:** This term indicates that the male is still macho but also in touch with his feminine side.

- **Retrosexual:** This term has been used to refer to men who reject metrosexuality and prefer to stay with the old-school style. They can be distinguished by their classical masculine identity.

As a society, we have caused a major shift in the perceptions of men, and because of that we have created different market shares for the changing roles.

It's also becoming increasingly common for men to stay at home with the children while the woman focuses on her career. Similarly, our society has seen an increase in single dads having custodial care of their children when marriages end in divorce.

An increase in the number of males with the caregiver role has had implications in terms of widening the range of products that men regard as acceptable. Consider, for example, the commercials that now show men making dinner. Also present is a shift in the number of household products and children's products that target their market messages to the male market. I'm sure you've also seen commercials in which the father is changing a baby's diapers or giving a child a bath.

# Targeting Your Marketing to Specific Household Types and Roles

When you understand the common household structures and stages and keep on top of the current trends, you can use the information to create your marketing strategy and advertising messages. In other words, you need to define your product as it relates to each household structure and stage, and then you can create a marketing or advertising message to reach out to each.

I've talked about the household structure both from a traditional and nontraditional perspective. I've also spent some time on the different role changes that are occurring for consumers. You must take all these things into account when marketing to consumers. When you make your message more appealing to the market you're targeting, you can entice them to buy and use your products. If you don't do this, you could be missing out on gaining a larger market share. Marketing messages also must be sensitive to the consumer and their needs in order to be effective.

In this section, I show you how to take the information you've gained and create a marketing message that not only gets the attention of consumers that you're targeting, but increases your sales by doing so.

## Assessing your consumers' household income

Knowing the income of your consumers helps to ensure that you're actually marketing to people that have the means to buy your product. For example, if you're selling a car that's $75,000, you don't want to market it to a single parent who's only making $12,000 per year. You can also use this information to gauge the lifestyle of the consumers you're interested in. Refer to Chapter 7 for more information on the lifestyle of consumers.

Three types of income exist:

- **Disposable income:** This is the take-home pay of the consumer. It's the income the consumer brings home after deductions for taxes, social security, and insurance are taken out.

- **Real income:** This is the consumer purchasing power. It's the income after adjusting for inflation.

- **Discretionary income:** This is the consumer's disposable income that's left over after regular commitments, such as mortgage or rent and payment of utilities, are deducted.

It's important to recognize the difference in income so you gain a true picture of the consumer's spendable income.

## Factoring in family dynamics and disagreements

Every consumer goes through a decision-making process, and household structure plays an important part in this process. Because you're more than likely dealing with more than one consumer that has input into the decision-making process, you may find that the process is more difficult. You may even encounter conflict. When you understand the process, you can step in and help guide the consumers by answering questions, reassuring, and guiding them into the purchase.

When families are making decisions, they come to one of two conclusions:

- **Agreement:** This conclusion, which is called the *consensual decision,* is where the family agrees on the purchase and the only thing that may differ among family members is how the purchase will be achieved. They may not yet have a decision on the terms of the purchase or on the purchase place.

  A great example of a consensual decision within the family is the purchase of a pet. All family members have decided that they want to add a dog to the family, but they may not know where to get Rover or what kind of dog he will be.

- **Disagreement:** This conclusion, the *accommodative decision,* is where family members may have different preferences and can't agree on a purchase that will satisfy everyone within the family.

  Take, for example, the purchase of a movie. Children in the family may want to purchase a cartoon; dad may want a suspense movie; and mom prefers a drama flick. Not everyone in this situation will be satisfied, so the decision will accommodate only one or some of the family members.

Family decisions in particular are often subject to a great deal of conflict. Conflict occurs where there isn't a clear understanding of the needs and preferences of each family member. However, by understanding the two types of conflict, you can position yourself to solve these conflicts. The conflict is caused by either logical or social factors. You can use your knowledge of the degree of conflict to help in the resolution. Involve all family members in the process. And remember that in order to be successful in helping in the decision-making process, you must be able to identify the roles of each family member and understand the conflicts each may be encountering. By understanding and being able to identify the level of conflict, you can step in and address the family's concerns and needs.

### Logistical factors

Specific factors dealing with logistics determine the degree of conflict in the decision-making process. These factors include the following:

- **Interpersonal need:** This factor deals with a family or household member's level of investment within the group. Conflict can arise when members of the family have different levels of participation in the investment.

- **Product involvement and utility:** This factor pertains to the degree to which the product in question will be used or how successful it will be in satisfying a need. Consider, for example, when a family purchases a washer and dryer. Conflict can come up because perhaps the person responsible for doing the laundry feels as if he should have more say in the purchase because he will be the one using the washer and dryer the most.

✔ **Responsibility:** This factor refers to the person responsible for procurement, maintenance, and payment of the purchase. Consider the purchase of a car. Conflict may come up when there isn't an agreement on who will take responsibility for that car.

✔ **Power:** This factor represents the power that one family member may have over the others in making a decision. For example, a parent may express power over the children by making a decision and saying to them "because I said so."

### Social factors

Certain social factors affect families and households as well. These factors deal with the way the members of the family socialize and relate with one another. Consider the following:

✔ **Cohesion:** This factor refers to the emotional bonding between family members. Conflict can come up when a family member feels that she isn't being heard or that her opinion is being overlooked because she isn't as close to a family member as another member is.

✔ **Adaptability:** This factor pertains to the ability of a family to change its power structure, role relationships, and relationship rules in response to situational and developmental stress. Conflict can arise when new members enter the family structure and the other family members can't adapt to the change.

✔ **Communication:** This factor pertains to the ability that a family has to communicate, specifically regarding communication about a purchase. Conflict can happen when not all family members feel like they're being equally communicated with about a purchase.

## Dealing with interests and responsibilities

All consumers have different interests and responsibilities that they have to take care of. When marketing to consumers, take into consideration what they're interested in and what their responsibilities are. For example, if you're dealing with a father who's interested in golf, perhaps you want to market a family golf trip to him. If your consumer is a mother who works outside of the home and has three children, you probably want to take into account the workload that she carries and how your product can help her in feeling less tired and stressed.

As you know, consumers see hundreds of marketing messages daily, so you need to stand out from the crowd. Use the interests and responsibilities of the consumers to attract them to your product by appealing to those components in your message. Doing so helps them feel as if you have a genuine interest in their needs and are willing to help. It also makes them feel like you have really taken the time to find out more about them before releasing another marketing message.

# Chapter 10

# The Power of the Masses: Group Influences

*In This Chapter*

▶ Understanding the different types of groups

▶ Exploring consumers' reactions to groups

▶ Increase your marketing effectiveness to groups

*I*ndividuals identify with groups to the extent that they can take on the values, attitudes, and behaviors of a particular group. Consumers who belong to different groups often have similar tastes, traditions, likes, and dislikes of others within the group.

In this chapter, I take you through an in-depth look at the different types of groups that typically affect consumer behavior, how they impact it, and how you can adapt your marketing strategies to target particular groups of like-minded people. I also delve into the psychology behind the formation of those groups, as well as their communal behavior, so you can better understand the folks you're targeting with your marketing efforts.

## Getting a Glimpse of the Strength in Numbers

Consumers are social creatures who want contact with others. As a result, consumers often belong to a number of formal and informal groups. A *group* represents two or more individuals who share a set of norms, values, or beliefs. The group members have certain relationships that make their behavior interdependent. A group also has a collective identity; the members interact with one another, and they have a shared goal or interest.

When it comes to marketing, groups are referred to as *reference groups* because they provide consumers with a point of reference. This reference point explains a consumer's behavior. An individual uses the reference group's perspective or values as the basis for his behavior. The reference group provides an individual with a point of comparison for personal attitudes, behaviors, and performance. Major consumer reference groups include family, friends, social class, selected subculture, one's own culture, and other cultures.

In the following sections, I identify three categories of groups, explain how consumers behave in response to groups, and reveal the marketing opportunities that groups offer you.

## Recognizing the major types of groups

There are three types of groups, which can be broken down into more specific groups. Knowing what types of groups a consumer belongs to can tell you how much influence the groups have in a consumer's lifestyle and over the consumer's decisions. The types of groups include

- ✔ **Primary groups:** These groups are intimate, face-to face groups, such as family or peer groups. Family and peer groups are considered *informal groups* within the primary group category. *Formal groups* are highly defined in their structure, and they tend to interact less frequently. School groups, business groups, or work groups are examples of formal groups within the primary category. Examples of primary groups include the following:

  - **Peer group:** This is a group of individuals who share the same age, social status, and sometimes interests. In this group, individuals are relatively equal in terms of power when they interact with each other.

  - **Clique:** You can usually find these informal, tightknit groups in high school or college settings. The members seem to share common interests. This group establishes power among its members, but it can shift.

  - **Household:** This group represents all individuals who live together. This category can include traditional families, blended families, roommates, or people living in group homes.

- ✔ **Secondary groups:** These are groups that are seen less frequently; they're considered more impersonal than primary groups because they interact only occasionally. Examples include shopping groups, sports groups, alumni organizations, and technical associations. Here are some examples of secondary groups:

  - **Club:** A club can be dedicated to a particular activity, such as a car club or sports club. You usually have to apply to become a member.

- **Community:** This group represents individuals that develop a relationship based on a shared interest. They often have group leaders and a well-organized structure.

- **Gang:** A gang is usually an urban group that gathers in a particular area. They are similar to clubs, but they tend to be less formal.

- **Mob:** This is a group of individuals who have taken the law into their own hands. They usually gather temporarily for a particular reason.

- **Squad:** This is a small group, usually comprised of three to eight people. They work as a team to accomplish a shared goal.

- **Team:** This group is similar to a squad, but is typically made up of more people. The members work together to accomplish shared goals.

✔ **Symbolic groups:** These are groups that you never join, but you try to take on their values. Your favorite football team, basketball team, or baseball team would be considered symbolic groups.

By understanding the different types of groups and the extent of the influences they have on consumers, you can better understand your consumers.

## Seeing how groups influence consumer behavior

Groups carry significant weight when it comes to the influence they have on consumers. Consumers often believe that others hold a great deal of power over their own behavior. Because of this belief, social power can greatly influence the types of products that consumers buy, the attitudes they hold, and the activities they choose to participate in.

Groups influence consumers and buying patterns in two ways:

✔ **Individual decisions:** Groups can affect an individual's buying habits and purchases. Individuals often evaluate themselves by comparing themselves to others. Groups provide a reference point that consumers use to measure their behaviors, opinions, abilities, and possessions.

✔ **Collective decisions:** Group members sometimes make a decision as a group, usually as a result of discussion. The majority often rules, so even if an individual in the group disagrees with the group decision, the individual will often still side with the group.

By knowing how a group makes its decisions, you can determine where to focus your marketing efforts in order to have the best chance of influencing that group decision. For example, if you know a group focuses more on making collective decisions than individual decisions, you should focus on the group leaders in order to have a greater impact and influence on the group's decision. If the group is more focused on individual decisions, focus on the impact and influence you have one on one with the individuals.

Group influence doesn't just affect buying behavior. Consumer attitudes, opinions, and values are heavily influenced by reference groups, even if a specific purchase doesn't directly result. Groups that consumers belong to, want to belong to, or want to avoid provide them with information, rewards, and punishments that they use to shape their behavior and identity. This, in turn, influences purchases, consumption, and communication.

### What groups do

Reference groups influence behavior in three general ways:

- **Groups provide information needed to make decisions.** *Informational influence* gives consumers the information they seek and the advice that pertains to their purchases. Consumers use the reference group's behavior and attitudes to help them to make their own decisions, because they view the group as a reliable source of information.

  Informational influence can result from an explicit search for facts, but it's also present when a consumer isn't searching for information. For example, if a consumer is looking for a physician, she often asks friends for suggestions and recommendations. When a consumer isn't seeking information, her friend's behavior may influence her actions. For example, a consumer may see a friend drinking a new beverage and decide to try one.

  If the group has a negative perception of your product or service, you need to change that perception at the group level in order to gain a positive outcome from the individual consumers in the group.

- **Groups reward or punish behavior to encourage compliance.** *Normative influence* occurs when consumers conform to a group's expectations to receive a reward or avoid punishment. Compliance with these expectations often leads to valued rewards. For example, when a teenager wears clothing that her peer group approves of, she feels accepted, or rewarded. If she wears clothing that isn't accepted, she may feel shunned by the group; she considers this rejection a punishment.

  It's important to understand the standards of compliance within a group in order to ensure that you're providing the individuals in that group with products they'll be rewarded for; otherwise, the consumers within the group will avoid your product in order to avoid group punishment.

- **Groups project shared values to influence members to behave similarly.** *Value-expressive influence* refers to how consumers internalize a group's values or why an individual joins a group to express her own values and beliefs. Individuals seek membership into groups that hold values that are similar to their own. Also, they often choose to adopt the values that are held by the group.

Because consumers internalize the group's values, if your products or your marketing message doesn't support those values, you'll lose consumers in that specific group rather than gain them.

Many groups influence consumer behavior, but not all groups have the same influence. It depends on how much contact an individual has with a group. The degree to which a reference group affects a purchase decision depends on an individual's susceptibility to the group's influence and how involved she is with the group.

### How consumers respond

Individual consumers can react to groups in different ways. In other words, they can go through three processes of social influences. They can

- ✔ **Comply with the group's expectation.** When it comes to compliance, it's not uncommon for individuals to do something overtly, even though they don't necessarily believe in it. For example, someone may arrive to work on time, even though he'd rather sleep in an extra hour. But he arrives when he's scheduled to because, within the work group, it's a compliance issue. He complies to fulfill his role within the group.

- ✔ **Conform to the group's way of thinking, believing, and behaving.** Sometimes consumers find satisfaction from conforming. An individual conforms to the group by changing his behavior, views, and attitudes to fit in with the group's views. This often helps an individual find his identification within that group. That is why you often find that individuals dress like members of a group that they admire. Take a look at the students at your local high school and notice how they all tend to have the same style and fashion sense. This is one way students identify with their peers as a group. They conform to the style of the majority to fit in. (I discuss conforming in further detail later in this chapter in the section entitled "Why customers succumb to group influence.")

- ✔ **Internalize attitudes and behaviors that agree with their own values.** Group members internalize the group's teachings, particularly if the person teaching is viewed as an expert. Parents, teachers, and ministers are great examples of people within groups who can teach attitudes and behavior. An individual internalizes the information that's presented because of the respect he has for the person doing the teaching.

These processes help develop a consumer's attitude, which influences how an individual thinks and why he acts and responds as he does (see Chapter 6 for more on consumer attitudes). All three reactions can in some cases be prompted by a single reference group. The way that a consumer reacts or responds to group influences is really determined by the type of group, type of influence it has, and the amount of influence it has on the consumer. Figure 10-1 shows the influencing factors and possible purchasing behavior outcomes.

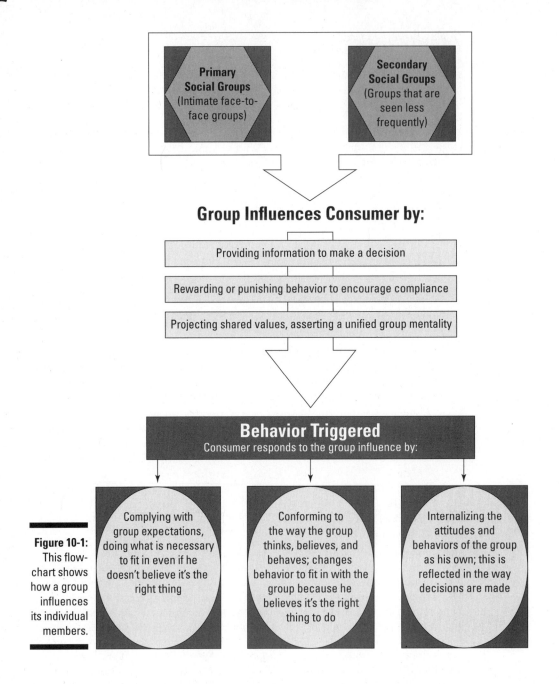

**Figure 10-1:** This flow-chart shows how a group influences its individual members.

## Identifying the marketing opportunities groups provide

By understanding the influences that a group has on the consumers you're targeting, you can adapt your marketing strategy to influence a number of people simultaneously. You can market to the group's commonalities as well as to their leadership. You also can influence the purchasing behavior of that group so it turns to you when it needs to purchase items and services for the group itself.

Information within groups often spreads by word of mouth. Individuals hear about what others are doing, what they are using, and whether they like certain products. Consumers share all kinds of information — both positive and negative — about purchases, services, experiences, and more. This information can have a major impact on consumer behavior. As I explain in the earlier "What groups do" section, individuals find out about new products from friends and reference groups by observing or participating with them as they use the product, or by seeking and receiving advice or information from members of the group.

When it comes to your marketing strategy, word-of-mouth information exchange can have a positive or negative effect (or both), depending on how a group feels about your product. If a group supports your product, selling it to the individuals in that group is much easier; if the group doesn't like your product, you'll have a tough time gaining market share from that group. Opinion leaders within groups have a great deal of influence over how a group feels about your product. (Refer to the later section "Targeting the leader of the pack" for more on opinion leaders.)

# Gaining a Deeper Understanding of Group Influence

It isn't uncommon for reference groups to change as situations change for individuals. For example, a college student's reference groups change during her years in college. Before a student begins college, her strongest reference group is her family. She relies on the values, beliefs, and attitudes that her family instilled in her while growing up. During her college years, however, her strongest reference group changes to her peers. This is especially true for students who attend college outside of their hometowns. Even though both of these groups can work simultaneously, one may carry more influence over an individual at certain times.

In the following sections, I explain how groups affect a consumer's behavior and why individuals follow the herd. I also discuss the amount of influence that groups have over their members.

## Where a group gets its power of influence

Groups carry a level of social power with them. _Social power_ is the ability of an individual or a group to alter the actions of others. Groups get their power because consumers respond to the following:

- ✔ **People they admire:** When consumers imitate qualities by copying behavior of a prominent person they admire, this is called _reference power_. Consumers are often persuaded by groups that are either similar to or represent someone they want to be like. Belonging to such groups allows consumers to feel as though they fit in.

- ✔ **People with information:** A group or individual can influence a consumer through knowledge of or experience with a specific subject. This is called _information power_ (or sometimes _expert power_). Consumers may alter their behavior based on the perceived expertise of the source of information. When a group provides superior expertise to consumers, it often increases the group's trustworthiness.

- ✔ **People with authority:** Groups gain _legitimate power_ by granting people authority, which is sometimes conferred by a uniform. In this scenario, the group has a legitimate right to try to influence the individual. Take, for example, religious leaders. An individual gives a rabbi or a priest the right to influence him.

  - **Ability to reward:** A person within a group can use _reward power_ to provide positive reinforcement. Parents and supervisors often use rewards. Advertisements use reward power to attract consumer groups. Groups frequently have the power to reward members for compliance with expectations.

  - **Ability to punish:** A group can use social or physical intimidation to give the perception that a consumer will be punished if he doesn't do what the group wants. This is called _coercive power_. When consumers fail to give in to a group's expectations or rules, disapproval can be harsh and may even result in the loss of membership.

It's important to understand the social power that groups have on consumers in order to gauge the type and amount of influence they have on their members. This tells you how you can use the social power of the group to influence consumers. If the group has a great deal of influence, you need the support and backing of the group in order for the consumer to purchase your product; if their influence is minimal, the support of the group may be less important.

# Why customers succumb to group influence

A group meets certain internal needs for its member individuals, including the following:

- **Desire for reward or fear of punishment:** When a group carries the perception that it can give rewards and punishment based on compliance, the group's influence on an individual is strong. Consumers usually comply with the group to receive a benefit; sometimes people do what the group wants to avoid negative consequences.

- **Need to protect or modify their self-image:** Group members often use their membership to protect their own self-image or self-concept. For example, an individual may join a group that represents a specific cause because she feels strongly about that cause. After she has joined, she begins to project the group's values as well.

- **Desire for social acceptance:** This type of influence comes into play when a consumer conforms to the group's expectations. Real or perceived pressures from a group on an individual can change the individual's beliefs or actions. To be accepted in the group, a person may conform to the group's wishes without necessarily accepting all of its beliefs or behaviors.

In order to become or remain part of a group, consumers oblige the group's expectations in order to meet their own internal needs; this outcome applies to the way they behave as consumers — what products they buy and where they buy from.

# What determines the strength of a group's influence

Individual loyalty and dedication to a group determines the strength of a group's influence in terms of the number of people it influences as well as the level of control it has over those people. By understanding how strong of an influence a particular group has over its members, you can identify whether you'll market to the group or to its individual members. The following sections show you how to assess the strength of a group's influence on its members.

## Members' attraction and commitment to the group

When you classify groups, you understand why consumers are attracted to the group, which helps to measure the depth of influence that group has on its members. Groups can be classified in three ways:

✔ **Nature of association:** This area of classification considers how consumers are connected to the group; this information helps you determine its members' dedication and loyalty to the group. For example, does the group require a paid membership? Is it a group of family members or peers? Groups within this category can be further separated into the following subcategories:

• **Membership groups:** These are groups that individuals already belong to. An example is a local gym that an individual belongs to.

• **Aspirational groups:** These are often nonmembership groups. Individuals have a strong, positive attraction to these groups and an interest in joining them. Aspirational groups can have a strong influence on the purchase and support of products. An example of an aspirational group is the Olympic team. An individual aspires to be a part of that group.

• **Associative groups:** These groups include people who represent the individual's peers. Examples would be co-workers, neighbors, and members of a church, club, or organization to which the person belongs.

• **Dissociative groups:** These groups have values that an individual rejects or doesn't agree with. Individuals have a negative attraction to them and don't want to join them. People often go out of their way to avoid these groups or the products they promote.

• **Virtual groups:** These groups are based on virtual communities rather than geographic communities. Examples are social networking groups such as online forums, Twitter, or Facebook.

You want to associate your products with aspirational groups, and you need to accurately represent associative groups in your marketing pieces. You should try to avoid referencing dissociative groups in your marketing materials and advertisements so you don't turn consumers off to your product.

✔ **Frequency of contact:** The frequency that group members have contact with one another often determines depth of information that they share and the amount of influence the group has on them. Members of primary groups generally have frequent interpersonal contact, while people in secondary groups generally have limited interpersonal contact. Larger groups tend to have less contact.

✔ **Attractiveness:** Attraction refers to how appealing (or unappealing) a group is to an individual. Individuals can be interested in specific groups for different reasons. When you understand why individuals are attracted to a group, you can use the information to market to those members with specific interests.

For example, suppose a young professional is attracted to a group that has an interest in wine. He feels that this group is a great source of wine education and assists him in donning sophisticated social graces in situations where wine is served. You know that he's attracted to sophistication; knowing that, you can research the group more in order to home in on his personality and find out what attracts his interest. If this is a group that you see as having an interest in your product, you want to take these personality cues to create your marketing message. In other words, your marketing message must carry a sophisticated, upper-class, graceful tone in order to gain the attention of the group members.

### Need or desire that a product or service fulfills

The influence that reference groups have on a consumer to purchase a specific product varies. There are four categories of influence, which involve product and brand, and you can put each purchase of an item or service into at least one of these categories. The categories are as follows:

- ✔ **Public necessity:** These are products that are a necessity to the consumer and easily seen by the public. Examples of a public necessity purchase include a wristwatch, automobile, or man's suit. With a public necessity, the influence a group has is weak for the product, but strong when it comes to the brand.

- ✔ **Private necessity:** These are products that are a necessity to the consumer, but not easily seen by the public. Examples of a private necessity purchase include a mattress, floor lamp, or refrigerator. With a private necessity, the influence is both weak for the product and weak for the brand.

- ✔ **Public luxury:** These are products that the consumer feels are a luxury and are often in view of the public. Examples of a public luxury purchase include golf clubs, skis, or a speedboat. The influence of a group on the purchase of public luxuries is both strong for the brand and strong for the product.

- ✔ **Private luxury:** These are products that the consumer views as a luxury, but they aren't often seen by the public. Examples may include a video game, an undercounter wine cooler, or an icemaker. The influence of a group on the purchase of private luxury items is strong for the product, but not for the brand.

When you understand these categories and can place your product into one of them, you can measure how much influence a reference group carries and how you should cast your marketing message to reach the consumer. You can cater your marketing message by classifying your product and gauging how much influence reference groups have on the purchase of your product. This information tells you whether you need to be concerned with the reference groups your consumers belong to.

# Tailoring Your Marketing Strategy to Groups

When you understand the factors that groups implement to encourage like-mindedness, you can better understand your consumers' preferences and allegiances as well as the amount of influence the group has on them. By implementing into your own marketing strategy the same tactics that the group does, you can often see great results — especially when reaching out to specific groups and understanding how they appealed to an individual to join them in the first place.

The following sections help you pinpoint the group concerns and interests that your marketing strategy should focus on. I also reveal how you can best appeal to those groups.

## Identifying what group members have in common

Groups have core characteristics that help you understand the individuals within a group. These core characteristics hold the group together. The characteristics not only tell you the influence the group has on its members, but it also can provide you with a basis of the members' belief systems, norms, and habits. Core characteristics include

- **Social status of group's members:** Have the members attained a certain status level? Are they wealthy or poor? Do they believe in luxury or necessity only? When you evaluate status within a group, you can identify what the individual members value. For example, if a group is wealthy and belongs to a specific country club, you can market golf clubs to their higher-end tastes.

- **Common values, attitudes, and behaviors among group members:** Members within a group develop particular ways of interacting with each other. They develop norms within the group. *Norms* are considered to be the rules that a group uses to determine appropriate and inappropriate values, behaviors, and attitudes. Are you violating norms within a group you're trying to reach? When you evaluate a group's norms, you can identify their traditions and habits.

- **The role the group fills for its members:** What is the role of the group to its members? Every member within a group has a role, in the same way the group plays a role in the consumption patterns of individuals. For example, some roles within the group relate to task aspect of the group; others may relate to social interaction. When you evaluate a group's role, you can identify what is important to its members.

✔ **Nature of social interactions among group members:** How do group members get along with each other? Where can they be reached? When you evaluate the social interactions of a group, you can identify how they communicate with one another.

✔ **Amount of social power the group holds over its members:** The amount of social power that a group carries measures its capacity to alter the actions of its members, who can sometimes influence those outside of the group.

You can use a group's characteristics to tailor your message. Making your message specific to the group members helps you speak their language. When you know how a group encourages conformity, you can use that information to help encourage conformity around your product.

## Assessing the strength of the group to understand its influence

An individual is attracted to a group based on the group's ability to satisfy the individual's internal needs. An individual looks for positive ways to conform with the group consciously and subconsciously. When working to create a marketing strategy toward a specific group, it helps to understand the group characteristics that an individual looks for, because then you can understand why the group appealed to the individual and focus on those appealing characteristics in your marketing strategy. Characteristics that affect the strength of a group's influence include

✔ **Attractiveness:** How interesting and engaging the group is for its members

✔ **Expertise:** How much individuals rely on the group for information and expertise about a specific area of interest

✔ **Credibility:** Whether and how much reliable insight the group gives individuals

✔ **Past success:** Whether and how much hope and trust the group gives individuals that they can claim the group's past successes as their own

✔ **Clarity of group goals:** Whether the group gives its members a feeling of accomplishment

If you aren't sure what groups to target, you can look at your individual consumers and the groups to which they belong. You can then determine whether that group is worth going after with your marketing strategy and, if so, how you can best do so.

# Determining how you can appeal to the group

You can gain a lot of information about consumers when it comes to the way that groups appeal to them. A group can encourage conformity by following these steps:

1. **Raise awareness of a specific brand, product, or service.** You can try several strategies to increase a group's awareness of your product or service:

   - **Target groups of interest for market research.** By doing this you can make sure that your marketing message accounts for the influence of reference groups within that target market.

   - **Offer product samplings and free trials to groups.** By offering free trials and samplings to groups, you can enhance the chances of positive word-of-mouth marketing that spreads throughout the group.

   - **Identify the opinion leader and use your advertising to motivate her to purchase your product or service.** Opinion leaders within groups carry a great deal of influence; sometimes you need only reach one opinion leader and sell her on your product, and then she'll turn around and sell your product to the entire group. This tactic is often a great way to reach the masses in a short amount of time.

2. **Provide the individual with the opportunity to compare her thinking with the group's attitudes and behaviors.**

3. **Encourage the individual to adopt attitudes and behaviors that are consistent with the norms of the group.**

4. **Legitimize the decision to use the same products as the group.**

How do you appeal to the group to gain an interest in your product? You can appeal to consumers with their reference groups by using

- ✔ Celebrities
- ✔ Experts
- ✔ The "common man"
- ✔ An executive or employee spokesperson
- ✔ A trade or spokes-character
- ✔ Other reference group appeals that consumers may be affiliated with

You often find that it is not only the messenger that's important in a reference group; sometimes it's also the message you share and how you share it that is of interest. You also can use different types of appeals by celebrities to attract group members' attention. Examples include the following:

- **Testimonials:** A celebrity attests to the quality of the product or service based on personal use.

- **Endorsement:** A celebrity lends her name and appears on behalf of a product or service for which she may not be an expert.

- **Actor:** A celebrity presents a product or service as part of a character endorsement.

- **Spokesperson:** A celebrity represents the brand or company over an extended period of time.

The way that you get your message to a group depends on the group itself and the target market you're trying to reach. You must do your market research to be effective and understand the group. (Refer to Chapter 12 for more information on market research.)

When you have the information that you need to gain a better understanding of who you're marketing to, you then need to create a marketing message that's specific and appealing to that group. (Refer to Chapter 16 for more information on drafting your marketing message.)

You can also locate group leaders or other prominent members to ask for advice on marketing specifically to their group. Opinion leaders are well respected in their groups, and many times they will accept promotional opportunities and act as a spokesperson for your product. (See the following section for more on opinion leaders.)

## Targeting the leader of the pack

An opinion leader can hold great sway over the members of his group. The *opinion leader* is the gatekeeper of the group; he is a knowledgeable, accessible individual who provides information about a specific sphere of interest to his followers. This person can be very persuasive.

Here are some characteristics of an opinion leader

- Knowledgeable about products
- Heavy user of mass media

✓ Early adopter of new products; he buys products when they're first introduced into the marketplace

✓ Self-confident and sociable

✓ Willing to share product information

For these reasons, you want the opinion leader to focus his attention on your product or service. Opinion leadership happens in a two-step process:

1. **The mass media delivers the message to the opinion leader.**

2. **The opinion leader delivers the message to the group.**

You must specifically target opinion leaders, use them in your marketing communication, and refer consumers to them. In other cases, you can use buzz marketing by enlisting or even creating opinion leaders to spread the word about your brand.

As a marketer or business owner in need of a strong group influence, you must figure out how to reach opinion leaders. In order to find an opinion leader in a group, look for the top influencer — the person that everyone knows. This person may have written articles or books or may have spoken or held training sessions and seminars. You can find this information by conducting your own marketing research on the targeted group. The answer may even be as close as a search on the Internet. (Refer to Chapter 12 for more information on market research.)

When you've found the opinion leader, it's time to reach out. But I caution you: Reach out to this person tactfully and professionally. The majority of the time, opinion leaders — especially those of large groups — are bombarded with companies trying to sell products, so make sure you reach out and just have a conversation to see if in some way your product can benefit the group. If so, then you can take the next step forward, but don't do so without permission — if you do, you could start a negative word-of-mouth marketing campaign that you wish you hadn't.

# Chapter 11

# Defying Legislated or Moral Laws: Consumer Misbehavior

*I*n this chapter, I focus on *consumer misbehavior,* which is behavior that violates laws and generally accepted norms of conduct in today's society. It's important to be familiar with consumer misbehavior because it disrupts the flow of consumption activities. And this disrupted flow can cause loss to your business by the way of time and money. This loss can be caused by theft or by distractions or disturbances that chase consumers away.

Consumer misbehavior is a big problem nowadays. More than $13 billion worth of merchandise is shoplifted from retailers each year. And more than 10 million people have been caught shoplifting in the last five years. The software industry alone loses billions of dollars annually due to pirating of licensed material, both software and entertainment media. Identity theft has become a huge problem as well. More than 15 million individuals were victims of identity theft in 2006 alone. Even though lawmakers have begun to combat the problem with laws created to protect individuals from identity theft, it hasn't slowed this category of consumer misbehavior. In fact, it's growing annually. I share these alarming statistics with you in order to put consumer misbehavior in perspective and so you can see the importance of marketing your intolerance of consumer misbehavior.

Understanding the motives behind consumer misbehavior can be difficult. This chapter is designed to help. In it, I explain the different types of misbehavior and discuss the common motives that cause those behaviors. I also discuss how the morals and beliefs of consumers influence the choice of whether to engage in consumer misbehavior. Finally, I show you how you can adapt your marketing strategy to aid in minimizing the occurrence and effects of consumer misbehavior — at least, as far as they affect *your* business.

# Discovering What Consumer Misbehavior Is All About

Consumer behavior is all about value; the ironic thing is that consumer misbehavior is also based on value. The difference is the way that consumers attempt to obtain that value: morally or immorally.

For instance, consumers who shoplift or keep excess change that's accidentally given to them, think they're receiving value. (They're getting something for nothing after all!) Consumers who purchase items with bad checks also feel they're getting value. The truth is that other consumers suffer because of these consumers who are exhibiting misbehavior in exchange for what they consider value. Consumers who break societal norms and laws usually have no remorse for how it affects other consumers.

Some folks consider consumer misbehavior to be a division of *human deviance,* which is behavior that's considered unacceptable and not in line with accepted social standards. This classification is often due to the fact that human deviance has a long history of research behind it and consumer misbehavior has only begun to be recognized, making the research on this topic difficult to find. You'll notice that throughout this chapter, the topics that I discuss are similar to the topics studied in sociology and human deviance research.

## Recognizing the difference between misbehavior and problem behavior

To get a complete grasp on consumer misbehavior, it's important to note that misbehavior isn't the same as problem behavior. *Misbehavior* describes behavior deliberately harmful to another party in the consumption process; *problem behavior* refers to behaviors that are outside of the consumer's control. Even though the line of misbehavior and problem behavior can be blurred, the deciding line has to do with the issue of self-control.

This difference is important to recognize because if it's a problem outside of the consumer's control, there isn't much you can do to prevent it. These are problems that individuals would like to stop, but they find difficult to do so. Examples include drug addiction, compulsive shopping, and alcohol problems. You can't do much to detour these situations; it takes professional help to intervene. However, you can take some preventive measures to stop the misbehavior — or at least lessen the effect it has on your business.

Table 11-1 shows some of the common misbehaviors and problem behaviors. Notice that the behaviors in the left-hand column affect more than just the person who's participating in the behavior, and the behaviors in the right-hand column affect only the person participating. (Also note that the behaviors in each row don't correspond with one another.)

| Table 11-1 | Common Misbehaviors and Problem Behaviors |
| --- | --- |
| *Consumer Misbehavior* | *Consumer Problem Behavior* |
| Shoplifting | Compulsive buying or overspending |
| Fraud | Eating disorders |
| Abusive consumer behavior | Problem gambling |
| Dysfunctional sports behavior | Binge drinking |
| Aggressive driving or drunk driving | Drug abuse |

## *Understanding the common forms of misbehavior and their effects*

Consumer misbehavior disrupts the consumption process. In order for the process to occur in an orderly fashion, the expectations of the consumers, marketers, business owners, and other consumers must coincide with one another. If they don't, conflicts can occur between the parties involved. These conflicts can often cause frustration and sometimes even the loss of a sale.

For example, when you go shopping the day after Christmas, you expect to wait in line to make your purchases. You hope that your wait won't be a lengthy one and that management does all it can to ensure that the wait isn't long. Management expects customers to conduct themselves in an orderly fashion, keep their places in line, and wait their turns to check out. Customers expect the same from each other. When you see consumers become disruptive and abusive by cutting in line or exhibiting rude behavior, it makes you feel uncomfortable — the nice, tidy process is disrupted. Similarly, the process is disrupted by shoplifters and consumers that write bad checks, because these behaviors increase your costs.

Some of the most common acts of consumer misbehavior include the ones I explain in the following sections.

### Shoplifting

*Shoplifting* is officially understood to be theft of goods from a brick-and-mortar store. Thousands of dollars are lost daily from the act of shoplifting. This misbehavior affects all consumers because it increases the prices to cover store losses.

### Computer fraud

*Computer fraud* refers to any activity conducted illegally by using a computer and Internet technology. Here are some of the main forms of computer fraud:

- ✔ **Identity theft:** This is the theft of another person's name and private information by another individual for the sole purpose of stealing their identity to open credit card accounts or other financial accounts. The increased reliance on the Internet and technology has contributed to the rapid spread of identity theft. This type of fraud costs businesses thousands of dollars. Businesses also suffer because of liability suits, fines, and the loss of clientele that occurs when their security is breached.

- ✔ **Illegal downloading of electronic material:** Improvements in technologies have enhanced the ability for consumers to participate in the sharing of illegal software, video games, and music. Consumers often can illicitly download electronic material from a number of sources, such as peer-to-peer networks. Consumers have been provided with alternatives to purchase immediate downloads, but they still continue to share music and software in illicit and illegal ways.

  This misbehavior costs businesses thousands of dollars in theft. They not only lose money from the direct sale of the product, but they also lose money from the product being passed on from consumer to consumer for free. This sharing obviously decreases the demand for the purchase of the product.

- ✔ **Computer hacking and virus spreading:** Literally thousands of computer viruses are circulated from computer to computer. Unfortunately, viruses range from being mildly annoying to devastating for individuals and businesses. Hacking and virus spreading are devastating because they affect critical daily business functions, thereby drastically affecting the business's bottom line.

### Consumer fraud

*Consumer fraud* is a deceptive practice or scam that results in financial loss for innocent consumers. Examples of consumer fraud include fraudulently obtaining credit cards, opening fraudulent bank accounts, using someone's identity, and submitting bogus insurance claims. It's extremely difficult to estimate exactly how much consumer fraud ends up costing innocent consumers. The price of this misbehavior is the price of trust for consumers.

Consumer fraud has made consumers cautious and leery to make purchases over the Internet or sometimes even over the telephone.

### Hostile behavior

Some consumers become so incredibly upset when they don't get their way that they become obnoxious and belligerent. When you encounter rude or aggressive consumers, they're usually abusive. They may be

- Verbally or physically abusive
- Uncooperative
- Drunk
- The type of customer who breaks company policy with no regard to how it may affect others

Abusive behavior often has a negative effect on employees. It affects their self-esteem and morale. It can do the same to other consumers. For example, if an individual comes into your store upset about a specific situation and they're loud and belligerent around other consumers, those consumers may feel uncomfortable and leave without purchasing. In fact, those consumers may not return because of the emotional impact it has had on them.

### Alteration and destruction of marketing materials

I've seen an increase in what's called *culture jamming,* an attempt by individuals to disrupt advertisements and marketing campaigns by altering messages put out by marketers. Defacement of billboards is one example. The defacement changes the message and delivers it in a way that's different than it was intended. This can cause negative reactions by consumers, especially if the defacement is vulgar, if it offends consumers' cultural beliefs and heritage, or if the changed message attacks specific groups of consumers. This can cause consumers to be turned off by your message and not purchase from you, even though you had nothing to do with it.

### Unfounded complaints

Consumers complain about products and services even when there isn't a problem. You can do everything imaginable to meet their needs and they still complain. This has an obvious effect on other consumers; when they hear negative word-of-mouth marketing from consumers that spew unfounded complaints, they may be inclined to not purchase from you because they may believe those complaints.

### Product misuse

Consumers often try to use products in ways they weren't meant to be used, and when the use doesn't work out you have a situation on your hands.

Consumers become injured and sometimes die due to misuse. These injuries can be costly to the economy and the companies that produce the products.

The motivation behind the misuse of products is simply not as cut and dried as it is with other misbehaviors. It can be the result of ignorance, ego, thrill, or just plain deviance.

### Compulsive buying or shopping

*Compulsive buying* can be defined as chronic and repetitive purchasing behaviors that are often the result of negative events or feelings. Consumers use the act of buying to rid themselves of the feelings associated with negative events. A compulsive buyer usually suffers from low self-esteem and feelings of inadequacy. He may suffer from obsessive-compulsive tendencies, fantasy-seeking motivations, and materialism. The sad fact about compulsive buying is that the individual experiences the same feelings before and after purchases are made. The results of compulsive buying include high levels of debt, domestic problems, and feelings of frustration. Compulsive buying is truly a vicious circle.

*Compulsive shopping* is a manifestation of compulsive consumption that is related to compulsive buying, but it isn't the same thing. When it comes to compulsive shopping, consumers are more drawn to the *function* of shopping — anything that will provide them with a mental high or escape in regard to the hunt. They frequently shop four to seven days per week and they often think about shopping nearly nine hours per day. They will typically spend two or more hours shopping during each trip. Compulsive shopping is not only a problem for women consumers, but recent studies also show that it affects men.

Regardless of whether a consumer is a compulsive buyer or shopper, the effect of the misbehavior is the same: He will likely face buyer's remorse on a regular basis. When this happens he usually will bring the product back to the store. The problem with this is that there are times when you can't resell the product or you must mark it down and take a significant loss due to the product being opened. This can end up costing you a lot of money. These two behaviors are the reasons that many stores set very strict return policies.

## Seeing how marketing efforts can derail misbehavior

If you take the time to understand the motivations behind consumer misbehavior, you still may not be able to avoid all the misbehaviors that affect your business. However, you can avoid some. Most of the time, misbehaviors aren't personal; usually they're internal issues that consumers deal with. At times, these issues come with no explanation.

Use the information and knowledge that you've gained from studying your consumers to better understand and deter their misbehaviors. Just as you market great prices and products, you must market the fact that you won't tolerate misbehavior. Do so by applying deterrents such as signs and policies. If you don't have a no-tolerance policy that's public, some consumers may think that misbehavior won't be punished.

For example, if you want to deter shoplifting, you not only have to be aware of the signs of a shoplifter, but you must show that you have a no-tolerance shoplifting policy. You show off your policy by having security cameras and signs within your store that state you won't tolerate shoplifting. If you own a large store, you may even want to consider a security guard.

Just as you can classify behavior into areas of consumer misbehavior or problem behavior, you can do the same by categorizing them into immoral and illegal categories. Behaviors that are considered immoral — but not illegal — limit the action that you can take against the individual involved. It's important to understand the differences between these categories, because the knowledge can help guide your response when encountering such behaviors.

For example, shoplifting is considered illegal and almost always considered immoral. Speeding, on the other hand, is illegal, but it's often considered an acceptable behavior. Keeping excess change that a retail employee has mistakenly given you isn't illegal but is viewed as immoral. As you can see, consumer misbehavior can be illegal and immoral (or one or the other), but it can also be viewed differently by individuals and society.

Many behaviors can be considered misbehaviors, but it's important to realize that what one person or culture views as a misbehavior may be seen as perfectly fine to other individuals or cultures. The term can be somewhat subjective based on your own moral standards and what society considers acceptable conduct. Behaviors are often cautiously classified because opinions regarding what's acceptable or normal depend on individual ethical beliefs and ideologies. Keep this in mind as you handle certain behaviors, because while you may not see a behavior as appropriate, it could be very normal to the person that was involved in the behavior.

# Examining the Tale behind the Act

It's difficult to avoid consumer misbehavior altogether, but you can be aware of it and know it when you see it. Each misbehavior reflects specific signs and activities that you can watch for. Consumers also conduct misbehavior due to internal reasons, and that's what I take a look at in this section.

## Why do they do it? Considering the underlying motivations

There are many motivating factors behind consumer misbehavior, and the fact is that a consumer can be motivated by more than one reason.

Understanding the motivation doesn't necessarily make the misbehavior easier to handle or avoid, but it does provide you with the knowledge that helps to make sense of the behavior. This knowledge, in turn, helps you to be aware and take preventive measures to avoid the misbehavior when possible.

In the following sections, I discuss several common motives to give you an understanding of the reasons behind the actions.

### Unfulfilled aspirations

Unfulfilled aspirations are often the influence behind consumer misbehavior. Consumers experience *anomie,* which is the state that occurs when a disconnect exists between cultural goals and norms and the capacity of society members to act within the norms to achieve those goals.

Consider, for example, the emphasis that the United States puts on attaining material possessions and getting ahead in life. You could argue that not all society members have the necessary tools, skills, and resources to get ahead and enjoy the things that we as a society deem as important. As a result, these consumers turn to deviance in order to achieve what society sees as important and teaches them that they should enjoy. They might write bad checks or shoplift to get what they want. They believe that it's the only way to acquire the products they desire.

Anomie doesn't mean that all consumers turn to illegal acts when they feel deprived, but it does help to explain some of the misbehavior exhibited by consumers.

### Thrill seeking

Even though it seems absurd, some consumers misbehave just for the simple thrill of the action. For example, some consumers may shoplift items even though they don't need or want them. They do it just for the excitement. Yes, that's right. Individuals may steal for the excitement associated with the activity. Typically, most of the individuals that consider thrill seeking a motivation are adolescents. They're especially susceptible to the influence that gives them a level of excitement in performing this behavior.

Emotions and feelings play a large role in shoplifting as well. The fear of being caught plays an important role in the ability to predict shoplifting intentions. There are often signs you can watch for in the actions of a shoplifter. She often will watch you, at first, more than you watch her. She also will be obscure and even have a difficult time looking you in the eye or carrying on a conversation. These actions are especially true of first-time shoplifters, though seasoned shoplifters may display them as well. The truth is that shoplifting intentions — especially among young consumers — are more heavily influenced by emotions than moral beliefs. The opposite is true for older individuals, however. It's also not uncommon for shoplifters to be acting from repressed feelings of stress and anger.

### Lack of learned moral constraints

Some consumers simply don't have a set of moral beliefs or even a conscience that keeps them from performing immoral acts. They're so disillusioned that they see no problem at all with their misbehavior. This is often true for younger individuals who haven't been taught anything different than to live by doing what feels good to them with no regard to moral beliefs, laws, or concern for others.

### Differential association

*Differential association* is the explanation of why groups of people replace one set of acceptable norms with another set that only a few others view as acceptable. By acting in opposition to the prevailing acceptable standards, group members can forge their own identities, and by doing so they strengthen their own sense of group unity. When differential association serves as the motivation behind consumer misbehavior, the consumer can view the deviate behavior as a way to belong to a specific group.

An example of differential association is gang members who often accept behaviors and ideals that other members of society would find unacceptable. Adolescents also often use this motivation. They steal to show off and gain acceptance into a particular group. They see shoplifting as a way to fit in, because the group they're involved with may see it as funny or cool.

### Pathological socialization

*Pathological socialization* refers to consumers that deviate from those in ownership or control as way of "getting back" at their success. These consumers have a desire to harm you as a service provider or company. This motivation occurs when a consumer sees misbehavior as way to get revenge against big companies. The sheer size of major companies sometimes produces feelings of resentment, and so some consumers view the misbehavior as a method to get back at big businesses.

An example of this motivation is when consumers justify shoplifting as a way of getting back at a bigger company, because they see the loss as being insignificant. They believe that the company can absorb the loss. These consumers are less likely to perform the misbehavior against a small, local company, because they feel it would in fact hurt the local company more so than the larger corporation.

### Situational factors

Factors like retail crowding, flight delays, excessive heat, or noise can all contribute to consumer misbehavior. These types of situational factors play important roles in guiding consumer behavior. For example, normally well-mannered, quiet people may lose their cool after having to wait in line for 20 minutes at a retail store. They may end up taking out their frustrations on the employees.

The best way to understand this motivation is to remember that although the behavior is deemed unacceptable, it's also seemingly beyond the control of the consumer as well.

Another situational factor example would be the consumer who's tempted because retailers present merchandise in an enticing way, and the consumer is then willing to steal to obtain the merchandise.

### Opportunism

Misbehavior can be the outcome of a deliberate, rational decision-making process that weighs the risk and rewards of the behaviors. Consumers may simply believe that the rewards associated with the behavior outweigh the risks or consequences. Opportunism focuses specifically on self-interest when weighed against all other consequences.

Consumers often believe that only a small portion of offenders actually get caught, so they feel safe performing the act (which is most often shoplifting). They strike when stores are busy and crowded so they won't be noticed.

Research reveals that how consumers view illegal downloading depends on the motivation behind the consumer. Motivation is primarily based on utilitarian value, or for personal gain. When a consumer views the motivation as morally ethical, justified, or socially acceptable, they find the behavior easier to be a part of than if the behavior was occurring just for fun.

When consumers make unfounded complaints, for the sole purpose of monetary gain, it's often because they're looking for discounts or perhaps free products as a resolution to their complaints. This is also a way for them to evade personal responsibility for the misuse of the product you sold them.

### Compulsion

Compulsive consumptions aren't the same as addictive consumptions. *Addictive consumption* has to do more with physiological dependency, whereas *compulsive consumption* refers more to repetitive and excessive behavior that's performed in order to avoid internal anxiety.

An individual who's addicted to a product physically needs that product or the body will suffer from withdrawal effects. When an individual has a compulsive need, it's more psychological. However, keep in mind that a compulsive need can be just as controlling as an addictive need. So both addiction and compulsion can be problematic to consumers. When you recognize the differences in individuals, you can better understand the reasoning behind the behavior and possibly assist them in getting the help that they need.

## The decision-making process that leads to misbehavior

Consumer behavior is guided by ethical decision making. In other words, consumers are influenced by their moral beliefs and how they evaluate those beliefs. This influence guides them in the decision-making process. When you understand the components of moral beliefs, you have a better chance of marketing your intolerance of misbehaviors in a way that can appeal to consumers' morals. A consumer's moral beliefs contain three components:

- ✓ **Fairness:** An individual's moral equity represents beliefs regarding an act's fairness or justness. For example, he may ask, "Is it fair that I write this check even though I know the money isn't in the bank and the store will never collect?"

- ✓ **Contractualism:** *Contractualism* deals with the beliefs an individual has regarding the violation of written or unwritten laws. He may ask, "Does my action break a law? Does it violate an unwritten promise of how I should act? Is writing this check really illegal?"

- ✓ **Relativism:** *Relativism* is representative of beliefs about the social acceptability of an action. For example, an individual may wonder, "Is writing a bad check acceptable in this culture? Does it matter to me if the action is socially acceptable or not?"

As consumers consider each of the alternative courses they can take in their actions, they bounce the decisions against their moral beliefs. Then they go through a two-step evaluation process. Just like understanding the decision-making process and being able to use that in your marketing strategy, you can do the same when it comes to misbehavior and how a consumer acts. The idea is to be able to recognize these phases in order to deter the consumer from the activity. Here's the process:

1. **Go through the deontological evaluation.**

   This evaluation focuses on the inherent rightness or wrongness of a consumer's anticipated action. It focuses on how he will accomplish his goal. The anticipation of "how" he'll accomplish a goal is actually more important than achieving the goal.

2. **Proceed through the teleological evaluation.**

   This evaluation focuses on the consequences of the behavior and the individual's assessment of those consequences. In this phase, the consumer considers four major issues:

   > What are the perceived consequences of the action for those involved?

   > What's the probability that the consequences will occur?

   > What's the desirability of the consequences of those involved?

   > Are the people involved important to me?

Here's an example showing a consumer proceeding through the process: Suppose an individual is considering shoplifting in your store. You realize that in the first step he has evaluated whether the act is right or wrong. He then enters into the second step in order to decide whether to proceed with the misbehavior or to walk away from the situation. If you have signs within your store that remind him that the misbehavior is wrong and that punishment will follow the behavior, he may be encouraged to forgo the shoplifting.

# Minimizing Consumer Misbehavior

Everyone is affected by consumer misbehavior. In order to protect your regular customers, it's your job to be aware of the misbehaviors and do what you can to deter and avoid them when possible. This section offers some tips for minimizing misbehavior:

## Exercising an ounce of prevention

Stay in tune with the consumers that enter your store. Recognize the warnings signs of misbehavior and apply strategies and techniques that deter that behavior.

For example, shoplifters often come in with large bags or oversized coats in order to hide the merchandise they're lifting. They also may work in pairs. One person distracts store personnel while the other lifts the merchandise.

Use strategies that deter shoplifting. Set up cameras in the building, post signs informing consumers of the prosecution of shoplifters, require receipts for merchandise returns where the customer wants cash, and encourage employees to check consumers' parcels when they enter your store. You want consumers to know that you're watching them, but you must check on them in a way that doesn't make your behaving consumers feel uncomfortable.

## *Setting up policies and consequences*

If consumers can continually get away with misbehaviors at your store, they will continue to visit and misbehave — your business becomes a delinquent's buffet. Instead, be sure to have consequences in place for when misbehavior occurs.

For example, if you have a consumer who continually writes bad checks, it's time to stop taking those checks. Make sure that other personnel are aware that you won't accept checks from that specific consumer. Employ services that provide you with information on bad-check writers so you have the right to refuse a check from a habitual bad-check writer. Also avoid taking checks without first seeing photo identification. You can even consider not taking low-numbered checks from consumers you aren't familiar with. And be sure to post notification that you prosecute those who write bad checks.

Similarly, set up policies and consequences to take control of abusive consumer behavior. Make sure that customers know you won't tolerate abuse. If a customer is reeling out of control, using obscene language, or threatening employees or other customers, ask her to leave. If the customer won't leave, call the police and have her escorted out. Tell the customer she's no longer welcome in your store.

# Part IV
# Crafting Your Marketing Strategy

"All right, ready everyone! We've got some clown out here who looks interested."

# In this part . . .

In this part, you get to put your knowledge into action. You find out how to use the information you've gained regarding internal and external influences in order to create a successful marketing strategy. I focus on the core pieces of marketing strategy, including conducting research, identifying your key segments, and finding new market opportunities. You discover why research is the key to getting a handle on why and how your customers make purchase decisions.

# Chapter 12

# Conducting Market Research

In This Chapter

▶ Understanding why market research is vital

▶ Exploring and planning the different steps of the research process

Consumers all have different tastes and ideas as to what's important in their lives. And they have different abilities to pay a particular price for what they want. So the days of relying on your gut instincts and intuition are over. In order to minimize risk and improve your chances of succeeding, you need sound and objective data. Market research provides you with that necessary data.

Market research is the key to getting a handle on how consumers behave. It's often needed to ensure that you produce what consumers really want, not what you think they want. In this chapter, I discuss not only the importance of market research and the knowledge you gain from using it, but I also explain how to conduct market research. I show you the different methods of market research and the benefits and difficulties surrounding each method.

# Recognizing the Vital Role of Market Research

In this day and age, most businesses can't afford to take chances on ideas without getting more information about what consumers want and what they're willing to pay to get it. Market research can provide you with that information. *Market research* is the systematic collection, recording, analyzing, and distributing of marketing data.

Market research consists of a plan that charts how data is to be collected and analyzed so the results are useful and relevant for making marketing decisions. The research helps you create marketing campaigns that are sturdy and effective. When you use research to develop your marketing campaigns, they'll be more effective because they'll be viewed more favorably by consumers (because you've done your homework first). Market research serves as the foundation of all areas of marketing, so all decisions should be supported by some level of research.

## Examining the purpose of market research

Regardless of the industry that you're in, market research provides the information that you need to make sound business decisions. Market research plays the following three functional roles for every business:

- **Provides a picture of what's occurring:** This is the *descriptive function*. It involves gathering and presenting statements of fact. In particular, good market research will inform you of

  - The preferences of your consumer

  - Information regarding your competition and what it's doing

- **Enables you to figure out the reasons behind what's occurring:** This is the *diagnostic function*. It involves taking the descriptive information and explaining the data so that it makes sense and is clear.

- **Helps you identify what's likely to occur in the future:** This is the *predictive function*. It involves the implementation of what your research has shown you. Market research encompasses all methods of gathering information to determine which markets have the best potential.

When research is done well, it offers you alternative choices. For example, good research might suggest multiple options for introducing new products or entering new markets. You use the information gained to determine which products and services to offer and which products would be profitable to introduce into your market. Good research also does the following:

- Determines whether you've been able to satisfy customer needs and whether any changes need to be made to packaging, delivery, or the product itself

- Allows you to formulate a valuable and effective marketing plan and measure the success of that plan

# Understanding how market research affects your marketing success

As I explain in the preceding section, market research is your key to marketing success. Specifically, market research

- ✔ **Reduces your chances of making costly mistakes in marketing, strategic planning, and even product design:** When you conduct market research, you gain a deeper grasp of what your target market is looking for. Then you can create a marketing message that pertains and appeals to that market.

- ✔ **Makes maintaining your customer base easier:** Gaining and maintaining consumers takes a lot of money, so understanding what makes some loyal and others not can contribute to the success of your business. When you ask questions, you increase your knowledge of your current customers. You gather that information to help in the development of loyalty programs that will actually work with your current customer base.

- ✔ **Uncovers gaps in services or product capabilities, which leads to new business ideas:** Market research allows you to ask consumers what they're looking for, enabling you to discover current gaps that consumers feel — even if you don't see them. Discovering these gaps puts you ahead of the competition because you're better able to serve the needs of consumers.

- ✔ **Helps you anticipate changes in the marketplace:** You can anticipate changes in the marketplace by conducting market research that gauges trends in the general population of your customer base. Gauging trends allows you to prepare for change and make any modifications necessary to keep your product viable in the marketplace.

- ✔ **Helps you assess whether your business is delivering on its promises:** You can use market research to effectively measure the satisfaction of your customers and determine whether they're happy with the products and services you're providing them.

- ✔ **Determines whether your advertising is effective:** You can use research to determine whether your advertising messages are attracting your target market to purchase your products. If not, the research will provide you with the information that you need in order to change the message and make it more effective.

# Using market research to your marketing advantage

Market research is the core of a great marketing strategy. You wouldn't take off on a cross-country trip without a road map, so why would you spend hundreds or even thousands of dollars on marketing without the tool that guides you in creating a successful marketing strategy? Market research brings to light the unknowns about the consumers you're trying to market to. You can use your marketing research to do the following:

- **Identify newly emerging trends in economic, social, and competitive environments and alter your marketing mix to fit them.** Market research enables you to gauge the needs of the consumers you're marketing to, which in turn allows you to target your message with the correct marketing vehicle. Sometimes consumers aren't vocal in their needs, but market research will help open them up.

- **Develop a long-run marketing strategy.** Research helps you create longer campaigns in order to get your message in front of your consumers multiple times. It has been proven that a consumer must see your message seven to eight times before deciding to make the purchase.

- **Identify external threats and opportunities.** Market research can inform you of competitors or other products that may prove to be a threat to the sale or acceptance of your own products.

- **Compare the potential of diverse markets.** You can use market research to evaluate opportunities that you may have in other markets.

- **Select target markets.** Market research provides you with the information to help select the group you will target.

- **Establish realistic missions and goals.** You can use market research to set financial and forecasting goals for your product.

- **Formulate and implement goal-oriented strategic plans.** Market research gives you the information you need to create a road map that helps formulate a marketing strategy that's successful in meeting the goals that you set.

- **Control market performance.** Market research helps you create marketing plans that provide you with predictions of how they should perform.

- **Identify and define marketing opportunities and problems.** You can use the knowledge that you gain from market research to help define where you should market and also to identify problems you may encounter when marketing there.

- **Generate, refine, evaluate, and monitor your marketing efforts.** Research helps you create a marketing plan that takes everything into account, allowing you to make the best of all your marketing efforts.

✔ **Improve your understanding of the marketing process as it pertains to your consumers.** You can use market research to understand the ways that your consumers think and the reasons they purchase specific products. Then you use this information in your marketing strategy.

✔ **Find where your products are most likely to sell.** Market research can show you the behavior of consumers, including where they make purchases.

✔ **Identify market segments and niches.** It's important to identify segments that you can market to in order to create pertinent messages that appeal and entice consumers; market research can help.

✔ **Determine who your competitors are.** With market research, you can ask consumers about competitors of your products. Doing so helps identify competitors and gain information on why consumers purchase from them.

✔ **Discover how to overcome barriers to market entry.** Market research allows you to gauge product apprehension from consumers. This enables you to create a plan to overcome those barriers that may hurt the sale of your product.

✔ **Establish fair market pricing for your products.** You can use market research to help gauge the market value of your product to consumers. Doing so ensures that you don't overprice or underprice your product.

Market research doesn't have to be elaborate to be effective. It can actually be quite simple and still provide you with usable and valuable information. Later in this chapter, I discuss the different methods of research and how to determine which ones fit your needs.

# Getting an Overview of the Research Process

Market research can sometimes seem daunting to marketers, but the key is to work through the steps of the process. Following the steps enables you to be clear about the information you're looking for. Here's how to make your way through the research process:

1. **Define the problem.**

   You never want to conduct research on things that you would *like* to know. Instead, make sure you're conducting research for the things you *need* to know. Use the earlier section "Understanding how market research affects your marketing success" to identify what it is that you want to gain from your market research. Identify the problem and make that the core focus of your research.

### 2. Determine the research design.

In this step, you identify what data you will collect and analyze to solve the problem. First you determine the information that you're seeking (whatever kind best supports your objective). Then you choose your data collection approach. You have two main options when collecting data:

- Acquire third-party research, which comes from companies that specialize in market research. They sell this research data for a price.

- Conduct new research (either conduct it yourself or outsource the research to a market research firm).

### 3. Gather third-party data if you're using it.

Third-party data may not be specific to the group you're targeting, but you still can glean information from it that's helpful in guiding you in your marketing strategy. The best part is that this type of research comes at a lower cost than primary research. Later in this chapter, I show you where to find the data and how to evaluate whether it meets your needs.

### 4. Create a plan for original research if you're doing it.

This step is the most intensive. In it, you do the following:

- **Determine your methods of collecting data.** Will you interview various individuals? Will you observe behaviors without direct interaction with the individuals?

- **Design data collection forms and questionnaires.** You want your forms and questionnaires to ask for the information that will provide you with the data that will help solve the problem you identified in the first step of the process. A questionnaire only has validity when the questions asked measure what was intended to be measured. Your data collection forms and questionnaires also must be properly written, formatted, and administered in order for them to be valid and reliable.

### 5. Determine sample plan and size.

A *sample plan* identifies how you'll conduct your market research, what questionnaires or forms you'll use, and what you'll do with the analysis. A *sample size* is the number of people you need to interview in order to get the results that reflect the target population as precisely as needed for an accurate sampling.

### 6. Collect the data.

All you're doing in this step is implementing the plan, which you don't need me to tell you how to do — hence the lack of coverage on this topic.

**7. Present, interpret, and report the data.**

After you've collected all your data, it's time to make sense of it. Before you can gain a clear understanding, you must examine the raw data to make sure that the information you need in order to conduct an accurate analysis exists as required.

After you have put the data in a form that's useful, you can begin the process of analyzing the data to determine what you've discovered. The method you use to analyze the data will depend on the approach you used to collect the data.

Finally you report your findings. The effort you put into your report will depend on whether you need a formal or informal report.

The remaining sections in this chapter detail what you need to know about each of the preceding steps.

# Clarifying the Problem at Hand

The problem you've chosen to focus your research on must be translated into a market research problem. In other words, you must set up the question in a way that can be observed and measured. You do this by formulating the problem into questions and analyzing what the resulting information means. Then you can use this information to determine the method you'll use to collect the data. Doing so allows you to translate the decision problem into a research problem. For example, a decision problem may be whether or not to launch a new line of products. The corresponding research problem might be to assess whether the market would need and accept the product line.

To ensure that the true decision problem is addressed, outline possible scenarios of the research results, and then formulate plans of action under each scenario. The use of such scenarios ensures that the purpose of the research is agreed upon before it begins.

# Settling on the Research Design

Determining how you'll design the research you're about to collect is really about selecting the method that works best for you. In order for the research to be accurate and efficient and provide you with the information you need, your design must reflect the problem you want to define and solve. It must also provide the details on how you'll obtain and gather the information that's needed.

# Classifying the focus of the research

By taking the time to classify what type of research you're looking for, you're better equipped to make a determination on whether to conduct the research yourself or use a research company that has already collected the data. Classifying helps in selecting not only how to do the research, but also in selecting what method will be most effective.

Market research can be classified in one of the following categories:

- ✔ **Exploratory research:** This is the classification of research that's used when a problem hasn't been clearly identified. It helps determine the best research design, data collection method, and selection of respondents. Exploratory research classification often relies on *secondary research* (research from an outside source, including research reports that are already finished, newspapers, magazines, journal content, and government and nongovernment organization statistics.)

  Exploratory research allows you to gain a greater understanding of something that you don't know enough about. The design of exploratory research is much more flexible and dynamic than the other classes of research, because the research you're doing is more general and not necessarily focused on specific statistics.

- ✔ **Descriptive research:** This class of research is also known as *statistical research.* It's used to describe the data and characteristics of the population that you're studying. It's often done in order to identify a problem or to study frequencies, averages, and other statistical calculations. You often use descriptive research to test a hypothesis and answer questions concerning the current status of the respondents involved in the research. It won't gather the causes behind your situation, however.

  In order to obtain the most useful and accurate results possible, descriptive research must comply with strict research requirements. In other words, you need to figure out who you're gathering your data from and where those subjects are located. In order for the results to be accurate, you must use the same sampling. For example, if you're trying to test pricing of your product, your sampling needs to be aligned with who you would be selling your product to. After all, what a consumer may pay for your product on the West Coast isn't necessarily what she'd pay on the East Coast. So, because the variables are too different to provide you with accurate results, you don't want to do market research using the East Coast price if you're selling on the West Coast.

  You can use two basic types of descriptive research:

  - **Longitudinal studies:** These studies make repeated measurements of the same subjects. They allow you to measure and monitor behaviors such as brand switching. Longitudinal studies are somewhat difficult to conduct, because they require your subjects to make a time commitment. This commitment is often a deterrent to participation.

- **Cross-sectional studies:** These studies focus on a sampling of the population to make measurements at specific points in time. A special type of cross-sectional study is called *cohort analysis;* this analysis tracks a collection of individuals who experience the same event within the same time frame. This analysis is useful for long-term forecasting of product demand.

✔ **Causal research:** This classification explores the effect of one thing on another — more specifically the effect of one variable on another. You can use this class of research to measure the impact a specific change will have on existing norms. It allows you to predict hypothetical scenarios, and it's designed to identify a cause-and-effect relationship.

These classifications are made according to the objective of the research. For example, it's possible that in some cases the research will fall into one of these categories, but in other cases different phases of the same project may fall into different categories.

## Deciding what type of info best supports your focus

Before you collect data, you need to decide what kind of data you need. Doing so will assist in accomplishing the goal you have set to achieve with your market research. Information types for market research are divided into quantitative and qualitative methods. I break down these methods for you here:

✔ *Quantitative methods* use mathematical analysis, which identifies differences that are statistically significant. The sample size used is quite large. This method relies less on interviews, observations, questionnaires, focus groups, subjective reports, and case studies, and focuses more on the collection and analysis of numeric data and statistics. Because it relies on precise measurement and analysis of identified and target concepts, it's the more objective method.

This data is more efficient and allows you to test hypotheses, but you unfortunately may miss contextual detail with this method. Because this research is presented in the form of numbers and statistics, it's less descriptive. The researcher in this role can remain detached, impartial, and objective.

✔ *Qualitative methods* are used to provide a base for quantitative research and help in quantitative research design development, because this type of research provides more descriptive information that can help you in determining the statistical data that you need. These methods help define problems, generate hypotheses, and identify determinants. They consist of one-on-one interviews to probe for personal opinion, beliefs, and values, and they serve to uncover hidden issues. The sample size used for this method is small. Qualitative methods rely less on numeric data and statistics and more on interviews, observations, focus groups, subjective reports, and case studies. This method is more subjective because it depends on the interpretation of the data.

If you use this method, your data will be richer, more time consuming, and less able to be generalized. Data is in the form of words, pictures, or objects. The researcher in this role is personally involved and may have some partiality. He may also portray an empathetic understanding to the subject.

## Determining the nature of your research methods

The nature of research — that is, whether it's brand new and tailored to your audience or current but not specific for your business — falls into two categories: *primary research* and *secondary research*. Your research could involve one or it could involve both; it simply depends on the needs of your business. Here's the lowdown on both types:

- ✔ **Primary research** involves collecting original data about the preferences, buying habits, and opinions and attitudes of current or prospective customers. Primary research can be costly, ranging anywhere from $3,000 to millions of dollars. This data can be gathered by using focus groups, surveys, and field tests.

  Primary research can be done by your business, but it's also common for companies to hire a firm to assist with the research. If you want to conduct the research on your own, try using online survey tools; these services usually charge you a setup fee plus a one-time fee, but they're well worth the money.

- ✔ **Secondary research** is data that a company collects indirectly from various sources, such as reference books, magazines, newspapers, industry publications, chambers of commerce, government agencies, and trade associations. Secondary research provides information regarding industry sales and trends as well as growth rates. It also can provide you with demographic profiles and regional business statistics.

  The unfortunate thing about secondary information is that it isn't uncommon for researchers to find that the information presented as a teaser is in fact the only information the research contains. You'll often come across this situation when a sample report is presented at no cost but the full report must be purchased. And usually the full report is extremely expensive to obtain.

Primary research isn't conducted as often as secondary research, but it still represents a significant part of overall marketing research. Secondary research provides you with a good starting place, and it's obtained at a fraction of the cost of primary research. It lays the groundwork and primary research fills in the gaps. In fact, some businesses first conduct secondary research, and then they fine-tune their findings with primary research methods. The use of both types of market research can give you a well-rounded view of the market. This balanced view provides even more detailed information that enables you to make important business decisions.

You also can use secondary research data to clarify questions you have before actually conducting the primary research. For example, if you aren't sure who your competitors are, you can use secondary data to gain that information. If you're using secondary research in order to gain more information on conducting your primary research, you may find that your question has already been answered. It's likely that you can find the exact information you were looking for, eliminating your need for primary research. It's also possible that secondary research can show you that conducting primary research may be difficult. How? Secondary research often shows you how data was collected, so this information could include discussions of the difficulties that were encountered when conducting the research.

Both types of research have their pros and cons. By being familiar with both of them, you can make an educated decision on which type of research works best for you and your situation. Table 12-1 outlines the advantages and disadvantages of both primary and secondary market research. Because secondary research is often the first method used, I cover it in the next section, before delving into the details of conducting primary research.

| Table 12-1 | Comparing Primary and Secondary Research | |
|---|---|---|
| *Factor* | *Primary Research* | *Secondary Research* |
| **Cost** | Very expensive; the expense of planning and carrying out the research can be high | Less expensive because the research has already been done; also less time consuming for the researcher; you can recoup costs by selling the research to multiple users |
| **Quality of data** | Provides detailed and specific information; usually based on statistical methodologies that involve sampling as little as 1 percent of your target market | Varied quality; could provide out-of-date information, which offers little value, especially if your business is competing in a fast market |
| **Time required** | Lots of time; requires the development and execution of a research plan from start to finish | Already available, so minimal time is required; easily obtainable because of how widely distributed it is |

*(continued)*

### Table 12-1 *(continued)*

| Factor | Primary Research | Secondary Research |
|---|---|---|
| **Applicability of data** | Tailored to your company's particular needs, allowing you to gain specific information about your target market | Not specific to your company; may provide information that doesn't pertain to you or that you don't need (for example, a report may show the age group as 14- to 18-year-olds, but you need information for all ages under 16) |
| **Practicality** | Varied practicality; the project or information may not be feasible or available; a project may be too large to be carried out (for example, hiring a large number of researchers will create an unrealistic expense) | Very practical; information is easy to access due to its widespread availability over the Internet |
| **Control over process** | Great control over how the information is collected; allows you to focus on issues such as size of project, number of responses expected, research location, and time frame for project completion | Much less control; research conducted is often controlled by the researcher; requires you to ensure that the data is valid and reliable by critically evaluating how it was obtained, analyzed, and presented |
| **Privacy of data** | Very private; data and research findings are yours, allowing you to keep the information hidden from your competitors; gives you an information advantage | Not private; access is granted to everyone, including your competitors; rarely gives you an information advantage |

# *Obtaining Existing Data*

Using existing data is often quicker and less expensive, which is why many businesses opt to go this route. You want to get the best data available, so it's important to be equipped with the knowledge you need to do so. You need to know where to find the information and how to evaluate whether the data is useful to you and your business needs. In this section, I cover both of these tasks. By the time you finish this section, you'll know how to get the most use out of secondary data.

# Knowing where to find secondary data

You can obtain secondary research from either internal or external sources. The majority of businesses and organizations collect information from their day-to-day operations. This information is considered your *internal sources* of secondary market research. This type of research includes sales data, financial data, transport data, and storage data.

You also can gain secondary research from *external sources,* such as the Internet, government statistics, trade associations and publications, commercial market research companies, and national as well as international institutions.

Here are some common sources you can use:

- ✔ **The Internet:** Many Web sites share product descriptions, summaries of services offered, locations, revenue information, and company specifications. Similarly, digital dossiers provide you with company profiles on public corporations, income statements, and balance sheets. You can use this information to research how your competitors are doing business and how successful their businesses are. You can even find out what products are selling best.

- ✔ **U.S. and state government sources:** You can gain statistical data and information from government sources. This type of data will help you gauge product sales and determine how your competitors are doing in the marketplace. This data often includes the following:

  - • Economic news

  - • Export information

  - • Industry trends

  - • Legislative trends

  - • Market trends

  - • Population demographics

  - • Product specifications

  Data collected by U.S. government agencies also can be accessed for free (or for a minimal cost), using the Internet. You can use this information to conduct your own research, which helps you make determinations about the previous data.

- ✔ **Specialized research companies:** These companies sell information that contains

  - • Business data

  - • Census information

  - • Consumer classification reports

- Consumer purchase information

- Demographic data

- Five-year forecasts

Syndication services often make this information available in both print and electronic formats.

✔ **Business publications and trade organizations:** Nationwide and state-wide trade associations often publish secondary research data in articles, reports, and books. You can use these publications and organizations to gather existing data.

## Evaluating the usefulness and accuracy of the data you find

The problem with secondary data is that you don't control the research, so it may not have the information that you're looking for. Or it could contain errors or be unreliable. So, when you use secondary data, it's important to evaluate the information for accuracy and the sources for reliability.

When evaluating secondary data, consider the following questions:

✔ Is the data useful in your research study?

✔ How current is the data and does it apply to the time period you're interested in?

✔ Is the data dependable and verified?

✔ Is there any bias in the data that can alter the quality of use for your research?

✔ What were the specifications and the methods used in collecting the data? What was the response rate? What was the quality of the analysis of the data? What was the sample size and sampling technique? How was the questionnaire designed?

✔ What was the object of the original data collection?

✔ What's the nature of the data? What was the definition of the variables? What units were used to measure the data? What categories were used? What relationships between the subjects and variables were measured?

If, after reviewing the information, you find that the secondary research won't provide you with the answers you need, it may be time to evaluate whether primary research is necessary to complete your research. See the following section for details.

# Creating a Data Collection Plan for Original Research

When acquiring original data, you can either do the research yourself or hire someone to do it for you. If you decide on the latter, you have several different types of firms you can use to outsource your primary research, and the level of services they offer can and do vary. These firms include:

- **Full-service marketing research firms:** These firms develop and carry out the full research plan for their clients.

- **Partial-service market research firms:** This type of firm offers expertise that addresses a specific part of the research plan, such as developing methods to collect data and design surveys. If you're willing to pay, they'll even go as far as to locate research participants and undertake the data analysis.

- **Research tool supplier:** This firm provides the tools used by researchers, including data collection tools such as surveys, data analysis software, and report presentation products.

If you go it alone, be prepared for some hard work — but remember that you're saving big bucks this way. The following sections outline what to do and provide guidance to help you along the way.

Even if you decide to hire the work out, you still want to be aware of the process in order to ensure that you're getting the information that you need from the research. While the company you hire knows market research, only you know your business in the way that you do.

## Picking your collection methods

Primary research can be collected using two different methods: survey and observation. You can use a variety of tools to gather that data. For instance, you can gather primary market research by using the following:

- Case studies
- Contacts with representatives, buyers and resellers, and end-users
- Field tests
- Focus groups
- Interviews

### Surveying select people

The *survey method* is a research technique in which information is gathered from people through the use of surveys and questionnaires. It's the most frequently used method of collecting primary data. Survey research can be conducted in person, by phone, by mail, or over the Internet:

✔ Personal interviews can be conducted in focus groups, door-to-door, or randomly in central locations. A major advantage when it comes to personal interviews is they get much better responses than mail, phone, or Internet surveys do. However, telephone interviews do serve as a quick and relatively inexpensive way to conduct an interview.

   *Focus groups* typically involve 8 to 12 people that are brought together to evaluate advertising, a product, a design, or a marketing strategy under a skilled moderator.

✔ While mailed surveys tend to have a low response rate, a successful survey can get a 10 percent response when you offer some type of incentive to complete the survey and return it. Incentives help convince more individuals to respond.

✔ Internet-based surveys are quick, and they eliminate the need for data entry, which is in itself a timesaver. A draw to using the Internet is that the surveys are limited to individuals that have access to the Web; however, this number is growing annually. Another drawback is that people dislike receiving uninvited e-mail surveys.

When you decide how to collect the information and conduct the survey, you then write the questions according to the specific needs of that type of survey. You need to carefully construct, format, and administer your questionnaires and collection forms because doing so allows you to obtain unbiased data and increase your response rate. (See the later section "Crafting and presenting questions effectively" for guidance in this task.)

Your administration of a questionnaire must be structured and planned. You must select participants in an unbiased way, and you need to explain the survey's purpose either in person or on the questionnaire. If you make a mistake in the way that the questionnaire is structured or administered, you may come up with inaccurate and unreliable results.

### Gathering information through observation

The *observation method* is a research method in which the actions of people are watched and recorded either by cameras or by observers. A *mystery shopper* is an effective observation method. A mystery shopper is a researcher who poses as a customer or client. The shopper observes the interactions between customers and salespeople to evaluate the effectiveness of sales staff. The mystery shopper concept is becoming popular among service offices such as physician and attorney offices as well.

One disadvantage to the observation method is that it can't measure attitudes or motivation. However, this method has two significant advantages:

- ✔ It's more time efficient than personal interviews.
- ✔ People are unaware they're being observed, so they act as they normally would. This candid behavior provides a clear picture of the interaction that takes place.

When using the observation method, you want to watch behaviors and take careful notes. For example, be sure to note the following:

- ✔ What are the participants saying and how are they reacting to the product or the situation?
- ✔ What type of language are participants using to express themselves, and what is their mood?
- ✔ How are the participants thinking and feeling during the process?

Sometimes these things are easier to observe in an interview process, so it's best to conduct on-site interviews whenever possible. Interviewing helps to put the participant in an environment where he can discuss the preceding items, thereby helping you gather additional data that may be needed in the research process.

*Point of sale research* is a form of research that combines natural observation with personal interviews to get people to explain buying behavior. Researchers observe shoppers to decide which ones to choose as research subjects. After observation, researchers approach the selected shoppers and ask them questions. This method of research provides fresh and accurate information from the consumer because the purchase has just been made.

The *experimental method* is an observation technique in which a researcher observes what happens when he changes one or more marketing variables while keeping the others constant under controlled conditions. This method isn't used as frequently because of the inaccuracy of the responses and the cost of setting up the research conditions.

## Crafting and presenting questions effectively

The way that you present or word a question can impact the way that it's interpreted by the participant. For this reason, it's important to make sure that you craft your questions so they're simple and easy to understand. It's also important not to use questions that lead a participant in a specific direction.

You want to craft your questions in such a way that if a question doesn't apply to the participants, they can choose not to answer. The following sections list some guidelines to help you in crafting your questions correctly.

### Selecting your question type carefully

You can choose from a variety of question types. For example, you can use any of the following:

- **Open-ended questions:** These questions ask respondents to construct their own responses. These questions are good for gathering opinions from participants and gaining a wider range of knowledge than you would when using a question that has fixed answers.

- **Forced-choice questions:** These questions make the respondent choose answers only from the possibilities presented on the questionnaire. Force-choice questions can be used to rate a product or service based on a scale.

- **Yes/no questions:** This type of question allows the participant to select only "yes" or "no" as a response. You only want to use yes/no questions when asking for a response on one issue. When you use yes/no questions that ask about more than one issue, the reliability and validity of the answer is decreased. That's because this type of question doesn't allow for a gray area with the participant. If they're in the middle on whether they would choose "yes" or "no," they must select one or the other, because there's no in-between answer.

- **Multiple-choice questions:** These questions give the respondent several choices. When you construct multiple-choice questions, it's vital that you make the options mutually exclusive and comprehensive enough to include every possible response.

    If you offer the choice of "other," you increase the reliability of the multiple-choice question. Why? Because, participants are able to make a selection that isn't necessarily listed. If the "other" answer isn't presented, they will only select one because they have to. Multiple-choice questions are great to use when asking about benefits they're interested in or regarding the competitor that they would select when faced with the decision.

- **Level-of-agreement questions:** These questions make statements and ask your subjects for their level of agreement regarding those statements. The commonly used options for these types of questions include strongly agree, agree, neutral, disagree, and strongly disagree.

    Answers to level-of-agreement questions can vary and cloud results, because they aren't absolute and they're based on attitudes and emotions rather than on statistical data. These questions are good when you're looking to offer a forced-choice question, such as asking them to rate the product or service you've provided them.

You need to be careful of the structure you choose for specific questions, because the way that you format or structure a question can lead participants in how they answer. Each question on your questionnaire must have a specific purpose or it shouldn't be included. The goal of the question is to obtain some piece of required information.

### Following basic guidelines

Here are some basic guidelines to follow when creating your collection forms and questionnaires:

- ✔ **Each question must be written so it's clear and as brief as possible.** It's important to choose questions that all participants can understand, because misunderstood questions produce unreliable and inaccurate results.

- ✔ **You want to use a consistent ranking scale for all similar questions.** Using an inconsistent ranking scale can be confusing to the participant and can lead to unreliable and inaccurate results.

- ✔ **Always avoid leading questions or introducing biases.** If you lead a participant to answer in one way or another, you don't know if she selected the answer based on her own viewpoint or if she selected it because she was led in that direction.

- ✔ **Don't use questions that make your respondent guess.** If your participants are guessing and not providing you with accurate answers, your results will be skewed and may not necessarily represent the true picture when analyzed.

You can use questions to establish rapport with your subjects, especially if you're seeking sensitive information. You position the sensitive questions in ways that increase the likelihood of an honest response. Consider the following techniques:

- ✔ **Place the question in a series of questions that are less personal.** This technique allows the participant to answer honestly without feeling like she's being personally attacked or judged.

- ✔ **State that the behavior or attitude isn't so unusual.** Participants often answer in ways that protect their own attitudes or viewpoints. By stating that a behavior or attitude isn't unusual, you make them feel more comfortable to provide a true answer, even if they feel that answer is against the norms of society.

- ✔ **Phrase the question in terms of other people, not your subject.** When you do this, you help the participants not feel as if they're being personally interrogated or judged by their answers.

✔ **Provide response choices that specify ranges, not exact numbers.** This helps the participant to feel as if they're still maintaining a sense of privacy. For example, instead of saying "I make $15,000 annually," it's easier for participants to say "I make between $15,000 and $20,000 annually." It helps them keep a level of anonymity but still provides you with the information that you need.

### Presenting questions effectively

When formatting your collection forms and questionnaires, be sure to use a dark ink on light paper and a font that's easy for your subjects to read. And use good-quality paper stock, which projects to the subjects that your questionnaire is important. Number the questionnaires in order to keep track of them. This way, you know if one has been lost.

Positioning and the order of questions can affect response. Here are some general suggestions to guide you:

✔ **Make your forms and questionnaires short enough that your subject doesn't get frustrated or tired while answering.** Try to keep your form or questionnaire under two pages. Beyond that you begin to lose the interest of your participant.

✔ **Use section headings and numbers on all individual survey sections, and number each question.** Doing so makes the organization and layout of the form or questionnaire easy for your subject to navigate and understand.

✔ **Group questions that pertain to demographics, such as age, gender, ethnicity, and education, together at the end of the survey.** This organization is effective because subjects are more likely to answer personal questions after completing other questions.

✔ **Place neutral questions at the beginning of your questionnaire to establish rapport and put your subject at ease.** These opening questions should be simple and nonthreatening.

# Choosing Your Sampling Group

Determining who you'll use as your sample group in your market research is crucial. If you don't take the time to identify the target market that will give you the answers you're looking for, you run the risk of introducing bias into the results. As a result, your data may be misleading and devalued. In this section, I discuss the steps in selecting a sample group and the things you should look for and be aware of when making your selection.

Not only do you have to evaluate the sample group in primary research, but you also need to evaluate the sample group used in secondary research.

Doing so helps you determine whether the research pertains to the target market you're focusing on.

Your *sampling group* is the pool from which your subjects are chosen — for example, from the telephone book, organization member lists, universities, or lists of past customers. You could use a telephone book as the sampling group from which you choose subjects, but there would be some shortcomings with this pool. Telephone books exclude those subjects who don't have home telephones or who have chosen not to be listed. It's also important to spend time evaluating the size of your sample group, because this too can skew research results.

No standards exist as to who you should include in your sampling group. And your sample size is subjective to your preference, your budget, and the consequences of your findings.

## Establishing a sample size

Your sample size depends on your trade, budget, and tolerance for error (which I talk about in the following section). Cost is an important factor when it comes to determining your sample size. If the ideal sample size and design methodology don't fit your budget, you'll have to make some trade-off decisions. However, it's possible that some of the trade-offs may compromise the quality and scope of your research. It's best to select a sample size that will provide you with as much accuracy in your results as possible. However, remember that even if you do find the need to compromise to stay within your budget, it's better to do so than to do no research at all.

Businesses make important, tactical, and strategic decisions based on research data that covers only 100, 50, or even 30 people. Even a small sampling of 1 percent can provide you with an accurate representation of a particular market. The sample size that you use is determined by the type of research you're doing.

Sample size is very subjective and I don't know the specifics of your market, so I can't tell you how large yours should be. If you need help determining your sample size, I'd suggest doing an Internet search for "sample size calculators." These calculators help you determine how big your sample size needs to be by taking into account specific variables of your market.

## Planning ahead for possible sampling errors

When choosing your sample group, you need to take into account the possibility of sampling errors. *Sampling errors* are due to the fact that data collected is from a part of rather than the whole of the population. There's a trade-off between sample size and cost. The larger the sample size, the smaller the sampling error, but the higher the cost. After a certain point, the smaller sampling error can't be justified by the cost.

While a larger sample size may reduce sampling error, it actually may increase the total error. A larger size sampling may reduce the ability to follow up on nonresponses. And even if you have a sufficient number of follow-up interviews, a larger number of interviews may result in a less uniform interview process, which could increase biases.

Your sample size is subjective based on your own market, the type of research you're doing, and the information you're trying to gain from that research. There are no absolutes — only the very general guidelines I provide in this section.

# Presenting, Interpreting, and Reporting Data

The information that you gain from market research can only be used if you put it in a format that really represents and interprets the data in a way that's useful to your business practices and operations. Formatting information properly allows you to take the information that you've collected and view it in a way that's useful to your own business and marketing strategy. Having this information in a way that's easy to understand enables you to make smart business decisions and forecast the future of where your business is going. It also makes you aware of issues that may need to be fixed or corrected and provides you with information about product changes or innovations that need to take place.

## Presenting the data

*Descriptive data analysis* is used to describe the results you've obtained. In most cases, the results are merely used to provide a summary of the information that has been gathered without making a statement on whether the results hold up to a statistical evaluation.

You present *quantitative data* (data that reflects numerical or statistical values) by using visual formats such as charts, tables, or the measurement of central tendencies. If you've collected *qualitative data* (data reflecting characteristics, opinions, and other consumer behavior attributes), you present the information with coded or summarized grouping categories.

Sometimes data may not be in the format that you need for further analysis, in which case you need to "clean" the data. This may require you to drop problematic data altogether or in part by excluding a specific question, depending on what depth the unclean data skews the research results.

You must also take into account sampling errors that occur. In the preceding section, I discuss how to avoid sampling errors. However, they still often occur, so in this section I show you how to recognize and handle those errors so that they don't affect the outcome of your market research. A few of the reasons data may be problematic include

- **Incomplete responses:** This error often occurs when the method of data collection isn't fully completed. For example, your subject may have skipped some questions or failed to provide you with necessary information.

- **Data entry error:** This error occurs when the information isn't recorded properly. For example, your subject may have marked "disagree" but it could have been entered as "strongly agree." These errors also can happen when data entry operators are fatigued or just careless in their entries. You must be aware of these not only with in-house staff, but also with market research companies that you outsource to. Data entry errors are difficult to catch. They're typically caught by supervising the entry at periodic times or watching for inconsistencies within the data.

- **Questionable entry:** These errors appear when there's an inconsistency in the subject's responses. You often see this when your subject doesn't answer honestly or doesn't understand the question.

## Interpreting the data and devising solutions

Inferential data is used when you want to move beyond simply describing the results and begin making judgments about specific issues. For instance, *inferential data analysis* allows you to use the information you've obtained from a small group to make judgments about a larger group. You can use this type of analysis to compare groups and see whether there's a difference in how they responded to an issue. You also can use this type of analysis to forecast what may happen based on the information you've collected.

In order to use inferential data effectively, you need a well-structured research plan that follows the scientific method. You'll benefit more by using the quantitative data collection method rather than the qualitative method.

Your solution recommendations must be clear and well supported by the research data. If you've done the research yourself, you're more than likely safe when following solution recommendations. However, when you use secondary data and base businesses decision on that data, you can run into problems. So you want to ensure that the secondary data you have collected is reliable and of good quality. You also want to make sure that it's collected from the same target market that you'll be providing your solutions and marketing to.

## Preparing a formal report

If you need to prepare a formal report, you must prepare a written report that outlines what was researched and what resulted from the research. In a formal situation, you'll likely be required to prepare an oral presentation as well.

A typical formal research report includes the following elements:

- ✔ Title page
- ✔ Acknowledgements of people who assisted
- ✔ Table of contents
- ✔ List of tables, figures, charts, and graphs

When recommending solutions to the problem, be sure to include the following contents:

- ✔ Introduction
- ✔ Review of the research information
- ✔ Procedures used
- ✔ Findings of your research
- ✔ Recommendations
- ✔ Summary and conclusions
- ✔ Appendixes
- ✔ Bibliography

If you've created an effective research report, you'll be able to use the report to make decisions about marketing strategies to address the researched problem or issue. And after the research is completed, you can implement changes that need to be made, and then you can carefully monitor and track the results in order to evaluate whether the changes you've made are a success.

# Chapter 13

# Identifying Target Markets through Segmentation

*In This Chapter*

▶ Breaking your market into segments

▶ Walking through the segmentation process step by step

The term *market segmentation* often scares business owners. They sometimes feel that if they segment their market, they're narrowing their chances for sales. This thought couldn't be farther from the truth. Instead, segmentation enables you to create specific market strategies that are geared toward specific markets. You'll find that by using segmentation, you can gain the highest return on your marketing and sales efforts. Developing a solid understanding of the purposes and processes behind market segmentation can go a long way toward positively changing the way you approach your marketing program.

In this chapter, I help you get a solid handle on market segmentation. I start out by explaining the basics of segmentation, clarifying what it is and why it's such an important part of a successful marketing plan. I also walk you, step by step, through the segmentation process, showing you how to apply knowledge of consumer behavior in order to narrow the range of customers you focus on.

## An Introduction to Market Segmentation

In simple terms, *market segmentation* is the process of dividing a total market into market groups that consist of people who have similar needs and desires. The process of segmentation purposely focuses on creating marketing strategies for consumers that have similar interest and needs, instead of the opposite, which is mass marketing and creating campaigns that treat consumers with a "one-size-fits-all" marketing approach. Segmentation enables you to target customers most effectively.

Your *core market* is the largest market that your business reaches. For example, say you have a golf course; your core market would be golf enthusiasts. If the customers within your core market have differences that require different target messages, you need to create a variety of small *submarkets* that you address individually.

The best way to gauge whether you should break your core market into submarkets is to evaluate whether certain groups within your core would have an interest in specific products or services that you offer. In the case of the golf example, your submarkets may include those interested in equipment, those interested in using your golf course, and those interested in golf camps or lessons. So your *target market* — the one you pitch your product or service to — can be either your core market or a subset of your core market.

Later in this chapter, I walk you through the details of applying market segmentation; for now, in the following sections, I explain why segmentation is a vital part of marketing efforts and provide you with a quick preview of the process.

## *Understanding why segmentation is important*

If you expect to use marketing segmentation properly, you must first understand why it's so important and how it affects your marketing efforts. Marketing segmentation has several main advantages:

✔ **You save time and money by focusing your efforts on the right customers.** When you segment properly, you ensure the highest return on your marketing investment, because you only market to those consumers who are interested in what you're offering and are, therefore, most likely to purchase your products or services.

Segmentation allows you to personally address the needs and expectations of that clearly defined group of consumers with a marketing mix that consists of product characteristics, price, promotional activities, and places to present the product. (For more on the four Ps of marketing, head to Chapter 3.) You will find that not only is segmenting your markets cost-effective, but it also actually makes your marketing easier.

✔ **Your marketing messages are more focused and, therefore, more effective.** When you create market segments, you can create different messages that cater to each individual segment. These messages are what the marketing world refers to as *positioning messages.* With these messages, you communicate your unique selling advantage or proposition in a targeted message to your segments. You must use positioning in every aspect of business, including in marketing, sales, and customer service.

If you accurately position your product or service, it should answer the following question: Why will someone in my selected segment buy my product or service rather than my competition's product or service? Additionally, the consistency of your marketing message helps your customer remember you.

✔ **You may be inspired with new product ideas.** By identifying and recognizing potential customer needs, you become equipped with information that you can use to create additional products and services that would be of interest to your customer.

To help solidify your understanding of market segmentation, take a look at the following scenario, which is an example of effective segmentation:

> You're thumbing through a high-end fashion magazine. You run across an advertisement for a vacation broker that features trips to New York, Paris, and Los Angeles. The advertisement appeals to fashion-centric individuals. You expect to see this type of ad in a high-end fashion magazine because, if a woman is interested in fashion, these advertisements may catch her attention and move her to book a vacation to view a fashion show.

> The next day you find yourself browsing through a magazine created for men who enjoy playing golf (you have eclectic reading habits, don't you?). You stumble across an advertisement from the same vacation broker, only this time it highlights vacation packages containing trips to some of the most exquisite golf courses in Las Vegas, Phoenix, and the Carolinas. This magazine caters to a different group of people, but the same broker is doing the advertising.

> On the third day, you're at the garage having your oil changed, and you pick up a magazine that discusses the latest cars. While perusing the articles, you come across an advertisement by the same vacation broker. It's a little different from the first two. This time the ad showcases vacation packages to Monte Carlo, Berlin, and Le Mans — destinations that are home to many exotic races.

Clearly this vacation broker is using market segmentation. It's advertising in three different magazines with three different messages. The company offers the same core product in each advertisement — the ability to put together a comprehensive vacation package — but it focuses its marketing messages in ways that best appeal to target markets that it has identified.

By creating these types of segments, you can speak directly to your customers' varied interests and needs. Would the vacation advertisements have worked just as well if the company had placed the fashion advertisement in all three magazines? The answer is no.

# Figuring out how segmentation works

The basic criteria that you use for segmentation are universal. So before you can start working through the segmentation process, you need to get a handle on those criteria, which are referred to as *variables*. Marketers use variables as guidance throughout the segmentation process. You could almost look at variables as the "qualifiers" of specific targeted markets that are identified.

## The variables

The key task is to find the variables that split the market into actionable segments. You generally use two sets of segmentation variables to split your market:

- **Customer needs:** *Customer needs* represent the needs that your customer has that your product or service meets. They're the most basic means of segmenting your market. In this case, you identify a product benefit that satisfies the needs of a particular group (or groups) of customers.

  For example, if you run a golf course and are segmenting according to customer needs, you could create three groups: Those who are interested in using the golf course services, those who are interested in purchasing equipment, and those who are interested in lessons.

- **Profiler bases:** *Profiler bases* are profiles you've created that contain commonalities that potential customers may have. When you use profiles to segment your market, you forgo customer needs and instead use more descriptive and measurable consumer characteristics, including demographic, psychographic, geographic, and behavioral bases.

  For example, if you're the golf course owner, you have to figure out whether you have customers that live in a specific region and whether they have specific demographics or behaviors in common. Here's why profiler bases work well: If you do own the golf course (and let's say you have multiple locations), you could segment your market by the area that the customers are located in. This would work especially well if you were marketing a special event in the same area that a group of your customers lives in.

To properly segment your market you want to look at both variables — consumer needs *and* profiler bases — in order to identify specific segments in your market. Say, for instance, you're having a special golf lesson event at a specific location. You can now use both variables to create your marketing message and identify where that message needs to be delivered. You want to segment using the customer needs to identify which customers are interested in lessons, and then you want to use the profiler base in order to identify which of those customers are in the location of your special golf lesson event.

### The process

To make your way through the process of segmentation, you follow these steps:

1. **Identify your core market.**

   This step is vital because it's the foundation of creating your segments.

2. **Determine whether your core market qualifies for segmentation.**

   You must follow through with this step to identify whether your core market fits in with segmentation criteria.

3. **Evaluate your core market for potential success.**

   The idea of segmentation is to create marketing messages that perform better, so in this step you evaluate that potential.

4. **Identify potential customer needs.**

   In order to speak directly with your marketing message, you must identify the needs of your customers.

5. **Identify submarkets within your core market.**

   In this step, you determine whether you have small groups within your core market that would benefit from segmentation.

6. **Identify segment dimensions.**

   In Steps 4 and 5 you identify the variables that you use in the segmentation process; you use those variables to identify your target market, which represents your core market as well as submarkets within that group. Within these groups the customers will have similarities as well as differences. So within your core group, you can have different target messages.

7. **Evaluate the market segments.**

   At this point, your segmentation is already complete, and you're now evaluating the segments you've identified. Consumers don't always share the same reaction to marketing messages, so you first want to identify the behavior of each segment. This way you can create a marketing message that appeals and attracts them.

   Then you estimate the size and revenue potential of your market segments. Doing so is important because you want to gauge the size of a marketing segment before investing time, money, and resources that you may not get back.

In the remaining sections of this chapter, I explain the nuts and bolts of each step in the segmentation process. So read on for more details.

# Step 1: Identify Your Core Market by Using Profiler Bases

The process of identifying a core market can sometimes be easier for a business that's already in existence, because you can look at the data from your company's history and identify the most common customer needs and profiler base variables. However, if you're a new company, the process can be somewhat more difficult — but not impossible.

With a new business, the historical data to use when identifying your core market will not be available, so you need to use your own expertise in your business to determine which consumers will represent your core market. You identify your core market by using the profiler bases I mention in the "Figuring out how segmentation works" section, earlier in this chapter.

## Deciding which profiler bases to use

There are four basic criteria you can use to create your profiles: demographics, psychographics, geographics, and behaviors. Even though I explain only four basic profiles in the following sections, you may have unique bases that you want to use when segmenting your core market. Additionally, when segmenting with profiler bases, it's possible to use more than one profile in order to narrow down segments of your market and gain a better perspective of the commonalities in that core market.

The easiest way to determine what profile to use is to sit down and evaluate the consumers you're selling your products to. Are their commonalities surrounded by geographic data, behavior data, psychographic data, or demographic data? If you don't have a current market, your profiler base will focus on the commonalities of your ideal market.

When selecting a profiler base to segment your target market, keep in mind that demographic and geographic bases aren't as useful as psychographic or behavior bases in determining what actually motivates people to buy products or use services. The demographic and geographic bases are less subjective (or more objective). If you do use these objective bases, use them when you first start segmenting, and then develop a marketing mix that triggers motivation by using the psychographic and behavior bases.

I find it easiest to identify a core market by making a list of customer groups on a piece of paper and then identifying their common traits in one column and differences in another. You can also then create submarkets with that same list. For example, in Table 13-1, I've created a list for a core market called "golf enthusiasts." As you apply the profiler bases to identify your core market, make a list like the one in Table 13-1 so you can see your consumers' differences and similarities at a glance.

#### Table 13-1  Common Traits among Core Market of Golf Enthusiasts

| *Differences* | *Similarities* |
| --- | --- |
| Age | Enjoy golf |
| Location | Median income of $80,000 annually |
| Ethnicity | |

When you try this exercise, you may only have two groups or you may have several. There are no right or wrong answers, because the number of sub-groups is dependent on your business.

During the beginning stages of the segmentation of your market, it's important that you not make general assumptions or start with narrow-minded thoughts about who represents your core market. There are many variables to consider in the segmentation process, and uncovering all the dimensions takes creativity and methodology. You want to use your knowledge, experience, and common sense in determining these variables.

## Applying the demographic base

The *demographic base* attempts to segment your market with descriptive characteristics such as gender, age, ethnicity, education, occupation, life cycle, and income level. For example, in evaluating demographics, perhaps you find that the majority of consumers that purchase from you work as physicians. You can use this as a profiler base and create a segment of physicians that buy from you. This allows you to create a targeted marketing message to physicians that purchase your product or that are potential consumers of future purchases of your product.

The demographic base is the largest of the four segmentation bases used by marketers. It's also the easiest to quantify and understand. However, the byproduct of all this simplicity is that demographics aren't all that useful in predicting specific buyer behaviors. Demographics rarely allow you to predict buyer behavior because the characteristics are often so similar that it's difficult to differentiate the needs of each segment. You'll often find that the segments within this base have similar brand preferences, consumption patterns, and media exposure patterns. So the segments aren't of much predictive use if most folks behave similarly.

Marketers use this base as a way to create a cut-and-dried method of segmentation that's less subjective than the other bases. You can always identify age and gender, which helps when fine-tuning your marketing message. That's because what may appeal to a man may not appeal to a woman, and in the same fashion what may appeal to someone who's 65 may not appeal to someone who's 21.

To determine the demographic base of a given population, all you need to do is get the answers to the following 13 standard questions:

✔ What is your age?

✔ What is your gender?

✔ What is your primary language?

✔ What is the highest level of education you have completed?

✔ What ethnicity group would you classify yourself with?

✔ What country do you currently live in?

✔ How long have you lived there?

✔ What is your current household income?

✔ Do you rent or own your home?

✔ How many children under 16 live in your household?

✔ What is your current employment status?

✔ What is your individual annual income?

✔ What is your religious affiliation?

You can use the answers to these questions in order to create an in-depth report on the demographics that your core market represents. You then use that data to focus on deeper submarkets that you can market specifically to, using the absolute data you've gathered. For guidance in soliciting the answers to these questions from the right people, head to Chapter 12.

## Applying the psychographic base

The *psychographic base* focuses on the customer's state of mind and its direct influence on buyer behavior. Characteristics that are included in the psychographic base are social class, values, personality, and lifestyle. For instance, perhaps you find that a large percentage of those that purchase from you are in the upper social class and live a wealthy lifestyle. You could segment this group and create a message that specifically pertains to its lifestyle and why those that live that lifestyle purchase your product. Doing so would help you create a message that was targeted toward that specific social class and lifestyle, making your message personally appealing and enticing to them.

The psychographic base is more subjective than objective. So your answers aren't as cut and dried as they would be with the demographic base. Because this area of creating a segment will be more subjective, you want to make yourself more aware of the attitudes that surround the psychographic base that you decide to market to. Refer to Chapter 6 for more information on consumer attitudes.

The characteristics of psychological bases are measured by Attitude, Interest, Opinion surveys, or *AIO surveys.* AIO surveys are designed and implemented by outsourced market research companies. These companies ask customers if they agree or disagree with a series of statements describing various activities, interests, and opinions. The data from these surveys allow companies to develop lifestyle profiles, which are representative of your core market and what interests that market has. It also helps in identifying the subjective behavior that your consumers represent. You can then use this information to create marketing messages that appeal to the motivations of your consumers.

Because the psychographic base can be costly to implement, most small businesses avoid using it.

## Applying the geographic base

The *geographic base* focuses on the location of prospective target markets and distinguishes characteristics associated with each location. The geographic base looks at characteristics such as region, climate, population density, and population growth rate. You can use this information to create marketing messages that appeal to consumers in specific geographical areas.

For example, let's say that you realize that the majority of your customers that purchase are in a warm climate. In other words, you realize that you actually sell more to the people of the West Coast than to those on the East Coast. Your product may not even be seasonal, but for some reason it's receipted more in warmer climates. So you make the decision to create a marketing strategy specifically for those climate areas.

As you can see with the example, this base of segmentation allows companies to focus on a single area, a few areas, or many areas depending on certain considerations, such as the size of each geographic area and the cost of serving it. It's possible to serve many geographic locations with success. You can use the geographic segments to tailor to different natures and needs in each area.

Consider again the warmer climate scenario I mention earlier. If you were in this situation, you would take a deeper look into your product to find out why that product sells to a client in a warmer area. Create some bullet points that represent why your product sells in those warmer climates and create a marketing message around those bullet points. This exercise can help you in tailoring your message directly to those climates.

## Applying the behavior base

The *behavior base* defines a target market by how a group behaves, as consumers, toward a seller's offering. The behavior base looks at characteristics such as usage rate and patterns, price sensitivity, brand loyalty, and benefits sought. An example of the behavior base would be how often customers use a product or service, how loyal they are to it, and what benefits they seek from it.

The behavior base isn't as absolute as the geographic or demographic base, but it does provide you with useful information. You can use the behavior base to determine the following:

- The benefits that consumers are interested in
- How much they use your products or your competitor's products
- What their readiness to buy is
- The occasions that stimulate the purchase of your products

This information is helpful in creating marketing messages that appeal to the motivations of your consumers and that trigger positive consumer behavior toward your product.

# Step 2: Determine Whether Your Core Market Qualifies for Segmentation

After you identify your core market (see the previous sections for details), it's important to find out whether your core group qualifies for the segmentation process (because not all do!). To find out whether your core market qualifies, ask yourself the following questions:

- **Is your core market group large enough to support your objective?** This is a crucial question. It's especially important if you find that you're serving a competitive market. That's because you'll have competition in gaining market share. You answer this question by measuring the potential of that market (based on those consumers' buying behaviors) and identifying the size of your core market to ensure that it can support you, even if you experience a large volume of competition.

- **Does your core market group show signs of growth?** You don't want to enter a market that's flat or declining, especially if you're going head-to-head with other competitors.

✔ **Does your company have the necessary skills, knowledge, and expertise to serve this core market group?** A company's skills, knowledge, and expertise sell a product to consumers. Make sure that you can communicate with your customers in the segment; otherwise you may find yourself facing a learning curve in understanding how to effectively market to a particular segment. Evaluate and take note of not only your own knowledge, skills, and expertise, but also that of your competitors.

✔ **Does serving the needs of the group that you identified meet the mission of your company?** You don't want your segment to extend too far beyond the direction that your company has chosen to take.

Were you able to answer yes to all the previous questions? If so, congratulations! You're ready for the next step in segmentation. If not, take a look and evaluate what areas you're lacking in. Then make a plan to rectify those areas so you can either make a determination that the core market isn't right for you or create a plan to bring the company up to par when it comes to serving the core market you've identified.

Keep in mind that while the questions and research are important, it's equally important to go by your own intuition and judgment — you know your company better than anyone.

# Step 3: Evaluate Your Core Market for Potential Success

During this step, you determine whether the core market you have chosen is a successful market for you. After all, you never want to choose a core market that runs a risk of going flat or that shows no sign of upward growth. The ideal core market

✔ Is strong and showing signs of growth

✔ Is static and financially holding its own

✔ Has a high product demand and isn't showing signs of decreasing

If your target market meets these criteria, you're set. You have the ability to reach your business and financial goals by going after this core market.

The biggest challenge in this step is making sure that the breadth of your core is appropriate — not too narrow and not too broad for your business.

The following five questions can help you determine whether you've selected a core market that can be successful for you. When answering these questions, take into consideration your experience, your knowledge, and your common sense.

- ✔ What's the potential of increased profit in this target market?
- ✔ What are the similar needs of potential customers in this segment?
- ✔ What are the different needs of potential customers in this segment?
- ✔ What's the ability to attain consumer purchase action by marketing to this segment?
- ✔ How difficult will it be to get buyers in this market?

The answers to the preceding questions will help you in determining the viability of the core market you're looking at going after. I call these the "hard" questions because they require more than a yes or no answer. Businesses often pick a target market without analyzing the "hard" questions. Big mistake. After answering the questions, you'll have a clear picture of current and future potential for the core market you've selected. Without that information, you could end up losing out on some big business and big bucks.

If you find that the core market you've decided on has potential, keep moving through the following steps. If you've found that the core market doesn't carry enough potential for success, spend some time going back and evaluating the variables of segmentation.

# Step 4: Identify Potential Customer Needs

Consumers make purchases on the basis of benefits and how a product helps them either by making their life easier or solving a need that they have identified. If you don't understand that need, you can't use it in a marketing message that will speak directly to consumers and motivate them to purchase.

You have to do some brainstorming in this step. I want you to switch places with your consumer and think about what you need. Right now, you're no longer the business owner; you're a consumer in your core market. The more needs you can come up with here, the better. When you started your business, you likely had ideas of what your customers needed. Do you remember what those needs were? If you've been in business for any amount of time, I'm sure that you've become even more aware of needs that you didn't know of in the beginning.

In Step 1, you focus on the profiler bases where you identified your core market. With that core market in mind, answer the following questions:

✔ Why should your customer buy from you?

✔ What is it that you offer that should persuade your customer to make a buying decision?

✔ What benefits and features that you offer appeal to your customer?

You can use the answers to these questions to help construct your marketing message in a way that helps consumers relate to the message. (Chapter 16 helps you create a targeted marketing message.)

# Step 5: Segment Your Core Market into Submarkets

In this step, you come up with ideas for any submarkets that represent groups within the core market or segment you've identified. Just remember to segment smaller markets only when you have the ability to satisfy each group's needs by using the same marketing mix.

The best way to work through this step is to use the core market that you identified in Step 1. Really spend some time focusing on the characteristics of the customers that are within that core group — specifically on a major need that they have. After that, it's time to think outside your "core" box. What needs do they have in common? Are there specific benefits they all look for when evaluating your product? The idea is to begin to evaluate submarkets within your core market so that you can create specific marketing messages based on their needs (rather than an "all-for-one" marketing message).

Try creating a new list that consists of customer-related benefits that you offer with your products or services in order to help consumers see value in your product or service. An example may be that you offer car wash services, but you're a traveling business. You go to the location of the customers to wash their cars while they're at work. This setup saves your customers time. You benefit by being able to charge a premium because of the convenience that you offer. Your demographics for this car wash service include:

✔ Professionals who work a minimum of 65 hours per week.

✔ Owners of swanky cars. (Maybe most cars that you wash have a value of $50,000 or more.)

You may have initially targeted investment firms as a submarket. One of your major resources of clients has over 150 employees with a median salary of $90,000 per year. Now, consider where else you can find a company with more than 150 employees with that kind of median salary: I'd say that leading law firms may be the next submarket for you to explore.

# Step 6: Identify Segment Dimensions

Consumers view specific dimensions of a product as important to them when purchasing. They place varying levels of importance on the dimensions that carry more value for them. When you understand the dimensions that your target market views with a higher level of importance, you can better position your product when marketing it to them. In other words, you can craft your message to the specific dimensions. Ideally, a product market will be described in terms of customer behavior, customer urgency to satisfy his or her needs, and customer geographic location.

Segmenting by using dimensions as a way to target multiple submarkets with different marketing messages can help in guiding your marketing mix planning. You can use the different dimensions to focus on four key factors when marketing to specific submarkets and segments that you've identified, including:

- ✔ Purchase behavior that's relevant to your product
- ✔ Consumer types that are relevant to your product
- ✔ Purchase influences that are specific to your product
- ✔ Attraction that's relevant to your product and to your brand

## Recognizing the two main types of dimensions

Different dimensions are available for you to use when segmenting your markets. There are actually two dimensions; however, those dimensions can encompass different factors, but they fit into only one of the following categories:

- ✔ **Qualifying dimensions:** *Qualifying dimensions* are those dimensions that are required in order to include a specific customer in a product market. For example, customers must have enough money to afford a specific product in order to qualify as a potential market or submarket member. Qualifying dimensions help identify the core features that must be offered to everyone in a product market.

> ✔ **Determining dimensions:** *Determining dimensions* are those dimensions that actually affect the customer's purchase of a specific product or brand in a product market. For example, customers in need of something in a general product category can be further segmented into groups depending on which features are most important to their needs. In the car market, for instance, "sporty" and "economical" may be different determining dimensions for different consumers.

## Calling out category-specific dimensions

You must take two categories into consideration when dealing with dimensions: the consumer market category and the business market category. In other words, is your market a business-to-consumer market or is it a business-to-business market? It's important to identify which market you're selling to, because the needs and determining dimensions for each group are different. Consumer and business markets differ in two very distinctive ways:

> ✔ **Business markets are more likely to be price driven than brand driven,** which means that your marketing message must focus on the sensitivity of price in order to attract the business market.

> ✔ **Demand in business markets tends to be more volatile than in consumer markets,** which means that your competition can be tough. You must create a message that's consistent and really focuses on the dimensions of interest in your target market in order to gain the attention you need to sell your product.

Each dimension refers to what marketers must evaluate when marketing to specific segments. These are the dimensions consumers often use to make the determination to purchase or not to purchase. Flip to Chapter 21 for more on the differences between business-to-business markets and business-to-consumer markets.

### The consumer market

In the consumer market, you need to take the following dimensions into consideration:

> ✔ **Attitudes:** Consumers have attitudes about specific products and brands, so it's important to understand the dimension that they have about your product or what type of attitude you would like to create about your product when marketing to them.

> ✔ **Brand familiarity:** Consumers often buy products they're familiar with, so you can use this dimension when marketing your product. The more you create familiarity, the more apt consumers are to remember and buy your product.

✔ **Geographic location:** Consumers look for convenience and whether your product is available in specific locations. Use this dimension when marketing in order to make consumers aware that your product is available to them at convenient locations.

✔ **Income:** It's important to consider this dimension when marketing your product, because you don't want to select a specific segment if your product is out of that segment's price range.

✔ **Needs:** Consumers buy on the basis of benefits and needs. So, when marketing, you can use this dimension to make consumers aware of what need you solve for them.

✔ **Purchase relationships:** Consumers buy on the basis of relationships. So when evaluating this dimension, you want to weigh the importance of a relationship with the segment you've selected. This way you create relationships through marketing with the segments that find this dimension important.

### The business market

In the business market, pay attention to these dimensions:

✔ **Buying situation:** Business consumers purchase based on need and convenience. You want to evaluate whether you're providing them with a convenient buying situation; if so, you want to focus on this when marketing to them.

✔ **Closeness of relationship with customer:** Business consumers find that relationships are important to them when they purchase. So, if this dimension is of high priority to them, you must work to create a relationship, using your marketing message in order to encourage them to purchase from you.

✔ **Geographic location:** Businesses, just like consumers, look for convenience. So if your product is available in specific locations, you want to use this dimension when marketing. This way you know the business is aware that your product is available to them at a convenient location.

✔ **North American Industry Classification System codes (NAICS):** Businesses often evaluate the NAICS in order to determine who they'll purchase from. If this is a dimension that's important to your potential business consumer, you want to market your participation and industry classification.

✔ **Reciprocity:** Business consumers strive to work with companies that reciprocate in purchases or send referral business, so you need to evaluate the importance of this dimension.

✔ **Size:** Business consumers often look at the size of a business they're purchasing from. So be prepared to explain the size of your business in a positive and optimistic manner. Be sure to emphasize the benefits of working with a company your size.

✔ **Source loyalty:** Business consumers like to work with companies that are loyal to them. If this is a strong dimension for your prospective business consumer, be prepared to explain your view on loyalty and how your company works to keep that loyalty.

✔ **Type of organization:** Business consumers often like to do business with specific types of organizations, so be well versed on the stance of the segment you're selling to when it comes to dealing with this dimension.

✔ **Type of product:** When purchasing, business consumers often evaluate the types of products as well as the quality of them. Evaluate this dimension to make a determination of the different types of products that you offer that will be of interest to your potential business consumer.

# Step 7: Evaluate Your Market Segments

It's time to determine which of your segments have the greatest potential to fulfill your overall business goals. Your goals probably include revenue, profits, and cash flow — as most business goals do.

Not all of your segments will satisfy these goals. Instead, when evaluating your segments, you'll more than likely come to the conclusion that some of them may be money drains at the present time. They'll cost the company more money to service and support than the segment actually makes in revenue. This doesn't mean that the segments won't be prosperous later; so even though you may put them on the back burner for now, always remember to evaluate them for future potential.

## Predicting consumer behavior within a specific segment

The best way to evaluate the behavior of a specific segment is to gather enough information about the segment that you can create a clear picture of a typical member within the segment. Then create a buyer profile. A *buyer profile* paints the picture of the buyer's motivation, location, and buying habits. It does this by exploring the following questions:

✔ How do they buy?

✔ Why do they buy?

✔ When do they buy?

✔ Where do they buy?

When reviewing the typical buyer's buying habits, also consider past and potential future economic issues and how they might affect the frequency and value a consumer places on the purchases of your products and services. When you're determining the segment you want to target, first look at the economic stability of that segment. You do this in order to ensure that you aren't entering into a dead end that will cost you resources with no return. If you do find that there are economic issues, such as layoffs, bankruptcies due to an economic downturn, or low economic resources, take some time to research how those issues could affect your business if you do decide to proceed into the segment anyway. You always want to make an educated and well-informed decision.

Considering these economic issues gives you a greater grasp on evaluating the success of a specific market segment and how the buyers within it will respond to your offer. When evaluating market segment behavior, know that it takes three to four weeks to build a buyer profile of a particular segment's behavior toward a particular product. And keep in mind that research shows that customer behavior tends to shift over a three-month period. This is important to remember because you want to have three months of data in order to accurately evaluate the segment.

The truth is, you really can't predict the buying behavior of your customers. However, you can gather as much information as possible to lower the risk in specific segments by evaluating the segments before entering them. Because there are so many unknowns to new markets, it's important to evaluate every angle — from buying behavior and consumption patterns to economic issues and difficulties you may not have considered.

## *Estimating segment size and revenue potential*

It's important when evaluating and developing segments that you take a hard look at the size and revenue potential of that segment. In this section, I discuss how to evaluate and estimate the segment's value as it pertains to time and money.

### Using the market segmentation estimation formula, the preferred method

The *market segmentation estimation method* is useful when you have general data about the segment you're entering. I always advise using this method, because with general data, you're gaining a clear and accurate estimation; with the other formulas, you'll spend a lot of time guessing and estimating figures that you'll more than likely not have access to. The market segment estimation method seems to be the quickest and easiest one to use. The formula is as follows — all the numbers pertain specifically to the segment demographic:

> Estimated population
> × % of people in target gender
> × % of people in target age group
> _____
> # of consumers in your segment demographic

After you calculate the number of consumers in your segment, you can calculate the potential revenue you'll earn from that segment by using this formula:

> # of consumers in your segment demographic
> × % of people that will use your product
> × price (in dollars) of product or service that you're selling
> _____
> potential revenue (in dollars) from that segment demographic

To use this evaluation method, you need the following figures, which you gather by conducting market research:

✔ Estimate of population within your segment demographic

✔ Estimated number of consumers that match the gender of your segment

✔ Estimated number of consumers that match the age of your segment

✔ Price that you will sell your product for (or the price that your competitors are selling similar products for if you haven't yet determined your price)

Estimate the numbers to the best of your ability; the more specific your data, the better the accuracy of the estimate you will have.

Use those figures as you work through the following steps to estimate the potential of your market segment:

1. **Estimate the population of your segment demographic.**

   This is the population that you have estimated that represents the segment demographic that you have identified and will be marketing to. Suppose I'm selling lipstick and I know that within my demographic there are 52,000 people in my segment area.

2. **Multiply the number from Step 1 by the percentage of the gender of segment you will be marketing to.**

   This will tell you the number of consumers within that segment that are the gender you'll be marketing to. For example, if you're marketing to only women in that population, you want to take the percentage of the population that is women and multiply that by the population estimate in order to gain the number of consumers in that area that are women. Of those 52,000 people, 35 percent of them are women. So the math goes like this: $52,000 \times 0.35 = 18,200$. In the segment area, 18,200 people are female.

3. **Multiply the number from Step 2 by the percentage of the consumers in the age group that you're targeting.**

   This will tell you the number of consumers within that segment that represent the age group that you're targeting. My segment market includes women who are from 18 to 25 years old. Of the 18,200 women in my demographic only 15 percent of them are 18 to 25 years old. The math is as follows: $18,200 \times 0.15 = 2,730$. Of the number of females in my segment area, 2,730 are in the age group I'm targeting.

4. **Multiply the number you get in Step 3 by the percentage of those consumers that you think will purchase your product.**

   Of the 2,730 females between the ages of 18 and 25 in my demographic area, I estimate that 65 percent wear lipstick. I have a potential audience of 1,174 consumers ($2,730 \times 0.65 = 1,774$).

5. **Multiply the number you get in Step 4 by the price that you'll sell it for.**

   You have determined that you'll have a potential customer base of 1,774 in Step 4, and you know that you'll sell your product for $11.50. The potential revenue is $20,401 ($1,774 x $11.50 = $20,401$)

   This will give you an estimation of sales revenue that you can gain from that segment. Last year in my area approximately 30,000 tubes of lipstick were sold at an average price of $13.50. My current competition has about 33 percent of the market share. Based on my features and benefits and consumer market feedback, I estimated a total unit sales potential of 12,000 tubes of lipstick at a retail price of $11.50. $12,000 \times $11.50 = $138,000$. I can estimate that this segment will bring in $138,000.

I can now use this information to determine whether I have selected a segment that has enough people and revenue to be worth my time to enter. If it does, I can begin to position my product specifically to this market by tailoring my marketing message to appeal and entice them to purchase from me.

### Resorting to other methods

Suppose there's very little information available for you to determine the size of a selected market segment. If that's the case, how can you estimate the revenue potential? You can use secondary research to gather specific information (see Chapter 12 for an explanation of research types), but if you're trying to keep cost down there are a few alternatives that you can use to estimate the market segment size:

- **Total the sales revenue of your competitors in the segment.** You can use this method to gain a general idea of how many products you should sell based on the sales of your competitors.

- **Total the purchase dollars spent by the customers in your segment.** This method is good to use when you know how many purchases consumers in that identified segment made when purchasing like products.

- **Take your estimated number of sales in the segment, estimate your share, and then multiply.** If you can accurately estimate how many products you'll sell and the percentage of the market share you'll own, this is a great method to use in order to gain a clear picture.

- **Total the sales number of key suppliers into the segment and estimate the sales revenue this represents.** If you have access to supplier information and can get the sales revenue for the segment you've identified, this is a good method to estimate the potential sales of your product in the area because it isn't limited to one supplier.

# Chapter 14

# Unearthing New Market Opportunities

*N*othing is more important to businesses than finding and exploiting untapped markets and opportunities. Gaining market share and creating stability by not having all your eggs in one basket, so to speak, is crucial for success. Sure, efforts to take advantage of untapped opportunities come with increased investment and risk, but the long-term benefits can outweigh any temporary setbacks that you encounter. When done correctly, entering into untapped markets or creating new ones can help you experience sales growth, increased reputation, and bargaining power.

When exploring new market opportunities, your goal is to identify what opportunities are out there and then figure out how you can take advantage of them. And last — but definitely not least — you need to evaluate what the opportunity means to you in terms of value to your company. In this chapter, I show you how to do all three, using your consumer behavior knowledge as a guide during your strategic planning phase.

It's important to remember that your ultimate goal when it comes to marketing is to not only grow your business by attracting new customers, but also to use it to discover untapped marketing opportunities that will help you retain your current customers. So in this chapter, I also provide insight on finding opportunities to protect your current market share.

# Finding and Recognizing Areas of Opportunity: A How-To Overview

Although opportunities in and of themselves are endless, they generally fall into three categories. Because the categories focus on different aspects of business, it's helpful to conduct your search with an eye toward one at a time; otherwise, your mind may very well spontaneously combust, because you've cast your search over far too wide a terrain.

When seeking out opportunities in these categories, you should certainly conduct market research, but rely on internal resources as well — these resources offer a different perspective of the opportunities, because they help you examine the behaviors of your current customers.

## What to look for: Opportunity types

New market opportunities come in three forms: marketplace, product/service offerings, and marketing activities. Here's the rundown on each:

- ✔ **Marketplace opportunities** are opportunities to change where or how consumers can purchase your products or services. An example of a new marketplace opportunity may be offering your product online rather than just in physical store locations. These opportunities don't arise out of luck. Instead, you discover them by recognizing the various forces that change the way a marketplace is governed. These forces include additional competition, laws and regulations, economy cycles, and social change. In order to identify these opportunities, you must understand what's possible based on resources of both your company and the market itself.

- ✔ **Product/service opportunities** are opportunities that you can use to add new features or benefits to your current products or services. These also can represent opportunities for new products or services that you can offer to an existing customer base. You can often find opportunities in product offerings by evaluating your current consumers and the circumstances that surround them. Your objective is to determine the types of opportunities that exist within your products only. Your business may need to add, modify, or eliminate product features or even products.

  For instance, I can create a product and offer it to my consumers. It offers them an added convenience and in return increases my revenue by being able to sell the new product to existing and new customers alike.

> ✔ **Marketing opportunities** are simply new ways that you can reach an untapped market simply by crafting your message to different groups and evaluating different placements of your marketing message. For instance, you may want to create a new marketing message specifically showcasing your product benefits for a group that hasn't yet used your product. Or you may want to place your current marketing message in a different marketing vehicle. An example of this would be advertising in a different magazine or newspaper that reaches a new market.

## Where to look: Information sources

When searching for opportunities, you can find the information you need from the following sources:

✔ **Consumer knowledge and feedback:** The best way to find untapped markets or identify whether a market idea has potential is by using the knowledge of your current consumer base. You can ask your consumers questions regarding the products they're using or about needs that they feel aren't being met with the current product. Their answers give you the information you need to understand whether the development of more features or benefits in your current product would be beneficial or if you need to evaluate the creation of a new product to fulfill an unmet need that your consumers are experiencing.

✔ **Market research:** If you don't have a consumer base, you need to conduct some market research in order to find untapped markets and identify whether your idea has merit. In other words, you want to make sure that it isn't just a no-brain whim you thought up in the middle of the night.

✔ **Sales team knowledge:** It's also important to use the knowledge of your sales force. Salespeople are normally the first to know about new products that are needed or solutions that your consumers may be looking for.

You don't need a huge sales team to do this. In fact, you can probably do it yourself by simply listening to your consumers. Find out what they need that you can provide.

Use these sources and the information throughout this chapter to help find opportunities in your marketing that not only reach untapped markets, but allow you to monitor your marketing initiatives, awaken customers that haven't used your product in a while, and gain new business by trying new marketing methods.

# Conducting the Search

In order to find available opportunities, you must conduct a search that's detailed and informational. By detailed, I mean evaluate all three opportunity types in your search. This way you'll walk away with a clear understanding of which opportunity will be the strongest for you when it comes to finding new customers. By informational, I mean a search that provides you with the knowledge you need in order to assess the opportunities by evaluating the needs and exploring how you can fulfill those needs. This evaluation will help you determine whether the opportunity is in fact viable and worth pursuing from a business standpoint.

## Seeking out unmet needs in the marketplace

It's easy to make finding marketplace opportunities more difficult than it should be. When evaluating opportunities within the marketplace, you simply need to assess whether an opportunity to enter that market exists right now. You can do this by walking through the following process:

1. **Identify the marketplace opportunity.**

   Look for opportunities that will help you gain the competitive edge against competitors.

2. **Focus on the consumers in that marketplace.**

   Identify the typical consumers in that marketplace and evaluate their consumption patterns for the product you're offering.

3. **Assess the current competition in that marketplace.**

   Identify the competition that already exists in the marketplace. Determine why your products are different from your competitor's and why a consumer should purchase from you instead.

When looking for new market opportunities, you must focus primarily on patterns and trends within that marketplace. And you want to evaluate patterns and trends not only of present customers, but also of previous and future customers as well. You'll be looking at the consumption patterns, sales patterns, customer satisfaction, and the trends of similar products within the marketplace. Usually with this information, you can discover whether a customer need exists because the customer isn't being satisfied by current products offered by the competition.

You can use the information from this process to determine whether entering into a specific marketplace opportunity would bring the potential of success. It will either cause you to feel comfortable about entering a marketplace or it will make you feel uncomfortable because the data doesn't prove that you'll have success. If you look at this information and don't see a need, it's probably wise to seek out other opportunities.

Here's an example to help you understand marketplace needs. Say that my marketplace is the university campus. I've looked at patterns and trends and have determined that the students order pizza from one business but are frustrated with the wait. I've also found that they would be willing to pay a little more for the convenience of quick delivery time. Here's the breakdown of the marketplace info:

- ✔ **Opportunity type:** I've identified an opportunity for a pizza shop located close to a university. The closest pizza shop is 45 minutes away. The business will deliver to the university, but the pizza is subpar and it takes nearly two hours for delivery. This information came from a survey I conducted with the potential customers that I identified.

- ✔ **Consumer:** My consumers are university students. With this group, I know that my prices must be competitive and that I'll need to keep the shop open late in order to serve the students' needs. I also gathered this information from the informal survey that I conducted.

- ✔ **Competition:** I've evaluated the competition and found that the closest shop is 45 minutes away. None of the other shops will deliver to the university due to the distance. This information came from market research that I conducted concerning my competition in the area.

As you can see, I've identified a marketplace opportunity. I can open a pizza shop near the university campus, provide the students with competitive prices, and deliver directly to the university. I will acquire business from my competitors, because I'll meet a need that they aren't meeting. Because this information shows me that my opportunity has potential for success, I can now begin to take steps in seizing this opportunity.

## Looking at your products for new or improved product ideas

You can expand your market by finding new users of your current product, new uses for your current product, or ways for consumers to use more of your current product.

For example, think of all the different uses of baking soda: cooking, cleaning, deodorizing, and so on. You can use each of these functions to market baking soda in a different way. You haven't changed the product; you've simply created the awareness by marketing the benefits of baking soda to showcase the multiple ways that consumers can use the product. You could market baking soda in a cooking magazine by showing the benefits of its uses when cooking. You also could market baking soda in a commercial that shows how to use it to clean stains out of a porcelain bathtub. Finally, you could market the benefits of using baking soda to deodorize a refrigerator. Marketing in this way increases the value perception as well as sales, because now consumers understand all the ways that this universal product can be used.

When you evaluate a product opportunity, you want to evaluate the following in order to validate the opportunity as credible and assess the potential success of that opportunity:

> ✓ **Product features:** You want to identify the features of the product that make the opportunity of interest to your customers. A product feature is what a product *does*. In a competitive market, when a consumer needs to make a decision between two comparable alternatives that provide the same benefits, he will base his decision on the features of the product.

> ✓ **Product benefits:** It's important that you identify the product benefits that will be of interest to the consumers. Then you can make a decision on whether they would purchase based on that benefit.

After evaluating the product features and benefits, you'll have the information you need to determine whether this opportunity holds merit for you and whether your customers would really see the value. In other words, you'll have the answer on whether you should pursue the opportunity.

As an example, say I own a jewelry store and I recognize an opportunity to offer an add-on product that will benefit my consumers. The customers who come to my store to have their jewelry cleaned always comment on how my jewelry cleaner enhances the appearance of their jewelry. I know they can't afford my high-tech machinery to clean their jewelry, but what if I could provide them with a solution that would make their jewelry sparkle? And what if that solution allowed them to clean their jewelry at home when they're unable to make it to my store?

I gained the knowledge of this opportunity from the many times my customers came in to have their rings cleaned. The comments they made after I had cleaned their rings helped me identify an unmet need. Here's where the evaluation comes in:

> ✓ **Product feature:** My customers could use this product to keep their jewelry clean and shiny. I recognized that the innovation of jewelry cleaner would meet a need that currently was unmet for my customers. I knew my consumers would enjoy a product that was cost-effective, portable, and as effective as if they had it done professionally.

✔ **Product benefit:** Customers can use this product in the comfort of their own homes when they can't make it to the jewelry shop. I knew that by providing my customers with the benefit of convenience and the ability to keep their jewelry looking its best, they would see this as a valued benefit and purchase the product.

When you evaluate a product opportunity, you get the full view of the potential that the product opportunity carries with it. In the preceding example, I recognized a need and, within that need, an opportunity. I created the product, satisfied the need of my customers, and increased my bottom line by generating additional sales of the jewelry cleaner.

## Assessing whether new marketing activities will reach more folks

In order to seek out new marketing opportunities, you need to consider who you will market to and what methods will best reach your customers. Begin by identifying the opportunity as usual. Then evaluate the opportunity by assessing the following three factors:

✔ **The external point of view, which is your consumer base:** Identify the consumer that you'll be marketing to. If you were to create a profile of this consumer, what would she look like? Also be sure that you can explain her buying patterns when it comes to your product.

✔ **The internal point of view, which comprises product features and product types:** Identify the product you'll market and the features you'll focus on in your marketing message to attract the consumer you've identified.

✔ **Marketing operations:** Identify the marketing methods and initiatives you'll use to reach this consumer, and then determine how you'll schedule those initiatives.

You use the information you gather to determine whether you've identified a marketing opportunity that has potential for success. You use it not only to evaluate the consumer and the product you're marketing, but also to determine the features the potential consumers will be interested in and the methods you'll use to share your marketing message with them. You can use all this information to decide whether the product opportunity carries merit and, if so, how you should move forward in seizing that opportunity.

For example, suppose I have a lawn care company. I want to reach a new market, so I've gone through the process to identify who I'm going after and what initiatives I will use. I have a client base of more than 1,000 customers who I'm either servicing now or I have serviced in the past. I've never entered my customers' information in a database, but if I did I could continually market to them. So, I'm going to create a database to house customer information. This way I can stay in touch with my customers and remind them of my business, causing them to contact me for additional services. The opportunity I've identified is that by consistently marketing to my consumers, they'll be informed of additional services that I offer and be reminded of when their maintenance services are due.

I evaluate the opportunity by assessing the factors as follows:

✔ **External:** After I create my database, I'll send out postcards reminding my customers of the services that I offer during the winter — such as snow removal. Snow removal is an added service that many of my customers would enjoy if only they knew about it. I can use the database to continue to market to my existing consumer base and gain more recurring and additional business from them.

✔ **Internal:** I can monitor my marketing efforts internally by tracking who contacts me. Doing so allows me to determine whether the postcard method of marketing produces new business. If my postcard method works, I can use this to gauge what services my current consumer base is interested in. It will also help me in determining whether I should consider additional services.

✔ **Marketing operations:** By implementing a new database, I can determine peaks of growth in my business and evaluate whether any of my marketing initiatives are working better than others. I can use this information to gauge the peak times of specific services that I offer. I also can use this information in the future to market to new consumers during those peak times.

When identifying new opportunities in marketing, I can gauge not only where and to what my consumers are most likely to respond but also when my services are needed most. The benefit of this opportunity is that it keeps me in front of my current customers and enables me to remind them of additional services at the appropriate times. Even though I didn't enter into a new market, I did introduce my consumers to products or services I provide that they may not have been aware of. The goal is that this marketing opportunity will increase my business with my current customer base and will hopefully help with my referral business as well.

# Determining Whether a New Opportunity Is Worth Pursuing

After you discover a new opportunity that you may be able to tap into, you must assess whether there's a need for that specific product or service in your marketplace. It doesn't matter whether you're contemplating a new product or a current product; when entering a new market, you must ensure that you're launching into an untapped market with little or no risk.

You need to consider attributes to each market segment that you're contemplating. Entering a new market sometimes can seem like a no-brainer, but it's still always a good idea to weigh the risks with the perceived benefits. In this section, I show you how to do just that.

## Evaluating an opportunity's chance of success

Before entering a new market, you need to assess the opportunity's chance of success. Luckily, you can follow a simple process to determine approximately how successful you'll be when entering a new market. You can measure the potential success of an opportunity and how solid the opportunity is by looking at the needs the opportunity meets and the problem the opportunity solves, and identifying those who would be interested in the solution that the opportunity provides. All three of these things are important when analyzing and measuring the strength and potential success that the opportunity presents.

To assess the opportunity, answer the following questions and then number them in order of importance. The importance is ranked according to which answers give the opportunity strength.

- ✔ What are the needs within the opportunity?
- ✔ What is the problem that creates the opportunity?
- ✔ What is the opportunity for you based on the needs and the problem?

After you answer the questions, weigh them by what's most important when evaluating the opportunity. If the problem is stronger than the need, the opportunity can still represent strength. That's because it could simply represent that consumers aren't aware of the need; they just know that they have a problem that they aren't sure how to solve. The ultimate goal in this exercise is to be able to walk away with a clear understanding of the viability of success when it comes to the opportunity you've selected.

## Weighing the costs against the potential rewards

Moving into untapped markets means that you must make some business evaluations to ensure that you've done your homework. Doing so ensures that you're prepared to take on the extra work and competition in order to make the opportunity a success. After you determine whether your new market is a viable source for your business, you need to consider whether you can fulfill — and will benefit from fulfilling — the needs of that market. You need to evaluate the following:

- **Your competitive advantage:** Make sure that you have the competitive advantage in cost, growth, and price.

- **Internal company functions and procedures:** Make sure that your company house is in order. You need to be able to handle the new functions and procedures that entering this marketing will entail.

- **The characteristics of the new market you're targeting:** These characteristics may differ greatly from your current market, so make sure you take the time to evaluate and understand the characteristics within that new market.

These are business evaluations that you must make in order to determine whether you're ready to enter the market from a business perspective. The following sections tell you exactly what to evaluate. Use this information to tie up any loose ends and take note of what it is that you need to do to be prepared before entering the market; otherwise you may experience devastation from an operation standpoint.

### Sizing up the competition you're working against

If you can be first into an untapped market, opportunity can easily abound. On the other hand, if you find current competitors in the market you're considering, you'll have more issues to evaluate.

If you enter a new market unaware of the competition that will greet you, you're asking for sudden death of your business. Before entering a new market, evaluate the following:

- **Number of competitors:** If you find only a few competitors, it may more than rationalize your market entry. You may also find that it can be less expensive to steal existing consumers than to try a new approach.

  If, on the other hand, you find that a large pool of competitors exists in the market that you're entering, it's extremely important to have benefits that will stand out to consumers and persuade them to purchase from you. If they can't distinguish a difference between you and the competition, success won't come easy in this market. Differentiation is key when it comes to competition.

- **Number of products and services that will be required to effectively compete in the market:** If you're adding a new product to serve a need, remember that consumers love one-stop shopping and the value of full service — those features create loyalty with consumers. The same is true when it comes to services: The more that consumers can do in one place, the more consumer loyalty you'll gain. Consider the retail stores that have now added groceries. They moved into this niche to create not only increased sales but also loyalty from the consumers that shop with them.

✔ **Competitors' marketing techniques:** It's not uncommon for new entrants into a current market to be greeted with competitive marketing tactics by businesses that are already established in the marketplace. For example, be aware of pricing levels when you enter the market and then continually monitor price changes. You may come across competitors who drop their prices in order to keep consumers away from the new competitor in the marketplace.

✔ **The amount of time it will take you to get into the new market:** Product life cycles represent a sequence of stages that a product follows, starting with the introduction of the product to the time that sales of the product begin to decline. It's important to understand timing because life cycles can sometimes last only a few months and then the demand for the product begins to decline. (Flip to Chapter 18 for more on product life cycles.)

If you've found an untapped market, it won't be long until one of your competitors also notices the opportunity. One more thing: Untapped markets generally don't go unnoticed. The fact is that some companies just won't take the risk to enter them, because when they do it can often take too long and someone else breaks into the market. So be sure to evaluate the time it will take you to enter the market, and then decide if it's soon enough to gain market share within the market.

### Speculating about the effects on your business

Just because you're entering a new market doesn't mean you're free to neglect the current bread and butter of your business. Be sure to find out how the new market will correspond with your current business resources. Then determine whether you can absorb the additional costs to effectively compete within the new market. You must be able to use current resources without putting your current business at risk.

When you're studying the effects that entering a new market would have on your current business, be sure to keep the following issues in mind:

✔ **Money:** When entering new markets, you need money in order to compete successfully. You need funds to develop, market, and launch your product or service. It isn't uncommon for businesses to enter new markets and promptly go bankrupt because they didn't keep their costs in mind. So be sure you know your costs before you even begin to count on the revenue the new market may produce.

Have a clear picture of each of the following costs to ensure that you can cover the extra weight until the revenue of the new market begins to trickle in:

- Product development costs
- Marketing costs
- Operations costs
- Customer service costs

✔ **Relative profitability:** You have to run the numbers in order to determine the profitability of your new venture. Determine whether your return on the investment of entering the new market will be greater than your initial cost.

It's proven to be less costly to grow profits from customers within an existing market than it is to pursue new customers in new markets.

✔ **Ease of distribution:** You need to consider whether your potential market will fit with your current distribution structure. If not, you may face additional costs. Consider whether you'll need a different location and how you'll deliver products to your new market.

### Eyeing consumer tendencies within the market

You must evaluate how your current consumer base will perceive your new market entry. You don't want to give up your current market share, so you must protect it. To begin, define and evaluate your existing consumer base and its perceptions on all strategic moves. Then you can protect market share by developing new products, improving your customer services and distribution effectiveness, and reducing prices.

It's also important to evaluate consumer loyalty. However, don't focus solely on consumers' loyalty to you. Consider also their loyalty to the competitors within the new market. Every market has a varying degree of consumer loyalty, often depending on the number and quality of the competitor products and services. So be sure to determine whether consumers within the market that you're evaluating have well-established relationships with current competitors. If you find that they do, create a plan to gain their loyalty.

# Part V

# Implementing Your Strategy with a Marketing Plan

The 5th Wave          By Rich Tennant

©RICHTENNANT

JUST CAKES
AND PIES
AND ICE CREAM   AND BURGERS
& Deli Wraps

JUST CAKES

Coming Soon!
SALAD BAR

# In this part . . .

In this part's chapters, you embark on a journey through the implementation process. I begin by taking a look at marketing ethics and explaining what your responsibility is when it comes to upholding those ethics. Then you dive in, discovering how to get consumers' attention by effectively positioning your product or service to your target market. I help you create positioning strategies and draft your positioning statement so you get your message across to your consumers.

The second piece of the implementation process is understanding how to educate your consumers about your products and services. Your goal is to persuade your consumers to choose your product or service over others. You do this by drafting your marketing message and choosing the right marketing vehicles to reach your target market.

The third part of the process is new product adoption. I show you how to increase your chances of consumers adopting the new products that you introduce as well as any changes to your current offerings. You find out what holds consumers back and how you can drive them forward in adopting change. Last but not least, I show you how to encourage repeat buying and customer loyalty — not just customer satisfaction.

# Chapter 15

# Understanding Marketing Ethics

. . . . . . . . . . . . . . . . . . . . . . . . . . . . . . . . . . . . . . . . . . . . . .

. . . . . . . . . . . . . . . . . . . . . . . . . . . . . . . . . . . . . . . . . . . . . .

**M**arketing ethics impact both the consumer and your business. So you must build trust with your consumers in the marketing system. In other words, you need to market your products appropriately and for their intended and promoted uses. Ethically, your responsibility is to use advertising that isn't deceptive or misleading. You're expected to embrace, communicate, and practice ethical values that improve the confidence of your consumers.

In this chapter, I help you understand the importance of marketing ethics and explain how deceptive marketing practices affect consumer behavior. I also show you your ethical responsibilities and how to create your own code of ethics.

# A Primer on the Role of Ethics in Marketing

Having a set of ethical standards in marketing helps you do the right thing regardless of your product or market sector. You use these standards to identify acceptable practices, foster internal control, and deal honestly and fairly with consumers. *Ethical marketing* is an approach to marketing in which businesses set high ethical standards and communicate those standards positively.

As a marketer or business owner, it's your responsibility to accept the consequences of your marketing activities and make sure that the decisions you make and actions you take in marketing satisfy the needs of your consumer and the needs of society.

## Exploring the fluidity of marketing ethics

Ultimately, you must follow your own code of ethics and gut instincts on many issues. There's a list of issues marketers are legally responsible for abiding by (I discuss them in the "Recognizing a Marketer's Ethical Responsibilities" section, later in the chapter). Two of them, however, create the most criticism from the public and possible legal action: product harmfulness and consumer vulnerability. These two issues are often intertwined.

When it comes to ethics, most public criticism occurs when marketing strategies target vulnerable consumer groups with harmful products. For example, a brewery targeting segments that have a large proportion of consumers with alcohol addiction and problems might be considered unethical.

However, the definitions of "harmful" and "vulnerable" are up to the interpretation of the individual. For instance, one person may think that by marketing fast food, companies are simply increasing the obesity problem that we face in the United States. However, that school of thought is arguable. After all, other folks feel that fast food is less harmful when not consumed in large quantities and when individuals exercise regularly.

Similarly, most people would agree that children, undereducated consumers, and elderly consumers would be considered vulnerable. But at the same time, others would disagree with these categorizations. There are now laws that affect children and marketing, whereas with seniors that isn't the case. As you can see, it's difficult to come to a complete agreement on both product harmfulness and consumer vulnerability.

As if the explanation of what is and isn't ethical weren't fluid enough, it's important to also remember the importance of intent when settling on a verdict of "ethical" or "unethical" behavior. There's a difference between simple marketing mistakes and truly unethical behavior.

Unethical marketers *intend* to act negligent, manipulate consumers, and generally do harm to others. Average marketers, on the other hand, may simply make an innocent mistake that only appears unethical. For example, consider a company that produces children's toys. It releases a toy, markets it, and introduces it to consumers. The consumers love it and begin to purchase the toy. After two months of being on the market, however, a defect is noticed and the company recalls the toy. In this case, the company didn't intentionally put this toy onto the market knowing it was defective and could cause harm to the consumer. Instead, it was an innocent mistake. But if this company knew that a defect was present in the product and it still introduced the product, it would have an unethical case against it.

In order for a business to cross the boundaries from ethical into unethical behavior, it must be aware that an action will be considered unethical. Then it must act with deviance to cover the true intent of the action. In other words, the business doing the marketing must know that the actions are considered inappropriate and carry through with them anyway. However, in order to prove that an action is unethical, it must be proved that there was intent to mislead the consumer. Proving intent isn't an easy thing to do.

There's a difference between marketing ethics and actual laws. Marketing ethics represent rules of conduct that have been put into place to protect the interests of consumers. However, if you market in a way that breaks actual laws, you're in for legal issues. These written laws have been approved and are enforced by the government in order to protect consumers. The labels of right and wrong are dependent on personal perspectives, morals, ideals, and cultures. It's a different story when a company breaks laws and violates the trust of the consumer, however.

## *Understanding how unethical marketing affects consumer behavior*

Unethical marketing behavior affects the emotions, attitudes, and perceptions of consumers, whether it happens to them directly or they just hear about it. Consumers often feel the impact when they experience a lack of trust or a feeling of disbelief in regard to marketing. Then they're hesitant to purchase. You've probably heard the phrase "If it's too good to be true, it probably is." Well, it's just my guess, but you have to wonder whether a consumer who had experienced unethical marketing coined that phrase.

When businesses begin to take advantage of consumers, consumers lose, businesses lose, and society as whole eventually loses. Many people believe that the ethical treatment of consumers is the basis of a fair and just marketplace. After all, when trust is violated, value perceptions held by consumers are harmed, and they may stop making purchases. And when a business misrepresents a product, consumers are led to expect more than is actually delivered. At that point, an unfair exchange results. A fair value exchange, on the other hand, results when consumers, business owners, and marketers act with good faith, complete disclosure, and trust.

Consider an example where a business knowingly deceives a consumer. In this example, a water filtration company salesperson knowingly contaminates a water purity test by adding certain minerals to a water sample. The consumer is alarmed by the poor quality of his water and the harm it may cause to his family, so he decides to buy a filtration system from that company.

The act of this one salesperson could have a detrimental effect on consumers, other employees, the business's hometown, and even the employee herself. For example, consider what would happen if that consumer later discovered that the water test was knowingly tainted. He would complain not only to the company but also to the Better Business Bureau. If the word got out that the salesperson acted unethically, the company could go out of business. Employees would lose their jobs, storefronts would suddenly become vacant, and consumers would be left with unnecessary products.

## Discovering how ethics affect the four Ps of the marketing mix

Because all areas of the marketing mix can be brought into question and construed as unethical by consumer groups, it's important that you use the tools in your marketing mix carefully. Marketing practices that potentially raise problems of ethics are associated with all four of the marketing mix variables: pricing, product management, promotion, and placement. (If you need a refresher, you can read more about the four Ps of marketing strategy in Chapter 3.) You can counteract the predisposed problems consumers may have by using these variables to identify and educate consumers, thereby building their trust and confidence in you. In this section, I examine each of these areas separately.

### Pricing

Pricing is one of the most visible elements of the marketing mix, and so pricing policies are constantly questioned by consumers. And when a consumer believes that prices are unfair, she's likely to leave the business and spread negative information to other consumers regarding that business.

It's also common for consumers to complain about marketing efforts that lead to overall higher prices. For instance, a company that pays millions of dollars for a Super Bowl commercial will often face criticism from consumers and push back on price. Marketers use the "price" as a statement of value received from an offering that may or may not be monetary; it's important that consumers see that same value.

An unethical use of pricing is to state that a regular price is a sales price. This practice is actually prohibited by law as well.

## Products

The largest ethical concern regarding the product portion of the marketing mix is whether the products are harmful to the consumer or to society as a whole. Products can often lead to short-term consumer satisfaction, but they also may lead to long-term problems for both the consumer and society.

The failure to disclose that a product won't function properly without necessary components is unethical.

Generally, products fall into four categories pertaining to social responsibility; these categories represent how long a consumer expects the benefits of the product to last:

- ✔ **Deficient products:** These products have little to no potential to create value of any type. An example might be a faulty appliance. Obviously you want to avoid offering products that are considered deficient.

- ✔ **Salutary product:** These products are good for both consumers and society in the long run. Salutary products offer practical value, but they don't provide pleasure value. For example, vehicle air bags have great value, but they don't necessarily provide pleasure or entertainment.

- ✔ **Pleasing products:** These products provide pleasure value to consumers, but they can be harmful in the long run. For example, consumers enjoy cigarettes and alcohol, but these products obviously can be harmful to your health and the health of others.

  The pleasing products category is usually the one where ethical issues come up. But it's important to realize that individual responsibility and freedom are important factors when it comes to the consumer's decision to use these products.

- ✔ **Desirable products:** These products deliver high practical value along with pleasurable value. Plus they help consumers immediately and have long-running benefits. An example is weight-loss products, which give consumers immediate results by curbing their appetites. When used correctly, these products have the long-run benefit to consumers of losing weight.

## Promotion

As marketers we use promotion to communicate a product's value through techniques such as advertising, sales promotion, and word-of-mouth marketing. Unfortunately, many times consumers believe that products are promoted in ways that are "too good to be true." This creates skepticism and a decline in trust toward the promotional message.

Promoting an item as being on sale and then informing the consumer that the product is out of stock and that a more expensive item should be bought is unethical. This practice, which is known as the *bait-and-switch* method, is prohibited by law.

## Theodore Levitt's marketing contribution

In the 1960s, Theodore Levitt developed a marketing concept, called *marketing myopia,* that brought a new marketing perspective to businesses. Levitt believed that businesses should define themselves in terms of the consumer needs that they solved rather than the products that they made. In other words, businesses should stop thinking of themselves as producing products and services and instead start doing things that would make consumers want to do business with them. This concept is still taught today and used by businesses. However, Levitt's marketing concept has raised a problem for companies that produce such products as fast food, tobacco, alcohol, and gambling supplies. Many people target these companies and criticize them for marketing products that some consider harmful.

### Placement

*Placement* refers to how you distribute a product through the various channels of delivery. Placement becomes a concern to consumers when they're worried about how or where they'll get their product.

If you limit product availability in certain markets as a means of raising prices, you would be acting unethically.

# Recognizing a Marketer's Ethical Responsibilities

Marketing ethics consist of societal and professional standards of right and fair practices. These standards are expected of marketing professionals as they develop and implement marketing strategies. The problem with ethics as it pertains to consumer behavior is that not everyone agrees on what behaviors should be considered unethical.

Some ethical marketing issues lend themselves to strict law and are now cut-and-dried legal obligations; other issues, however, aren't so clear-cut. The broad definition of marketing ethics leaves a lot of room for subjective interpretation. In fact, you can define marketing ethics as the determination of how much tolerance one has for actions that take advantage of others. Because this represents a gray line, it's important to adhere to sound ethical principles.

Some issues crop up time and time again in the marketing industry, so I recommend that you avoid those issues entirely — even if they aren't legislated and enforceable. Consumer perceptions of questionable incidents are important; bad events can mean disaster for a business in terms of lost business, customer boycotts, and bad publicity. In this section, I fill you in on your legal liabilities as well as the gray areas I recommend you do everything in your power to avoid.

## *Examining the requirements*

Many years ago, companies simply didn't listen to the voice of the consumer, especially in the early days of mass production. Instead, the focus was put on production efficiencies and cost per unit. In the 20th century, consumers began to see a change, however. The collective consumer voice grew steadily, and the adoption of the Consumer Bill of Rights helped this consumer movement even further. Various groups began to develop for the sole purpose of protecting basic consumer rights and focusing on consumerism.

The Consumer Bill of Rights, which dramatically changed how businesses viewed consumers, was introduced in 1962 by President John F. Kennedy and still stands today as the foundation of the consumerism movement. When President Kennedy introduced the consumer rights bill in a speech addressed to Congress, there were only four basic rights. In 1985, however, the United Nations endorsed Kennedy's Consumer Bill of Rights and expanded it to represent eight consumer rights.

Consumers are legally protected by the Consumer Bill of Rights, and if they feel they've been violated, they can sue the company that violated them. The Consumer Bill of Rights includes the following rights:

- ✔ **The Right to Satisfaction of Basic Needs:** Consumers have the right to have access to goods and services that satisfy their basic needs, including food, water, public utilities, shelter, clothing, health care, and education.

- ✔ **The Right to Be Informed:** Consumers have the right to information regarding your product. This information must be adequate enough for a consumer to make a knowledgeable and intelligent decision regarding the purchase and use of your product. Your product and service marketing communication must not be deceptive.

- ✔ **The Right to Redress and Be Heard:** Consumers expect to have the right to voice their opinions and complaints and be heard in order to have an issue resolved efficiently and in a responsive manner. So you need to have the appropriate process in place to address any complaints. You also must be able to redress any grievances your consumers may have about their purchases and receive a fair settlement. Your contracts should be written in good faith and should be honored.

- ✔ **The Right to Choice:** Consumers have the right to free choice, so they expect to have a variety of options available to them from different sources. They want to be able to select who they want to purchase from. This means you can't force a consumer to purchase from you; they have the right to look elsewhere and buy elsewhere without being harassed or harmed.

✔ **The Right to Education:** Consumers have the right to obtain knowledge and skills that helps them make better purchasing decisions. You can't withhold this important information from consumers.

✔ **The Right to Service:** Consumers have a right to expect that they'll be treated with respect and courtesy and that they'll be provided an appropriate response to any needs they have and any problems that they encounter from a product they've purchased from you. You can't refuse a service to a consumer who has purchased something from you.

✔ **The Right to Safety:** Consumers can expect to be protected from hazardous products or services that they purchase from you, particularly if they have used the products and services as they were intended to be used. You can't sell or distribute dangerous products and services.

✔ **The Right to Environmental Health:** Consumers should be protected from devastating and harmful effects, such as air and water pollutants, that may be a result of marketplace operations. They have the right to live and work in an environment that doesn't threaten their well-being. You must provide a safe environment for your customers to be in.

By fulfilling these rights and duties and using them as guidelines in your business practices, you ensure that your business doesn't engage in unintentional unethical practices. I suggest that you create a policy that represents these duties and rights, and then place this policy where it can be reviewed by consumers and staff. The section "Developing Your Marketing Code of Ethics: Some Simple Guidelines," later in this chapter, provides some guidelines to help.

## Considering the gray areas

Many marketing practices are serious infractions and are legislated against in order to protect consumers (see the preceding section for more). Obviously these practices would be considered unethical. However, some issues aren't universally labeled as unethical or illegal, but they commonly draw a lot of public scrutiny. Some may consider this type of marketing unethical, but is it? It's a line that can become blurred very quickly. I explain some of these practices in the following sections.

### Misleading with deceptive marketing

*Deceptive marketing,* also known as false or misleading marketing, tops the list of dishonest practices that aren't illegal. *Deceptive advertising* is advertising that either contains or omits information that's important in influencing consumers to purchase your product. If the advertisement is likely to mislead consumers, it's also considered deceptive advertising.

It's important to understand the difference between deceptive marketing and puffery. *Puffery* is the practice of making exaggerated claims about a product and its superiority in the marketplace. Puffery differs from deceptive marketing in that there's no overt attempt to deceive a consumer. Instead, it's an exaggeration about your product that's purely false and represents an outright misrepresentation of your product. Puffery isn't illegal, but it will diminish the trust consumers have in you. This loss of trust can haunt you in the future and affect the perception consumers have of you.

A popular tactic that marketers use is to advertise a product as being the "best" available. These claims are generally puffery. Are you concerned that you're engaged in puffery? This general guideline may help you decide: The more detailed a claim is regarding your product, the more it must be supported by practical evidence. For example if you claim that "consumers prefer your restaurant two-to-one over the competition" you would need to be able to support that claim with evidence. If you can provide the data to back up the claim, you're not engaged in puffery. If you can't and the statement is untrue, you're guilty of puffing up your product.

### Marketing to children (and other vulnerable consumers)

Children are considered to be vulnerable consumers because they lack the knowledge to behave as responsible consumers. As a marketer or business owner, you need to consider two issues when marketing to children:

- ✔ Children generally don't understand that some marketing messages offer a less-than-literal interpretation of the world.
- ✔ The sheer quantity of marketing messages that children are exposed to can be called into question.

These are important issues to understand when it comes to how children are affected by marketing, because you can use them as guidelines when crafting an ethical marketing strategy directed toward children.

In October 1990, legislators passed the Children's Television Act of 1990 to limit the amount of advertising to which children are exposed. The act limits the amount of commercial airtime during children's programming to 10.5 minutes per hour on weekends and 12 minutes on weekdays.

Some people argue that children today are growing up in a society that's far too commercialized and that the messages children receive harm their psychological development and lead them to focus too heavily on material goods. Others, however, believe that advertising and marketing messages simply add to the socialization process in which children learn marketplace skills that enable them to function properly as consumers later.

## What about social responsibility?

As a business owner, practicing social responsibility is one way you can attempt to gain respect from your consumers. Your *social responsibility* is defined as your organization's activities and status as it relates to societal obligations. In other words, your social responsibility is to make good decisions and do the right thing. You can use social responsibility to increase consumer awareness regarding not only your stance on ethics, but also your commitment to society. This leads to a positive perception on the behalf of consumers.

In recent years, businesses have experienced an increased pressure from consumer and media groups to be socially responsible in their activities. A few activities you can engage in to fulfill this obligation include:

✔ Making donations to causes of interest

✔ Supporting minority programs

✔ Ensuring responsible manufacturing processes to protect the environment

✔ Taking action quickly when product defects are detected

✔ Focusing on employee safety

✔ Encouraging employees to volunteer for local causes

What does social responsibility have to do with consumer behavior and ethics? Socially responsible marketing creates positive outcomes and is associated with more favorable consumer evaluations, increased consumer satisfaction, and the likelihood of more sales. This is especially true when a consumer identifies with the company and the causes it contributes to.

### Expiring a product prematurely

*Planned obsolescence* is the intentional phasing out of a product before its usefulness truly wears out. The purpose behind planned obsolescence is to guarantee that consumers are forced to purchase the product multiple times. Obviously, this increases the demand for the product. Take, for example, video game consoles. The manufacturers of these products have been criticized for releasing new and improved systems even when older models haven't been on the market for very long. The same is true for cellular phones.

Critics believe that it's both wasteful and greedy for marketers to engage in planned obsolescence. By participating in this practice, you run the risk of irritating consumers and developing a bad reputation. Both can affect future sales of your product with consumers. Consumers often feel as if they've been burned if they're required to make multiple purchases they didn't plan for. In my opinion, participating in planned obsolescence isn't worth the risk of losing customers or developing a bad word-of-mouth reputation, because these damages often can't be undone.

### Forcing artificial needs on consumers

It isn't uncommon for marketers to be criticized for imposing what are called *artificial needs* on consumers. These so-called needs are discussed in ways that make consumers feel that they must have a certain product in order to feel or look a certain way. In the end, however, the real issue is that businesses cause people to *want* a product, even if they don't truly *need* it.

In other words, many folks feel as if marketers and advertisements are responsible for leading consumers to confuse wants with needs. For example, does a consumer really *need* a 52-inch plasma, high-definition television? What about $175 tennis shoes when she can purchase a pair for $30?

The confusion between wants and needs is often brought on from marketing messages. Usually it's because marketing campaigns make consumers feel inadequate if they don't have a certain product. Instead of allowing the marketing message to focus on the benefits to sell the product, it works to manipulate the consumer into buying the product. Using these types of manipulative messages is unethical and causes the consumer to be confused and often regretful after making the purchase.

# Developing Your Marketing Code of Ethics: Some Simple Guidelines

Finding the balance between consumer protection and market freedom can be difficult. So how can you put your marketing ethics to the test and ensure that you're doing what's best for the consumer as well as what's best for growing your company? It's tough, but it can be done by creating a marketing code of ethics, which is simply a list of explicitly stated rules and codes of conduct when it comes to the ethics of marketing. Many organizations have a code of ethics; one such organization is the American Marketing Association (AMA).

The following guidelines are standard marketing ethics that can be used to help you make socially responsible decisions as you market and grow your business:

- ✓ Put your consumers first and consider the effects of their actions on all involved when using your product and services.

- ✓ Base your marketing standards on actions and go beyond the required laws and regulations to uphold those standards.

✔ Be responsible for the means and marketing vehicles that you use to achieve your desired goal. It isn't enough to simply focus on profit and motivation alone.

✔ Invest the time to focus on training your employees in ethical decision making.

✔ Embrace and publicize a core set of ethical principles that you will uphold as a business.

✔ Adopt an orientation and training program that leads to an appreciation of how marketing decisions affect all appropriate parties.

✔ Specify the protocols for ethical decision making within your business.

✔ Determine your company's policy toward attack advertisements and confrontational marketing.

✔ Stay clear of state and federal pricing guidelines by limiting price guarantees in your advertisements.

✔ Consider attaching legal requirements for disclaimers to your business ethics policy as you develop marketing campaigns.

✔ Detail permissions of marketing material that targets vulnerable populations in your ethics policy.

✔ Submit every piece of marketing copy for an extensive editing process to avoid breaking your ethics policy.

For businesses that want to gain an edge on their competition, marketing ethics can be difficult to stick to. With that said, however, you need to protect your business and your products by developing a marketing ethics policy. The previous guidelines can help. This policy can help you avoid ethics issues and keep the business of loyal customers.

# Chapter 16

# Evoking Awareness through Positioning

A challenge related to consumer behavior is the perceived value of your products and services to your customers. Consumers don't always accurately perceive the value that's being offered. And when a consumer doesn't believe that the product will deliver the value she desires or doesn't perceive the product in the way it's intended, she won't make the purchase. Your job, then, is to figure out what the consumers in your target market need and want and then determine what you have to offer, what benefits you provide, who your competitors are, and how you're different from those competitors. You use this information to create a positioning strategy and statement, which are tools you can use to reach out to your targeted consumers, identifying, communicating, and differentiating your company and products from your competition.

In this chapter, I show you how the concepts I cover in Parts II and III begin factoring into your marketing strategy. I begin by explaining what the process of positioning entails. Then I introduce you to some time-tested positioning strategies and guide you in figuring out which one is best for you. I cap off the chapter with guidance on putting your strategy into a concise statement that guides the rest of your marketing strategy.

## A Primer on Positioning

*Positioning* is the act of creating a unique identity for whatever it is that you're selling and then targeting a segment of the broader market by fitting your product or service to that segment's wants and needs. Positioning works for anything you're promoting, whether it be a product, service, or company.

The act of positioning requires a two-part process: devising a positioning strategy and creating a positioning statement. The *positioning strategy* is a tool that guides all your marketing communication, ensuring that you're integrating your position in all the parts of your marketing strategy. Positioning allows you to create a market-focused statement of value, otherwise known as your *positioning statement* — a simple, clear statement of why your target market should buy your product.

## Understanding the importance of positioning

Positioning represents the way you present your company and your products to your consumers. It works to create a perception within your consumers regarding who you are and what you offer. Positioning gives the consumer a unique statement of value that he can consider when it comes to making a purchase decision; without this statement of value a consumer can only judge what you offer by the price tag your product or service carries.

The goal of positioning, then, is to design products and services and present them to consumers in a way that occupies a meaningful and distinctive competitive position in your consumer's mind.

## Knowing what you're positioning

Generally speaking, there are two things you can position: your product and your company. Here's a quick explanation of each:

- **Product positioning** is the straight comparison of the features of a product. When working to position your product, you need to base that positioning on what the product can actually do for the consumer. This type of positioning also goes for services.

- **Company positioning,** on the other hand, deals with the perception a consumer has in regard to the entire company. It's similar to product positioning, but the objective is to create and transfer an image of the entire company rather than of one product.

When positioning a company, you have less control over the outcome, because you can't provide immediate influence to your consumers like you can with your product and its benefits. Instead, you have to work harder to create the desired perception of your company and what your company stands for. If you position your product for the consumer — and you do it correctly — your consumer likely will decide to purchase your product. In that case, you will have done all the company positioning that you need to do. For that reason, I recommend that most readers stick to product positioning and let the company positioning happen naturally.

Company positioning becomes extremely important when a company is trying to go public or position itself for acquisition. While the value of corporate marketing is perception, it's important to keep in mind that most companies are judged by their products, not necessarily by their name recognition.

You use different tools depending on whether you're positioning your company or a product. When positioning your product, you use marketing through various channels, including advertising, personal selling, and sales promotions; when you're focusing on positioning your company, you use publicity efforts and public relations. Just remember that positioning is really the same discipline either way. The difference is in "what" you're positioning rather than "how" you're positioning it.

## Getting a glimpse of the positioning process

In order to successfully position your product or service to your target market, you must do two things:

- ✔ Identify your target consumer as precisely as possible.
- ✔ Understand how that target consumer makes her buying decisions. For example, are her decisions based on frustrations, attitudes, values, challenges, likes, or dislikes?

These two things help you guide consumers (through both your positioning strategy and statement) to relate the benefits of your product or service to their needs. After you have a handle on the preceding two concepts, you begin the positioning process. The positioning process involves these three steps:

1. **Differentiate your product from its competition by crafting a unique selling proposition (USP).**

   Before you can position your product or service to your target market, you need to have a solid handle on what that product or service offers to the folks who buy it. Identifying your *unique selling proposition* means finding something meaningful and unique to say about your product offer that competitors either can't or won't say — and then presenting this difference to the consumer in the form of a proposition. Your USP represents the very core of what it is that you're offering; it can be an actual fact or just a perceived difference or specialty. It focuses on the key benefits or attributes of your product, service, or company.

You can have different USPs for products, but you should only have one USP for your company.

2. **Use your USP to address a common problem among consumers.**

   Consumers purchase solution-positioned products. So, determine how your product or service solves their problem, makes their life easier, and saves them money.

3. **Articulate the solution and the value of your product to the consumers by creating your positioning statement.**

   When a consumer tries to derive meaning from your message, comprehension occurs. *Comprehension* is the process where meanings are assigned to the stimuli. Of course, you want consumers to comprehend and interpret the information in the way you intended, but this isn't always the case. A consumer can encounter the same stimuli, but yet comprehend it in different ways. So, articulation of your position is crucial — it's your job to help consumers understand what you're offering to them and why they should care.

A *positioning map,* or what some call a *perceptual map,* is a useful tool for planning your position relative to your competitor's position (see Figure 16-1). It helps you map key attributes of your and your competitor's product, service, or business. Start out with a basic positioning map containing a graph that has two points: one being high quality and the other on the opposite side of the graph representing low quality. Rank yourself and your competitors on the graph based on the perception of consumers. Doing so enables you to see where you stand with your competitors from a positioning standpoint. If you want to get more detailed, which I often suggest, list in the graph the benefits and features that your product contains. Then rank your competition by doing a comparison of how your competitors are viewed and how you're viewed by consumers.

As you can see in Figure 16-1, Competitor A provides a high-quality product, but at a high price. Competitor B offers a product that is of lower cost and of lower quality than Competitor A, and Competitor C ranks the lowest on all points. Compared to the competitors' products, yours is of high quality — not the highest, but it does rank above two of your competitors — and you're able to offer it at a lower price, giving your consumers a better value than the competitors. These factors enable you to position better quality above two competitors and a better price above your third competitor.

### Step 1: Touch the pain point

In touching a consumer's pain point, you're lending urgency to your marketing message. Consumers won't act unless they feel an urgent pain that they need to remedy. So, as bad as it sounds, you have to use your marketing message to rub salt into the wound before presenting your unique solution.

Suppose my target market wants to lose weight. The pain point in this situation is the feeling of frustration with their current state of being and the experience of failing to find a sufficient remedy to fix the problem once and for all. Individuals who have tried weight-loss programs without success feel like they have failed. Additionally, many people are embarrassed about starting a new program in public. In my USP, I address that need, and in my marketing efforts, I'll find a way to touch the pain point to awaken consumers' attention.

Some of you may be thinking, "I just sell lip balm. I can't make anything of all this pain talk." Think about this way: If you've ever had chapped lips, you know that it's a painful experience. You keep licking them, it's difficult to eat, and it feels like the skin on your lips is being stretched to capacity. Your consumers must feel the pain in order to make the purchase. It can be a physical pain, an emotional pain, or even a pain because they continually run out of time. You must look at your product from the perspective of your potential consumer. Why do they care about your product?

### Step 2: Explain how your product or service eases the pain

If you identified your market's pain point or problem, but your product or service doesn't provide a solution to that problem, you may as well find a new business or target market. If your product or service *does* provide a solution, your task is to present that solution in simple but compelling terms.

You must identify the benefits of your solution, and determine how those benefits will improve your consumers' lives and situations. Reflect on how the benefits of your product relieve the pain and suffering they're experiencing. Consumers don't know your product like you do. So, you must tell them what your product will do for them and why they should buy it.

Say, for example, that your target market consists of folks who want to lose weight, and that you're offering an innovative online weight-loss program they can use in the privacy of their own homes. You even offer a money-back guarantee if consumers aren't satisfied. Your top three benefits in this situation are as follows:

✔ You're providing your target market with a weight-loss program that provides hope and diminishes the pain of being overweight.

✔ Your buyers can use the program within the privacy of their own homes, which diminishes the embarrassment pain point.

✔ Your buyers get a win-win incentive — they either achieve satisfaction or get their money back.

All the benefits that you claim regarding your product must be 100 percent true. You must be able to prove any statement you make about a product benefit to your consumer. If you can't, ditch the benefit, because it will only create future mistrust in consumers and risk of negative word-of-mouth marketing that will be difficult to recover from.

## Making sure your USP is effective

In the previous section, I walk you through the steps of developing your own USP. Now I want to share with you a few examples of effective USPs:

- **Dominos Pizza:** "We deliver hot, fresh pizza in 30 minutes or less or it's free."

- **M&Ms:** "Melts in your mouth, not in your hands."

- **Burger King:** "Have it your way."

These USPs are concise, specific, descriptive, and easy to remember. Can you create a USP that's just as effective? To create your own effective USP, follow these guidelines:

- **Be unique.** If your USP is unique, it will set you apart from your competitors.

- **Be specific.** You want your USP to be specific enough that consumers understand it and the benefits you're offering. If your USP isn't specific, you run the risk of consumers not being clear on what your proposition is.

- **Be succinct.** One of the biggest mistakes companies make when developing their USPs is that they're too wordy. Your USP must be a concise, one-sentence statement. In fact, the best USPs are so perfectly written that you can't change or move even a single word. Each word in your USP should sell your product or your service.

- **Make sure you can deliver on your promise.** If you can't deliver on your promise, don't risk your reputation on it — it isn't worth it. Instead, develop a USP that you can deliver, and be sure to stand behind it.

- **Offer proof.** Your consumers are already skeptical of the claims that businesses make, so by providing them with proof to back your promise, you're ahead of your competition. Proof can be testimonials, white papers, or success stories of past customers. (Refer to Chapter 17 for more information on using testimonials in your marketing message.) For example, it's a great idea to offer a guarantee to your consumers to support your claims.

# Using Your USP to Develop a Positioning Strategy

The key to positioning is understanding the factors that consumers use to compare you against your competitors and then make a purchase decision. After you have a handle on consumer perceptions, you need to select the best positioning based on the benefits that you offer consumers and then take steps to align the marketing program behind this positioning choice.

You can manage positioning by focusing your marketing activities on a positioning strategy. Pricing, promotion, channels of distribution, and advertising should all maximize the positioning strategy of your company and product.

Positioning is represented by what the consumer believes about your product's value, features, and benefits. The trick is to identify key attributes of your company, product, or service to show its value, features, and benefits. This section helps you do that.

## Positioning your product or service relative to its competition

Positioning with differentiating characteristics of your product will help you to stand out from the crowd of products that are similar to yours. You can differentiate your product or service in three ways:

- ✔ **You can position directly against a competitor.** You do this by claiming that your product is better than your competitor's. In today's market an effective positioning strategy focuses on specific competitors. This approach is similar to positioning according to product benefit, but in this case the competition is within the same product category.

- ✔ **You can position yourself away from the competition.** This strategy is useful if you can't compete with the competition because it's a strong and well-established player. To position away from the competition, look for consumer needs or market niches that position you elsewhere. Doing so helps position you away from the competing noise.

- ✔ **You can position yourself according to type of benefit.** This strategy of positioning has to do with positioning your product against others. The product categories aren't exactly the same, but the products all provide the same class of benefits. An example would be the positioning of airlines, trains, and buses. They don't provide the same means of transportation, but they do provide the same service — transportation.

Different differentiation strategy options allow you to create a variety of approaches geared toward targeted consumers. These approaches can be based on specific characteristics of each targeted group. For example, you have different differentiation strategies for specific demographics, household structures, or cultures. The strategies you create could focus on what's important to each group instead of having a "one-size-fits-all" strategy.

The best way to determine how many strategies you need is to evaluate who you're targeting and what's most important to them. If you find that your consumers have different pain points or unfulfilled needs, it may be best to try different differentiation strategies. If your targeted consumers have the same needs, you can simply focus on one differentiation strategy.

In the following sections, I focus on the process of creating a differentiation strategy as well as on what factors you can use to differentiate your product or service.

### The process

You need to do the following in order to make the development of your differentiating strategy go smoothly:

- ✔ **Define the criteria your consumers use to evaluate products that they buy.** This will help you in knowing what criteria are important to your consumers and how you can use those criteria to differentiate your product or service.

- ✔ **Identify your product's key benefits in customer terms.** Consumers make purchases based on benefits, so it's important that they can identify what your benefits are and that they have the information necessary to differentiate you from your competitors. Do you offer a better price, better customer service, or a better product? If so, you want to be clear about that with your consumers.

- ✔ **Identify your competitor's position.** You can't differentiate from your competitors if you don't have a clear understanding of their position in the marketplace. Evaluate where they stand on quality of product, price, and service and then determine where you're different.

- ✔ **Identify your competitive strengths.** It's important to have an understanding of your competitors' strengths so you can be aware of where they may stand out or fall behind in comparison to you. Doing so allows you to be prepared.

- ✔ **Select a position that gives you a unique and sustainable competitive edge.** You can use all the preceding information to determine the position you must create with your consumers and against your competitors. You must then take that information and create a statement that stands out to your consumers and gives you the competitive edge.

## The factors you can differentiate with

Differentiate yourself by identifying what your product does that others can't or don't. You're looking for the most persuasive, meaningful, and unique difference that your competitors can't claim. You can differentiate yourself by using these four factors:

- ✔ **Price:** You want to evaluate what your price is compared to your competitors. Is it higher or lower? One risk you take when differentiating due to price is that price isn't difficult to change. Plus, while some consumers will purchase based on price, most spend more time evaluating other differentiating factors such as benefits or service.

- ✔ **Focus:** You can differentiate yourself by using your focus. For example, are you specialized in a particular area? Are you viewed as one of the experts in an industry? Consumers often purchase from companies that they feel are experts or specialized in an industry rather than companies that are more generalized.

- ✔ **Product/service:** You can differentiate by using your quality of product or the benefits that you offer. How do they stand out from among your competitors? What benefits do you offer that they don't? Why is your product of better quality? These are the things that a consumer pays attention to before they look at a price tag. Differentiating a product from its competition is a bit different from differentiating a service. For example, if you're differentiating a product, you may want to focus on these common factors:

  - Design
  - Durability
  - Reliability
  - Reparability
  - Style

  On the other hand, suppose you're marketing a service. You may want to focus on the following common factors:

  - Customer consulting
  - Customer training
  - Delivery
  - Installation
  - Ordering ease

- ✔ **Customer service:** You can differentiate by the customer service that you provide. How does it compare to the competition? Do you promise service within a certain span of time? How do you follow up with consumers? Consumers take service very seriously and if you can show them how you stand out from among your competition, they will pay attention.

You can certainly differentiate yourself in more than one category, but you need to make sure that you focus on the one that contains the most compelling benefit for your targeted consumers. The best way to differentiate between you and your competition is to know your target and pick a blend of differentiation categories that truly sets you apart. And remember that your differentiation is about the consumer, so speak in terms that show the benefit to them.

## Addressing the need your product fulfills

After you've differentiated yourself, you must use the information you gained in the differentiation process to address the concerns and needs of the consumer. Determine what problems your product or service addresses: Are you saving consumers money, time, or energy, for example? They don't care if you have the best packaging or if they can find you in every discount store. They want to know what you can do for them personally.

This step is truly all about the consumer. It's about first positioning your product by addressing a problem and then being the solution to that problem. You can focus on one of the following factors as a positioning strategy in this step:

- ✔ **Product attributes:** Attributes often include price, quality, features, style, and design of your product. The attributes are specific to consumers and are often the basis for making a purchase decision. Many times a product can be positioned in terms of two or more attributes simultaneously.

- ✔ **Usage occasion:** When using this strategy, you work to position your product with a specific use or application. For example, you might say something like "This stain stick can be used when trying to get a stain out of clothes."

- ✔ **Users:** With this strategy, you associate your product with a particular user or group of users. For example, "This hands-free headset is designed for users of cellular phones."

In order for your positioning strategy to be effective, you must bring an element of differentiation to the table when you're clarifying how your product or service meets consumers' needs. The following positioning strategy guidelines will help you address the needs of your consumers most effectively:

- ✔ **Important to the consumer:** It must deliver a high-valued benefit to a sufficient number of consumers.

- ✔ **Distinctive:** Ideally your product isn't offered by a competitor. If it already is, at least ensure that the product is offered in a way that's extremely distinctive so it stands out.

✔ **Superior:** Show what makes your product superior when compared to the competition. In other words, show consumers that you help them obtain not only the same benefits as the competition, but also even more.

✔ **Communicable:** The difference between your product and your competitor's must be communicated and visible to the consumers.

✔ **Preemptive:** The difference can't be easily copied by your competitors.

✔ **Affordable:** Your consumers must be able to afford your product and be able and willing to increase their cost if your product is more expensive than your competitor's.

✔ **Profitable:** You must be able to make a profit by introducing this difference.

In order to gain competitive advantage, you want to use the strategy that proves true with the majority of the preceding factors.

## *Avoiding common mistakes*

You want to avoid the following common positioning errors, because they can cause consumer confusion and cause a negative perception of your company and the products that you offer:

✔ **Underpositioning:** You know that you haven't positioned enough when your target market only has a vague idea of the product you're promoting.

✔ **Overpositioning:** When you position too much, only a narrow group of consumers can identify with the product.

✔ **Confused positioning:** If you haven't been clear in your positioning, consumers can have a confused image of the product. It may claim too many benefits or the benefit claim may be changed too often.

✔ **Doubtful positioning:** Doubtful positioning occurs when consumers don't believe the product's claims in view of the product's features, price, or manufacturing company.

You can take the following measures in order to avoid the errors I just discussed:

✔ **Do** clearly communicate that the product attribute you're positioning is a benefit. Otherwise, it isn't a benefit.

✔ **Do** make sure that the benefit you're highlighting is important to the consumer. Otherwise, it isn't important.

- ✔ **Do** help your consumers perceive that your company and your product deliver the benefit. Otherwise, it isn't delivered.

- ✔ **Do** precisely define your target consumers. Otherwise, you could miss them completely and they won't know that the message is meant for them.

- ✔ **Do** include the reason that consumers should believe the benefit promise. Otherwise, it may not be clear to them what benefit you're promising them.

- ✔ **Don't** attack the leaders of competing companies. This only distracts from your message and the value that you bring to the consumer.

- ✔ **Don't** fall into the "everything" trap. In other words, don't try to be all things to all people. Doing so only waters down your message and diminishes its strength.

- ✔ **Don't** forget what has made you successful. Consumers love to hear success stories and endorsements that they can depend on.

- ✔ **Don't** position by using attributes that lack work or are unimportant. This will only take away from those important attributes that you want to be known for.

- ✔ **Don't** position by mimicking equality with your competitors. You must stand out in order to be remembered and to make consumers want to purchase from you. Equality isn't enough; you must offer them more to gain their interest and appeal directly to them.

- ✔ **Don't** list multiple differentiators and benefits. You want your benefit statement to be singular. Otherwise, it may confuse your consumers.

- ✔ **Don't** develop benefits that aren't unique or sustainable. It's the benefits that sell a consumer. If you don't offer them anything unique or sustainable, they'll see no reason to purchase your product.

# Crafting a Strong Positioning Statement

After you develop a positioning strategy and determine the problem that needs to be addressed, you have to take all that information and create your positioning statement. This is simply a no-nonsense statement of how you want your products to be perceived in the minds of your target market. Your positioning statement provides direction, and it focuses on your products and their position in the marketplace.

Your positioning statement is a great tool that can be used when you need a short description of who your company is or what products you offer. I like to think of it as a "fingerprint" that creates a perception in consumers, because it informs them of your company and products. It informs consumers of who you are, what you do, and why you're different and beneficial to them.

## Using a simple but effective formula

The key to creating an effective positioning statement is to remember that it isn't about what you do, but rather it's about the benefit you offer to your target market and the difference between you and your competitors.

When it comes to positioning statements, I like to use a special formula. It looks like this:

*(Product, company, service, person) is the one (category of your product) that provides (the target customer) with (product's key benefit) because (reason they should believe that your company can deliver the benefit).*

Here's a positioning statement that's created from the previous formula:

*Dazzling Toothpaste is the only toothpaste that provides kids with a fruity flavor that protects them from cavities because it was specifically formulated by the #1 rated pediatric dentist.*

Do you feel that creating this statement is difficult? It's okay. The truth is that positioning statements are rarely correct the first time. You must create and then rework them to ensure their effectiveness. You may also want to solicit the help of others to brainstorm your positioning statement. These sessions are especially helpful if you're feeling stuck.

## Paying attention to word choice and focus

Because your success depends on your positioning statement, you shouldn't take lightly the task of creating one. Your statement should

- ✔ **Be short and to the point:** By short, I mean your statement should be 12 words or less. However, you don't have to count the product name. Using concise words helps keep your word count down.

- ✔ **Use simple and clear language:** You want to use simple and clear language so that your statement is understood by consumers with no chance of misunderstanding. It's especially important to avoid jargon.

- ✔ **Be adaptable to various media types:** You must be able to use your statement in different forms of media, such as Web, radio, television, or print, in order maintain consistency.

- ✔ **Be a compelling statement of one important benefit that your product presents:** Benefits sell consumers, so your positioning statement is more powerful when it represents an important benefit that your product offers to consumers when they use it.

✔ **Serve as a conceptual statement, not necessarily a copy from a competitor that didn't put in much consideration or thought:** Your positioning statement must be powerful. If you create one without much thought, you won't receive the perception you desire.

✔ **Satisfy four evaluation criteria:** It should be unique, believable, important, and useable. Why? Because these are the things consumers use to evaluate and create perceptions of companies and products.

## Testing your positioning statement

After you create a positioning statement, you need to put it to the test. You test the statements to ensure that they make sense to your target market and will create the desired perception within your consumers. You also want to make sure that they will ultimately help in selling your product.

I like to test positioning statements by reading them out loud and then asking myself the following questions:

✔ Does my positioning statement contain a promise of an important consumer buying advantage?

✔ Does my statement give a clear differentiation between my product and my competitor's product?

✔ Is my company name or the name of my product ingrained in my positioning statement?

✔ Is there an inherent understanding of what my statement is saying to my consumer?

How did you do? If you answered "no" to any of the previous questions, you need to go back and rework the statement. If you answered "yes" to all of them, your statement is all set to be put in motion — you can now use it in your marketing message. It is also a great tool that you can use when creating your marketing collateral and campaigns in order to ensure that all marketing messages are consistent and effective. You will also want to share it with others within your company so that everyone understands it and is able to share it with potential customers.

# Chapter 17

# Leading Customers from Attention to Action

*B*efore you can persuade a person to purchase whatever you're selling, you have to get that person's attention. You attract attention to your product or service just like you attract attention to anything else — by engaging any one or more of your target consumer's five senses: sight, smell, taste, touch, or sound. When you place a stimulus along your target's path, you engage a sensation that requires the consumer's immediate response to the information he has just encountered.

After you grab the consumer's attention, you then have to educate him about your product by sharing with him information and advice on how your product or service can help him save money, find more time, and improve his daily life. You educate consumers by using brochures, pamphlets, seminars, or other publicity events. Any time you can provide consumers with information on how your product fulfills their needs can be seen as an educating opportunity.

You must understand your consumers in order to reach and educate them effectively. So in this chapter, I show you how to present your products to consumers and educate them at the same time. I also help you decide where to put your message so it reaches your target market. I have found that if you look at marketing as a tool to educate your consumers, you can actually end up answering their objections as well as increasing their chances of purchasing.

# Getting Consumers' Attention with Compelling Stimuli

Consumers can be motivated by marketing stimuli, such as product, price, place, or promotion. However, sometimes your stimuli may need to go a little deeper to gain a response, such as psychological, personal, social, or cultural stimuli.

Just because a consumer is exposed to any old stimulus doesn't guarantee that she'll pay attention — after all, a consumer can't pay attention to all the stimuli she's exposed to! For this reason, positioning (see Chapter 16) is key when it comes to consumer perception. You have to use the stimuli that consumers in your target market will notice and respond to. The stimuli that will work depend on what your consumers need and what they want. (Chapter 5 talks all about perception and stimuli you can use.)

To determine which stimuli to use and how to get your desired response, you really have to dig into the makeup of your targeted consumer and her individual behavior. The consumer you're targeting in one culture may not have the same needs as another consumer in another culture. The same goes for consumers in different household structures.

Marketing research can show you what motivates your consumer and can assist you in deciding what stimuli to use. To find out what it is that triggers a response from the consumers that you're targeting, you have to take the time to do the following:

✔ Ask your consumers questions to elicit the information you need.

✔ Study your competitors to determine what they're doing.

✔ Delve into the consumption patterns of the consumers you're targeting.

# Delivering an Action-Inspiring Message

The stimulus that you use grabs the attention of potential customers, but your marketing message educates them on your product. Your message allows you to present your unique selling proposition, or USP, and any additional benefits in a way that consumers can understand. In fact, your marketing message is critical to all your marketing efforts. An effective message combined with promotion draws in new customers. (Check out Chapter 16 for more information on creating a USP.)

When drafting a marketing message, I think of it as a note on a piece of scrap paper. You must grab a customer's attention quick — and hold it long enough to educate him with your message — or he's likely to wad it up and toss it in the trash can. Your marketing message should speak to that prospective customer personally. You have to appeal to his hot buttons by understanding his wants and needs. His hot buttons trigger an emotional decision. And after a consumer makes an emotional decision, he justifies it by logic.

You need to create urgency in your marketing message. A consumer won't act unless he feels an urgent pain that he needs to remedy. You have to use your marketing message to emphasize the pain and then present the solution. That solution must be backed not just by you but by former or current customers.

You also need to use your message to reverse any perceived risk that your potential consumer may feel regarding your solution. You must also position your solution as something that's easily implemented and that will provide immediate relief. Creating and delivering an effective marketing message is a crucial step — so really spend some time on it.

## *Educating consumers with a marketing message*

Education is seen as a value-add by most consumers. Taking the time and initiative to objectively educate your consumers about the products or services that you offer builds trust and confidence. Consumers want to make informed buying decisions, so they need guidance on how to purchase your product or service.

You educate consumers by providing them with information about not only who your company is and how your products benefit them, but also by sharing with them useful and easy-to-understand news about your industry. So be sure to stay informed and stay on top of trends. The key is to inform consumers about why they need your product and how it benefits them. Then you can guide your consumers into the action they need to take to obtain your product or service.

Consumers want and have a need for information that helps them. If you can give them this information, you'll create customers for life. The more information you can provide consumers — without selling to them — the deeper the emotional connection you will make with them. They'll feel that you genuinely care about their needs and that you want what's best for them. They'll believe that you aren't just interested in making a sale.

You're faced with opportunities to educate consumers on a daily basis. But don't worry; educating them is easy. You can create informative articles and how-to brochures, conduct seminars, send out informative newsletters, or simply have a conversation with a consumer. I suggest that you create an education piece by answering the one question you're always asked. Write about that question, providing information and guidance in an article, a brochure, or any other medium that educates your consumers in a way that builds the trust and rapport that eventually "sells" them.

When creating your educational marketing piece, it's important to refer to your USP and your positioning statement as a guideline for the message. Even though you're educating your consumers, it's important to still share why you're different from your competitors and why they need your products to fill their unmet needs. (Refer to Chapter 16 for more information on the creation of your USP and positioning statement.)

## Providing proof customers trust

Consumers expect companies to be able to support and prove their claims. After all, providing proof creates a level of credibility. When a company can't or doesn't provide proof, a consumer may become mistrustful of the claim and the company, often causing the consumer not to purchase from that company. In order to avoid this situation, it's important to have an arsenal of proof that supports your claims. This arsenal can include reviews, testimonials, and case studies. I explain each in the following sections. Evaluate the information to decide which works best for you and your consumers.

### Reviews by a third party

Reviews can be very useful in proving your claims, because third parties are the ones evaluating and reviewing your product or service. If your product or service stands up to the review process with raving results, you can show consumers that you have an outside party recommending it. A positive product review can increase sales and build consumer trust. Reviews are often published on the Internet or TV or in newspapers or magazines.

Here's the downside of reviews: If the product doesn't stand up to your claims, you'll have to activate immediate damage control in order to minimize negative publicity. Negative product reviews can diminish sales and create mistrust.

Reviews work well for products or services that provide immediate results that are visible to the consumer eye, because that's what reviewers are looking for.

### Testimonials

Great components to your marketing message are accolades or testimonials from current or past customers you've helped in similar situations. Telling potential customers that you have a solution simply isn't enough; you have to prove to them that your solution works. And the best way to do that is to use the voice of other customers who have achieved positive results by using your product. Consumers believe people who are similar to themselves.

The best testimonial is one that paints a before and after picture. A great product testimony follows this order:

1. Introduction of the problem

2. Presentation of the solution (your product)

3. Explanation of the result

A testimony following the previous formula may look like this:

> *While skiing in Colorado on vacation, I was hit with a severe case of chapped lips. It was difficult to eat or drink, and when the wind would hit my lips while skiing down the slopes the pain was excruciating. I purchased the L2 Lip Balm and experienced immediate relief. The pain disappeared immediately, and I was able to enjoy the rest of my vacation.*

### Case studies

A case study can demonstrate your benefits as well as illustrate proof of your claims. It does this by showing a detailed account of how your product or service solved a problem for a customer. Your case study should go into detail about your company, the industry you're involved in, the key people within the company, and an account of a project over time that benefits from the product or service that you offer. Case studies are great for service-oriented businesses or products that are used over time.

In order to use a case study to provide proof to a consumer, you need to thoroughly cover the project by discussing the objective of the project, the strategy you used, the challenges you faced, and the results you achieved. You also need to include in the study any recommendations you had during the project.

The problem with case studies is that they require a lot of upfront work. And while they can be beneficial, it's often difficult to get consumers to take the time to read through them. Usually only very analytical thinkers who need to view a product or service from a methodological approach read case studies.

# Perusing Your Options for Marketing Message Placement

After you have your marketing message drafted, you must decide what marketing media you should use. The marketing option that's best for you will depend on the target market you're trying to reach. After all, successful marketing is all about the needs of the consumer. For example, younger generations are generally more likely to appreciate marketing messages that are delivered via the Internet, radio, or television, while older generations may rely more on the telephone book and local newspaper.

Because you have many options to consider, the following sections give you a look at the pros and cons of each type: traditional and interactive. This way you have a greater understanding of which options may work best for you.

## Traditional marketing options

Marketers consider the options in this category to be traditional because they use traditional forms of media, such as television, radio, and print advertisements. New ways of marketing have been discovered, but many companies swear that the traditional ways still produce the best results. In the following sections, I explore the pros and cons of the different traditional marketing methods.

### Television

Television has been a popular method of advertising for large retailers since the TV set began appearing in living rooms. Because television allows businesses to reach smaller and more targeted markets, it has become a viable option for small and mid-size businesses as well the larger ones. Table 17-1 shows the pros and cons you can expect from television advertising.

| Table 17-1 | The Pros and Cons of Television Advertising |
|---|---|
| **Pros** | **Cons** |
| Reaches a larger audience in a shorter period of time than newspapers and radio. | Producing and airing television marketing can be expensive and eats up your marketing budget quickly. |
| Reaches viewers when they're most attentive. | Quick changes are difficult; updating requires changing scripts and reshooting. |
| Allows you to use the benefits of sound, sight, and motion, giving your business a personality and instant credibility. | New technology allows consumers to fast-forward through advertisements, causing target consumers to miss your commercial. |

### Phone book

There was a day when everyone went to the phone book — specifically the Yellow Pages — to find vendors and service providers. Some consumer markets still go that route, but the number is diminishing. Many folks in today's society are trying to be more environmentally friendly, and just about everyone else likes instant access, so most people tend to use the Internet more often than the phone book. Check out Table 17-2 for the pros and cons of using the Yellow Pages of the phone book to advertise.

| Table 17-2 | Pros and Cons of Phone Book Advertising |
|---|---|
| **Pros** | **Cons** |
| Considered to be the complete sourcebook for business listings with telephone numbers. | Ads are listed among competitors, so prospective consumers may be distracted by other companies in the same category. |
| Depending on the efficiency of your ad, consumers can learn a lot about your company. | Changing your ad is impossible; if it doesn't work, you're still stuck paying for the next 12 months. |
| Ads are generally listed by seniority in each category, so you can work your way up to a forward position. | Seniority can be trumped by bigger ads, so you may end up at the end of the line even if your company has been around a while. |

## Radio

Come on, who doesn't love radio? Many people still listen to the radio on their way to and from work or errands even though cars are equipped with other audio devices. Radio advertising won't be going by the wayside anytime soon, but it still has some cons. Refer to Table 17-3 to discover both the pros and cons of taking advantage of radio advertising.

| Table 17-3 | Pros and Cons of Radio Advertising |
|---|---|
| **Pros** | **Cons** |
| Quickly reaches a large number of people and allows you to narrowly define segments of your market. | Limits you to audio because visuals are obviously impossible. |
| Ads are easy to develop and relatively inexpensive (compared to television). | Listeners tend to scan stations in order to avoid commercials. |
| Enables you to reach additional audience segments and test new target markets rather quickly. | Requires multiple exposure spots in order to gain retention and exposure; consumers must hear a message 2 to 6 times to remember it. |
| Can make you look bigger than you are when you consistently run ads during a concentrated period of time. | The clutter of advertisements on the radio can be high and your message may get lost. |

*(continued)*

**Table 17-3** *(continued)*

| Pros | Cons |
|---|---|
| Because station personalities have great rapport with their audiences, they can give you an implied endorsement by announcing your commercial. | Exposure is short; you have 30 seconds to grab a consumer's attention. |
| Can support your printed advertisements, making them twice as effective; for example, you may say something like "Find our coupon in the Wednesday edition of the newspaper." | Can't be rewound or paused if message is missed. |
| Allows the use of music and sound effects, which create a personality behind the message; this personality helps make your company memorable. | Radio stations typically cater to a much more selective audience than other mediums, such as television, because they exhibit a much more unique and tailored personality. |

### Billboards

Billboards and other outdoor advertising are viable for businesses looking to send a simple visual message that can be read in a matter of seconds. Because most billboards are concentrated in heavily populated areas with high traffic flows, your company or product is sure to be seen. Take a look at Table 17-4 to find out the pros and cons of advertising with billboards.

**Table 17-4          Pros and Cons of Billboard Advertising**

| Pros | Cons |
|---|---|
| Achieves extensive coverage of the market with high frequency. | Makes conveying your message difficult; it must be brief and simple enough to fit in large letters on a billboard. |
| Offers the largest print ad available and generates attention-getting power. | Prime outdoor locations are often controlled by long-time advertisers. |
| Provides around-the-clock exposure. | Becomes background "noise" to consumers after they see the ad several times; they essentially become blind to it until a new ad is placed. |
| Allows you to target specific areas with your message by using different forms of outdoor advertising. | Creates great exposure but isn't generally very memorable. |

# Interactive methods

Interactive methods of marketing involve the Internet. These methods allow you to interact with your potential consumer in real time, which supports the "right-now" mentality that has been created in our society. Consumers no longer like to wait; they want what they want when they want it. These methods also allow you to change a marketing method on the fly within a matter of minutes. You can track your potential consumer with greater detail than when using traditional methods of marketing. In the following sections, I explain each of the interactive methods you have to choose from.

### Internet

If you ask me, I think all businesses need to have some type of online presence. After all, the Internet is becoming the Yellow Pages of today. Consumers use the Internet every day. So if you don't have an online presence, potential consumers may be turned off by your absence and will find your competitor instead. Internet marketing has pros and cons just as any other method. See Table 17-5 for a list.

An Internet presence or Web site paired side by side with more traditional means of marketing can show consumers that you're "with the times" and not stuck in the Dark Ages.

| Table 17-5 | Pros and Cons of Internet Marketing |
|---|---|
| **Pros** | **Cons** |
| Acts as a low-cost promotional strategy. | Doesn't build trust instantly; consumers have to rely on your message rather than physical evidence of your business. |
| Offers the ability to market globally because you aren't limited to a particular location. | Puts you in tough competition with businesses and prices worldwide; you won't be competing with your neighbor. |
| Reaches your target market quickly and easily (much faster than traditional marketing). | |
| Allows you to use audio and visual tools to create an unlimited amount of information regarding your product or service. | |

### Search engine marketing

If you want to be found online, you must participate in search engine marketing. *Search engine marketing,* also known as SEM, is a form of marketing that uses the Internet to promote Web sites and increase visibility in search engine results so that online users can find you when searching for specific services or products. *Search engine marketing* is the process of getting your potential consumers to see your marketing message by driving them to your Web site or advertisement. If your services or your products aren't found in the search engine results, online users won't find you. It's really that simple.

You can choose from two types of search engine marketing, including organic search engine marketing and pay-per-click search engine marketing.

#### Organic search engine marketing

*Organic search engine marketing* is natural visibility in search engine results; in other words, it doesn't require you to pay per click to be listed. This type of search engine marketing makes your site popular with search engines like Google. When focusing on organic search engine marketing, you work your Web site in such a way that consumers find it on the first pages of search results rather than in the later pages.

In order to boost your ranking in the results, you have to pay attention to *search engine optimization,* which is a set of guidelines that helps you create the best chance of your Web site being found in the search engine results. You can find many books and Web sites to help you with this task.

Organic search engine marketing is theoretically free, and it sounds easy, right? Well, not exactly. If you aren't familiar with search engine marketing from an organic perspective, you're better off hiring a company that can take on the task for you. (But, of course, that costs money!) Organic search engine optimization takes a lot of skill and talent in order to get the results you desire. And unfortunately, search engine optimization can't be guaranteed.

Check out Table 17-6 to see the pros and cons of organic search engine marketing.

### Table 17-6    Pros and Cons of Organic Search Engine Marketing

| Pros | Cons |
|---|---|
| Delivers free traffic; because you aren't paying a bounty for each click, visitors cost you nothing. | Takes time (at least 3 months) to start seeing results that are even close to the first page. |
| Provides long-lasting results; after achieving a certain ranking, it isn't difficult to keep it (as long as you follow search engine optimization guidelines ethically). | Requires professional skill and technological expertise, and therefore costs money to get top rankings. |

### Pay-per-click search engine marketing

When you market using *pay-per-click search engine marketing,* you pay when a consumer clicks on your advertisements. This payment could be anywhere from $0.05 to $25, depending on the audience you're marketing to and how strong the competition for that market is. This method is targeted and focused, but as you can see, it will cost you money — and possibly lots of it. Table 17-7 shows the pros and cons of this marketing method.

| Table 17-7 | Pros and Cons of Pay-Per-Click Search Engine Marketing | |
|---|---|
| **Pros** | **Cons** |
| Provides fast results — sometimes within an hour — for those who are in a hurry to be found in the search results. | Competition is tough, and as people catch on to this method, prices will go up. |
| Allows you to change things on the fly to cater your message to your target market; even though this method is labor intensive, you get up-to-the-second results of how your ad is doing. | Requires a steep learning curve, so you must gain as much knowledge as possible before starting out; or you may need to hire an agency that can help you or train you in the basics. |
| Makes creating a marketing campaign that gives you every chance at success easy; no guessing is required because you can use online tools to estimate your traffic and calculate how much you want to spend. | |

## Affiliate / strategic marketing partnerships

*Affiliate marketing partnerships* and *strategic marketing partnerships* help you align yourself with businesses or individuals that serve the same target market that you do. These partnerships are popular online. To take advantage of this method, you find a business that has a Web site that serves your target market, and then you pay that company a flat rate or a percentage of revenue that's produced by a sale initiated by the business. Check out Table 17-8 to see the pros and cons of these partnerships.

| Table 17-8 | Pros and Cons of Affiliate / Strategic Marketing Partnerships | |
|---|---|---|
| **Pros** | **Cons** | |
| Offers you a wider place to sell your products and services; the more Web sites that promote your product, the more sales you'll create. | Makes protecting your brand difficult; partners may not represent your brand correctly or in the way you'd like it to be represented. | |
| Works as a low-risk, cost-effective method; if sales aren't made, you don't pay for the advertisement or marketing. | Causes you to lose control of your marketing message and sometimes brand; you can monitor your affiliates and partners, but doing so takes time that companies often don't have. | |

### Social media

*Social media marketing* is a fairly new method of interactive marketing, but it's doing wonders for many companies. Social media marketing is the use of low-cost tools — typically Internet or mobile based — that are used to combine technology and interaction with the use of words and/or video to promote your products or services.

Social media is a great way to get to know your consumers; and even better, it enables them to get to know you. A few examples of these tools include Twitter, Facebook, YouTube, and Digg. There are new social media marketing tools being introduced daily. The best thing is that the majority of them cost little to nothing to use. Table 17-9 shows the pros and cons of using social media as a marketing method.

Social media can serve as a product marketing channel, but it must be done properly. It's all about the interaction — not only sharing but also listening. If your only interest is to market your product and not to interact with others involved in the social media marketing circle, I wouldn't suggest that you use this method, because you may actually lose consumers rather than gain them. The effectiveness of social media marketing is based on your involvement and interaction.

| Table 17-9 | Pros and Cons of Social Media Marketing |
|---|---|
| **Pros** | **Cons** |
| Provides you with great (uncensored) insight into what consumers really feel about your product or service. | Requires you to participate every day (and sometimes more depending on the topic of the day). |
| Builds your brand and visibility and allows you to provide information to potential consumers. | Results aren't immediate because you have to build relationships first. |

| Pros | Cons |
|------|------|
| Requires no specialized technical skill, so it's easy to use. | Brand control is lax; you can't always control what is said about your brand, product, or service. |
| Costs you nothing but the time it takes to participate. | |

# Choosing the Best Media Outlets for You

In today's world of marketing, you have many media outlets to choose from. I always suggest choosing two forms of marketing: one traditional method and one interactive (or online) method. (You can read all about the many methods in the earlier section "Perusing Your Options for Marketing Message Placement.") Mix it up and find what works for you in reaching your target market. If you drafted your message and know where to find your target market, you'll see success. Benefit from trial and error, and then stick with what works for you.

Before you try an outlet, you need to determine which of your options meet your objectives. To know which outlets meet your objectives, you obviously have to know what your objectives are. For example, do you want to create awareness, gain new customers, or promote an event? You first need to determine your objective and then make a decision as to whether the marketing option you're considering can achieve that objective. Choose only the marketing outlets that can meet your objectives. Doing so helps you narrow down your best marketing options. (Refer to Chapter 3 for more information on determining your marketing objectives.)

When selecting a marketing outlet, you want to evaluate how easy it will be for you to measure the results from that option. After all, it's your return on investment that will be crucial when determining and spending your marketing budget. You never want to select a marketing outlet that doesn't provide you with the capabilities to precisely track and calculate your results.

After you've rolled out your marketing campaign, you'll know whether the outlet you have chosen is successful by the response that you receive from consumers. If consumers aren't responding to your chosen media outlet, it may be time to revise your strategy or try a different outlet. Evaluate your message and make sure that the consumers you've targeted can relate to the message you're sending them. Tweak the message if necessary to see whether you can get an increase in responses; if that doesn't work, it may just be the wrong outlet. In that case, it may be time to try a new one.

After you determine which marketing options work best for you and give you the best return on your marketing investment, you can increase your investment and maximize your returns.

# Chapter 18

# Convincing Consumers to Adopt New Products or Changes in Terms

*In This Chapter*

▶ Exploring the reasons consumers avoid change

▶ Understanding the product life cycle

▶ Helping consumers adopt new products or changes to products

*W*hen you introduce new products or ideas to the marketplace, they're initially only adopted by a small group of people. Only later are those innovations spread to other people — and even then not all of them survive. Some cultures tend to adopt new products more quickly than others. If consumers don't adopt your new products or the changes you make to existing ones, your sales will diminish and eventually you'll no longer be in business. Growth only comes from consumer adoption. So in this chapter, I provide you with a deeper understanding of the adoption process and the product life cycle.

## Realizing the Challenge: Aversion to Change

As you may know, 80 to 90 percent of new products fail. But why is that? The lack of new product adoption by consumers always has been blamed on price, but the truth is that consumers reject new products for many other reasons as well. New products often fail because of

✔ Failure to meet customer needs

✔ Poor timing

- ✔ Market conditions
- ✔ Ineffectiveness or inconsistent branding
- ✔ Technical or design problems
- ✔ Overestimation of market size
- ✔ Poor promotion
- ✔ Insufficient distribution

If the new product or service you're selling offers significant improvement over its competition, or if a product or service you've changed (either in form or in terms) is an improvement over what's been on the market until now, your task is to understand why consumers often reject new offerings that clearly provide them greater benefits than they're currently enjoying. I help you understand the relationship between consumers and change in the following sections.

## How change affects consumers and their behavior

New products — or even just changes to a current product you're selling — force consumers to change the way they do things, whether the change be an actual external behavior modification or an internal adjustment in attitude, intention, or motivation. (These internal changes are at times more difficult than a simple change of procedure.) Changes on the seller's part often represent more than just changes in cost; they also include gains and losses for the consumer. If a new product has any chance at success, it must offer gains to the consumers; these gains include new benefits to be obtained or existing costs that can be avoided.

However, the problem with most new products is that while they may offer gains to the consumer, they also come with losses, which represent opportunity costs of switching. The losses are often viewed by customers as existing benefits that they must give up or new costs that must be incurred.

These gains and losses represent a significant psychological switching cost for the consumer, and the majority of consumers are opposed to undertaking that type of switch. (Refer to the later section "Addressing issues consumers face during the adoption process" for more information on handling opposition.)

# What affects a consumer's acceptance of change

Why are consumers hesitant to give up old benefits and often resistant to incur new costs when they're either retaining the benefits they currently enjoy or gaining new benefits? The answer, like all things related to psychology, is fluid. However, the influences that lead to resistance generally boil down to the following few fundamental truths:

- ✔ **Humans are sensitive creatures.** Chalk it up to the law of survival — people are poignantly aware of the concept of give-and-take. You can see this sensitivity clearly in almost any toddler; even though adults aren't so uninhibited, the sensitivity remains — humans don't like to lose things, and they sure do like to gain things. As a result, the greater the required changes, the greater the potential of resistance.

- ✔ **What people perceive in the world is a response to individual reference points they hold.** These reference points often come from culture influence or social groups that people surround themselves with.

- ✔ **The bad outweighs the good.** As individuals, people often focus more on the negatives of change than they do on the benefits that come with that change. It's easier to remain the same than it is to modify behavior.

When you look at these three components you can see that the adoption of a new product is more about the adjustment a consumer has to make in the gains and losses of abandoning the current product that she's using.

Say, for example, that I have a company called Grocery-Overnight, which sells groceries online. Leslie, who has been a consumer of mine for years, loves the convenience of shopping online and has enjoyed my company's service. Unfortunately due to the higher cost of shipping, I must increase my shipping charge from $2.95 per order to $10.95. In order to absorb these costs for my consumers, I expedite shipping. Most consumers find this benefit worth the extra cost, but Leslie is a single businesswoman who doesn't need the expedited shipping because she plans her weekly menus in advance. The expedited shipping is intended to be a benefit, but Leslie views it as a loss, and so I may lose her as a customer. She simply can't justify the extra $8 to place her grocery order online — it doesn't make economic sense to her. Going to the grocery store will be an inconvenience for her, but paying the $8 is an inconvenience that she sees as a bigger loss. So, Leslie won't adopt my new enhanced product.

In the following sections, I expand on the three factors that lead to consumers' aversion to change.

### The human sensitivity to gains and losses

When you provide a consumer with a new benefit, it will be perceived as a gain; take away an existing benefit, and it will be viewed as a painful loss. The same is true for cost. If you reduce a current cost, it will be perceived as a gain; and if you impose a higher cost, it will be treated as a loss.

Suppose, for example, that a consumer finds a new dry cleaning service near his home. Not only is the service convenient, but it costs less than it did previously, when he had to drive 15 minutes to reach the nearest dry cleaner. He experiences a great deal of happiness, because the costs he's used to paying for have decreased — therefore, he considers the change as gain.

Another man, however, has received notice that his television cable company will be increasing his cable rate and raising his monthly bill. His costs for the very thing he's been purchasing for years have increased, so he counts the change a loss and experiences displeasure.

Regardless of the degree of change, the simple factor of whether a person perceives the change as a gain or as a loss plays a big role in how he'll respond to that change. The perception that a consumer has concerning a change in the product or service that you offer determines whether he will adapt to that change and often whether he will continue paying for your product or service. When you present your consumers with what they can view as a potential loss, you must balance it with something that they can see as a gain; otherwise you run the risk of losing their business, because the feeling of loss wins out.

### One change, many interpretations: The role of reference points

The gains and losses a consumer experiences are evaluated with respect to a relevant reference point. Typically that reference point is represented by the individual's status quo or current state of being. Additions to that individual's status quo are seen as gains, and subtractions from that state are viewed as losses.

Here's an example: If status quo is represented by a consumer's current state, and she goes out one Saturday to purchase a new car that's an upgrade from her current vehicle, she'll have a sense of gain. However, say that on the same Saturday, the consumer doesn't purchase a new car. Instead she's involved in an accident that destroys her current car. In this case she'll feel a loss that she didn't earlier that day before the accident.

It's important to realize, however, that status quo isn't the same across all individuals. Status quo comes from individual situations and perceptions. This is important to recognize because what one consumer may see as a gain another consumer may see as a loss.

For example, take a look at the price of gasoline around the world. In France, I may pay $4 per gallon, and in the United States I may pay $2 per gallon. If the price of gasoline were to change to a universal $3 around the world, the French people would be ecstatic, while those located in the U.S. would see the change as a huge loss. People use the prices that they're currently used to paying for their gasoline as reference points to determine whether the price of gasoline is a gain or loss to their status quos as a consumer.

### The scales are tipped: Loss is heavier than gain

Consumers don't treat comparable size gains and losses the same. Instead, losses seem to loom larger than gains. At times, losses outweigh the gains when it comes to adopting a new product. In other words, when a consumer is forced to give up a specific benefit, the loss creates significantly more pain than the pleasure that's gained from a new benefit.

Research shows that losses are two to three times more painful than comparably sized pleasurable gains. Why the imbalance? The reason boils down to an issue of value: Consumers value items that are in their possession more than they value items that aren't in their possession. Behavior economist Richard Thaler labeled this theory as the *endowment effect.*

The idea behind Thaler's theory is that when a person has possession of something (meaning he owns it), he tends to value it more. In fact, he may value it so much that if he were required to sell it, he would want to ask the buyer to pay more than it's worth. For example, consider the vehicle that you own, and then ask yourself the following questions:

- How much would you sell it for?
- How much do you think people would pay for it?
- How much would you pay for it if you saw it for sale at a car lot?

If the endowment theory is true, you would see your vehicle as being more valuable to you than it is to other people — that is, the amount you would want to sell it for is higher than the amount you would be willing to pay for it.

# Tracing the Typical Life Cycle of a New Product

All new products — whether they're original products, product improvements, or product modifications — go through the product life cycle. You can apply the product life cycle to analyze product class, product form, and brands of product.

Fads, style, and fashion are three product areas that don't necessarily follow the product life cycle. The reason they don't follow this cycle is because they start off with a great deal of momentum, but then the interest of the consumer often diminishes just as quickly.

The product life cycle consists of the following four stages; however, remember that not all products go through each stage:

1. **Introduction:** During this stage of the product life cycle, a business seeks to build product awareness and develop a market for the product by using promotion. The need for immediate profit isn't of concern in this stage.

2. **Growth:** The focus in this stage is on building a brand preference and increasing and stabilizing the market share. Competitors are attracted to the market, and they begin to offer similar products. At this point, products become more profitable because of the growth in sales and because companies form alliances and strategic partnerships to take each other over. Advertising and marketing spending is high during this stage.

3. **Maturity:** The growth in sales begins to diminish during this stage. A product that survived the first stages tends to spend the longest time in this stage. Sales are still growing, but at a much slower rate. Because more competition begins to appear in this stage, it's extremely important to differentiate your product. You may begin to notice that the market is saturated and that price wars and intense competition begin to occur. It's common to begin to see businesses leave the market due to poor margins.

4. **Decline:** In this stage, you often see a decline in the market of the product. This decline is often caused by the introduction of more innovative products. It also can be due to the changing tastes of consumers. You often see intense price cutting in this stage, and even more products are withdrawn from the market.

The product life cycle represents not only the life of a product, but it also can offer guidance in the way that you market, affecting sometimes differences in strategy and the method of marketing that you use. Sometimes a new marketing approach can breathe new life into your product life cycle. For instance, you may notice a breath of fresh air when you begin to evaluate your target market and consider entering a different segment with your marketing. Or, your marketing may be reenergized after implementing a new method, perhaps going from television commercials to radio spots or going from a more traditional method to a more nontraditional method, such as interactive marketing or social media marketing. These are all things to evaluate throughout the life cycle of your product. (Refer to Chapter 16 for more information on marketing methods that you can use.)

# Encouraging Consumer Adoption throughout a Product's Life Cycle

As a business owner, it's important for you to understand the adoption process that consumers go through when purchasing new products and services. The adoption process is the psychological process that a consumer goes through to make a determination on whether to adopt a product. After you understand this process, you can help the consumer work through each phase, moving her closer to the final phase — adoption of your product. There are things you can do in each phase to increase the chances of consumers adopting your products.

Consumers don't adopt change at the same rate, so you use the five adopter categories to understand how and why consumers adopt innovations at different rates. In the last half of this section, I introduce the five categories as well as help you explore the characteristics of each category.

When a consumer evaluates a product, she's confronted with an overabundance of product attributes and choices. Her decision of whether to adopt a new product or a change in terms is based on the following:

- **Level of prior use:** This involves how much a consumer has used the product before the changes and how much she'll use a new product after. The consumer evaluates the usability of the product that meets her needs. For example, if she's evaluating a new shampoo, she would realize that she'd use this product daily. If the product is new or has changed, she'll determine how that will affect her use and satisfaction with it.

- **Involvement with the product:** With this factor, consumers evaluate their involvement with the product. Their involvement either serves as a motivator or it acts as a deterrent in their adoption of the new or changed product.

- **Understanding of the product offering:** A consumer purchases products based on the benefits they offer. So, when evaluating a new or changed product, she must understand what benefits that product offers her.

## Addressing issues consumers face during the adoption process

For consumers, deciding whether to adopt a new product is a process. A series of factors prompt them to consider their current condition and the alternatives that will improve it. You can use these factors to guide your consumers to adopt your product by simply alleviating the roadblocks that may stop them from moving through the process.

You also have to provide information that meets their needs. The more helpful information they receive, the more inclined they are to adopt a new product. Lack of information, on the other hand, will detour adoption. Just remember that successful adoption of your new product depends on your ability to help consumers move through the process.

The rate of adoption can differ significantly among products. The rate often depends on five characteristic factors of the product. These factors determine how quickly a product is accepted by consumers:

- ✔ **Communicability:** One characteristic of quickly adopted products is a high rate of communicability. In other words, their benefits are easily communicated and understood by consumers. The best way to create communicability with your product is to make sure that its benefits are well known and easy to see. This communicability helps consumers understand why they need your product and makes them want to purchase it.

- ✔ **Compatibility:** In order to get consumers to adopt a product, you first have to find out how well your innovation fits with existing traditions, cultures, values, needs, and past experiences. A product that's compatible with existing values of consumers will be adopted more quickly than one that isn't. Take Quaker Oats, for example. When the company first introduced oatmeal, consumers were skeptical because they thought oats were for horses. (Refer to Chapter 13 for more information on segmenting your target market and identifying its needs and values.)

- ✔ **Complexity:** If a product is perceived as being complicated, consumer acceptance will be delayed. Consider computers, for example. When they were first introduced, they were perceived as complex and consumers didn't adopt them quickly. So, be sure to take the time to simplify your product in terms that consumers can understand. And remember that the more difficult a consumer thinks a product is, the slower the adoption rate will be. (Refer to Chapter 16 for more information on product positioning.)

- ✔ **Divisibility:** Consumers prefer to try things on a smaller scale when they're new. They want to be able to purchase a trial product before purchasing the full product. So, if at all possible, ensure that your potential consumers can try your products before buying. For instance, consider the car dealer who allows consumers to test-drive cars over the weekend before making a decision to purchase.

- ✔ **Relative advantage:** Products that offer a significant advantage over the products they replace are often adopted more readily. A digital camera, for example, has a significant advantage over a disposable camera.

All these characteristic factors play a part in whether your product is ever adopted and how quickly it is adopted. The more characteristics you can include in your product, the better your chance of success. Compare your product against each characteristic and evaluate how well it fulfills that characteristic. If it's missing the mark, it's worth taking the time to evaluate how you can fulfill that characteristic better. After all, it really means success or failure when it comes to adoption.

## Reaching the right consumers within your target market

Consumers generally fall into five categories according to how quickly they adopt new products and other changes. These categories are largely based on the personalities of consumers. You can use the adopter categories to understand that the customers who buy first are likely to be significantly different from those who buy the product much later. You can then use this information when working to develop your marketing mix.

Table 18-1 shows the five categories, along with a description of each and the percentage of the target market that they typically comprise.

| Table 18-1 | | The Five Adopter Categories |
|---|---|---|
| *Category* | *Percent of Target Market* | *Characteristics* |
| Innovators | 2.5 | First users of a product. Want to be first to own new products, even if those products don't make it through early stages of product life cycle. Aren't always taken seriously by peers. Venturesome; able to cope with high levels of uncertainty; sociable. |
| Early adopters | 13.5 | Quick to buy new products; key opinion leaders for peers. Enjoy leadership and prestige. Integrated into the local social system; are looked at for advice from potential adopters; respected for use of ideas. |
| Early majority | 34 | First consumers in the mass market to purchase. Rarely leaders, though they usually adopt new ideas before the average person. Look to innovators to see if new product or idea works and begins to stand the test of time. May deliberate for some time before adopting. |

*(continued)*

### Table 18-1 *(continued)*

| Category | Percent of Target Market | Characteristics |
|---|---|---|
| Late majority | 34 | Usually skeptical of change and will adopt innovation only after a majority has tried it. Slower to catch on to the popularity of new products, services, ideas, or solutions. Skeptical; affected by peer pressure; adoption may be more of an economic necessity rather than a choice |
| Laggards | 16 | Last to purchase; some never adopt the products at all. Usually price conscious; traditional; conservative by nature; suspicious of change and new innovations; must be certain that a new innovation won't fail |

The key point in how to use this information is this: You must know which category you're targeting so you can understand that category's needs. Even though you can't cause a consumer to switch from one category to another (you certainly have the power to *influence* consumers, but you simply don't have the power to *change* their personalities!), you *can* market to the specific needs of consumers in each category. You'll find that you benefit the most by viewing each category as a static category that doesn't change; however, what does change is their needs and how you can market to them.

People in each of these categories have different personality characteristics, and each personality is comprised of the attitude that the person holds toward the adoption of a specific innovation. This attitude is what you want to use to gauge how to market to each category specifically. Here are some general guidelines:

- ✔ **Invite a select few innovators to participate in the development of your product, perhaps as a focus group.** The reasoning behind this is twofold. First you develop a relationship with the innovators, and then as a result they will endorse your product.

- ✔ **Involve early adopters by recruiting a few of them as trial partners.** It's important that in doing so you pay attention to the adopters' feedback; be sure to evaluate and implement their suggestions. You also need to take time to reward these early adopters. Promote them as leaders and provide them with ego strokes; you can do so with media coverage or publicity. It's important that throughout this process you maintain your relationship with these adopters, both by listening and providing feedback.

✔ **Attract members of the early majority with giveaways, lower costs, or performance guarantees.** To do so, use only mainstream marketing and media publicity, because consumers in this group tend to associate those marketing methods with credibility. Also, keep in mind that you must keep things simple for these consumers. The benefits of your product must be clearly communicated in order for them to purchase.

✔ **To gain adoption from the late majority, focus your marketing message on social norms rather than benefits.** That is, show them how adoption of your offering enables them to identify with whatever group they're in or desire to be in — their motivator for purchasing is a fear that they won't fit in and that they'll be left behind if they don't purchase. (See Chapter 16 for lots of group-specific guidance.)

✔ **Give laggards a high level of control when it comes to the adoption process, meaning that they control when, where, how, and why they adopt your product.** For this group, you must use your marketing message to create a familiarity with the new product. It helps if they can see other laggards adopting your product.

Turn your attention to the laggards only after you have hit the late majority category. The reason being that the consumers in the late majority category share many of their fears and often listen and respond to the criticism of the laggards when it comes to product adoption.

Working to create a marketing strategy that reaches out to each of these categories creates stability in the adoption of your product. Your product will mature just as your consumers and their behaviors will. For this reason, you must understand what category of consumers you're marketing to in order to understand their needs and create a marketing message that appeals to them and causes them to adopt your product.

## *Offering strategic incentives according to the life-cycle stage at hand*

The product life cycle provides a great timeline that you can go through when evaluating the growth of your products; your marketing efforts will be much more effective if you adapt them to the needs particular to the life-cycle stage that your offering is in. For example, if your product or service is new, you need to consider what ways you can advertise or promote your product in order to gain awareness, which is the first stage. If your consumers have an interest in a trial or desire to sample your product, how will you facilitate that?

If you're changing a product or service you currently sell or are changing the terms associated with it (such as shipping costs), you need to consider how your customers will view that change. Then you use that information to create marketing strategies that address the concerns and challenges your customers may have with the changes. Your goal is to use these marketing strategies to help consumers with the gain or loss trade-off they may be feeling.

Figure 18-1 shows you a general representation of the merger of the product life cycle and the five adopter categories. The percentages shown in this figure reflect the approximate market size of each adopter group. Remember, though, that the product life cycle is just a *guideline,* not an absolute depiction of every product's popularity path. Not only can the length of each stage vary dramatically, but also the marketing actions you take can change the stage at hand. For example, you may go from the growth stage to the decline stage by hiking the price of your product when the market isn't ready. So be sure to use the product life cycle in combination with your own market knowledge and intuition. (You can read more about the product life cycle in the earlier section "Tracing the Typical Life Cycle of a New Product.")

### Stage 1: Introduction

Your goal in the introduction stage is to establish your market and create a demand for your product. If you're introducing a product in this stage that has no or few competitors, you'll likely implement a *price skimming strategy.* With this strategy, a marketer sets a relatively high price for a product or service at first, and then lowers the price over time. If your product does have competitors, you need to ensure that consumers can understand what differentiates you from your competitor. You can adjust your marketing mix so that consumers are clear on the differentiation.

Consider the impact on the marketing mix during this stage:

- ✔ **Product:** Branding and quality level is established during this stage. Intellectual property protection, such as patents and trademarks, should be obtained now.

- ✔ **Pricing:** In this stage, you may use a low penetration price in order to build market share rapidly. Then you might use high skimming pricing to recover any development costs.

- ✔ **Distribution:** The product is only distributed selectively, which allows you to measure the acceptance of the product from consumers.

- ✔ **Promotion:** In this stage, promotion is aimed toward innovators and early adopters. (See the earlier section "Reaching the right consumers within your target market" for more on these consumers.) Marketing is used to communicate and build product awareness and to educate potential consumers about your product.

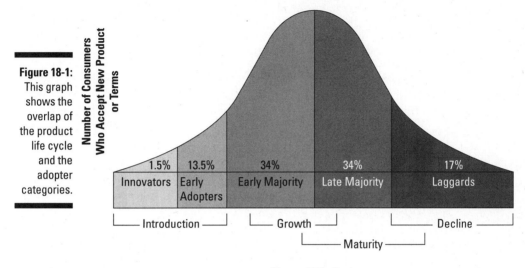

**Innovation Diffusion Curve: The Five Adopter Categories and the Product Life Cycle**

**Figure 18-1:** This graph shows the overlap of the product life cycle and the adopter categories.

## Stage 2: Growth

Your goal in the growth stage is to increase product sales and become the first choice of your customers. This is the stage where you'll more than likely see a period of rapid growth. Consumers become more aware of your product and as a result your sales increase. You want to make changes to your marketing mix to accommodate this growth.

Here are the impacts on the marketing mix during this stage:

- ✔ **Product:** The quality from the previous stage is maintained, though additional features and support service may be added.

- ✔ **Pricing:** The pricing strategy from Stage 1 is maintained during this stage because typically the demand is increasing and competition is low.

- ✔ **Distribution:** Distribution channels are added in this stage as demand increases and more and more consumers begin to accept the product.

- ✔ **Promotion:** Promotion and marketing are now focused on a broader audience.

## Stage 3: Maturity

The primary objective during the maturity stage is to defend your market share, extend the product life cycle, and maximize your profit. To do so, your promotion becomes more widespread and you begin to use a variety of media in order to get your message out.

Consider the impacts on the marketing mix during this stage:

- **Product:** During this stage, you'll likely enhance features to differentiate your product from the competition.
- **Pricing:** Pricing may be lowered because of new competition.
- **Distribution:** Distribution becomes more intensive, and you may offer incentives to encourage preference for your product over competing products.
- **Promotion:** Promotion during this phase emphasizes differentiation among competitors.

### Stage 4: Decline

The primary objective of the decline stage is survival or coasting until you run out of revenue. This is a tough stage to be in because you'll have to make some tough decisions. Make a decision on how you'll proceed with your product and then create a plan to act on.

Profit can often be saved or improved by reducing marketing and by cutting costs in other ways, such as reducing overhead costs that come from the development of the product. Your marketing mix is less important in this stage because your goal is to cut costs to survive. Your marketing mix would only apply if you had found new features or new uses for your product. And if that is the case, you would actually find yourself back in Stage 1 of the product life cycle.

Your action item during this stage is to make a decision. You have three main options, and in order for a company to stay on top, it must choose one and act on it:

- **Maintain and revitalize the product:** With this option, you keep the product going as is. You may enhance the product by adding new features or finding new uses.
- **Harvest the product:** You harvest a product by reducing costs and continuing to offer it, but you generally focus on loyal niche segments only.
- **Discontinue the product:** If you discontinue a product, you liquidate the remaining inventory or sell it to a company that's willing to continue the product.

# Chapter 19

# Cultivating Customer Loyalty

. . . . . . . . . . . . . . . . . . . . . . . . . . . . . . . . . . . . . . . . . . . . . . . . .

### In This Chapter

▶ Understanding consumer-business relationships

▶ Evaluating the different loyalty types

▶ Encouraging customer loyalty with a few strategies and methods

. . . . . . . . . . . . . . . . . . . . . . . . . . . . . . . . . . . . . . . . . . . . . . . . .

Consumers have to make choices every day; if you want to be the business they're loyal to, you must give them a reason to choose you. An enjoyable experience and exceptional service set the stage for customer loyalty, and an emotional connection and authentic relationship will seal the deal every time.

Creating loyalty within your customers isn't difficult, but it does take effort on your part. You must be able to provide your consumers with what they feel is that emotional connection; that connection comes from providing them with the best value, having the ability to satisfy their needs and desires, and taking the time to make them feel good about who they are. When you've done these things, you've laid the groundwork and cultivated the relationship that leads to the committed consumer loyalty that you're looking for.

In this chapter, I discuss consumer-business relationships as well as customer loyalty. Specifically, I show you how to recognize and foster loyalty from your customers.

## Waxing Romantic: A Primer on Consumer-Business Relationships

As a marketing manager, your goal is twofold: attracting new customers and retaining your existing ones. Getting business from current customers is easier and much less expensive than gaining a new customer. A regular consumer that's committed to your products doesn't have to be resold, so you save time, money, and effort. Marketing is a great tool that can be used to develop, nurture, retain, and maintain relationships with your customers. Marketers call this *customer relationship management.*

Business is based on relationships, and relationships are based on qualities such as trust, respect, appreciation, understanding, generosity, and open and honest communication. True customer loyalty is a continuing series of inter-actions and feelings of attachment between you and the customer. I provide the basics on customer loyalty in the followings sections.

## The difference between repeat buying and customer loyalty

There's a difference between a satisfied customer and a loyal customer. A satisfied customer is simply happy with the service and products that a com-pany offers at the moment. If something better comes along, however, that customer could be lured away. Loyalty, on the other hand, develops when consumers get involved with the company beyond the normal transaction. Customer loyalty usually develops when a customer has a problem and the company solves that problem by going out of its way to take care of the cus-tomer. This individual care causes the customer to feel an emotional connec-tion to the company.

It's important to understand the differences between satisfied customers and loyal customers because then you can use that information to be proactive in switching satisfied customers to loyal customers. Table 19-1 shows you the characteristics of both loyal customers and satisfied customers.

| Table 19-1 | Defining Characteristics of Satisfied and Loyal Customers |
|---|---|
| *Satisfied Customers* | *Loyal Customers* |
| Continue doing business with you until something better comes along (location, price, variety) | Understand and forgive minor problems they encounter with your company |
| Have not developed a relationship with you | Are not price sensitive and become repeat buyers of your product |
| Have no personal interactions with you | Help sell your business with word-of-mouth marketing — without you offering incentives |
| View business as impersonal; they do business with your company rather than with you as a person | Don't jump to competitors because they offer perks or products that may be seen as "better" |

Here's a personal example that will give you a clear picture of how customer loyalty works. One hot summer day, I accidentally locked myself out of my home. I had recently become a patron of a wine bar that's located not far from my house, so I decided to go there to see if I could use the phone to call a locksmith. When I walked in, the owner immediately knew that I was stressed. I explained the situation, and she let me use her laptop to locate a locksmith. The locksmith couldn't be at my house for 45 minutes, so the owner of the wine bar poured me a glass of white wine and invited me to wait it out there.

When it was time to leave the bar, I asked for my tab. The owner hadn't charged me for the glass of wine. As you can imagine, I have become a loyal customer of that bar. Even though a variety of wine bars are in my area and new ones are opening frequently, that one wine bar has become my "home." I not only visit there, but I also recommend the bar to others. When I have lunch meetings, I often take my guests there so they can experience the atmosphere and extraordinary care that the owners of this wine bar give their customers.

# Why loyalty is important for business

When a relationship between a business and a consumer is of high quality, the chance for ongoing business is increased, because both see value and mutual benefits in the exchanges. In other words, a high-quality relationship benefits both your business and the customer. Customers, for instance, have an easier time making decisions and their perception of practical value is enhanced. Your company benefits by not having to resell the customer. The pleasant nature of the exchanges between you and the customer are agreeable to both parties. You'll know when the relationship between you and your customer is strong, because you'll act as partners. Additionally, relationship building and staying in touch with your customers serves as a reminder of why they should buy from you and not your competitor.

Before you spend your time and money going after new customers that you aren't currently in a relationship with, consider the following statistics:

- ✔ Loyal customers spend 33 percent more than new customers.
- ✔ Referrals among loyal customers are 107 percent greater than among non-customers.
- ✔ It costs six times more to sell something to a prospect than to sell that same item to a loyal customer.

As you can see, your marketing dollars go farther when you use them to build, nurture, and develop your customer relationships and develop the loyalty of your customers.

Customer loyalty provides you with many benefits. For instance, loyal customers do the following:

- ✔ Purchase your products over and over again throughout time.
- ✔ Increase the volume of their purchases with you.
- ✔ Buy across product lines.
- ✔ Refer others to you with word-of-mouth marketing.
- ✔ Avoid being lured by your competition.
- ✔ Give your company the benefit of the doubt when something goes wrong.

# Digging Up the Roots of Loyalty

You may be surprised to find that there are different types of customer loyalty. General customer loyalty can create a certain level of stability, but committed loyalty is what creates business success — it's the type that doesn't build false hope in success but instead builds a strong commitment from your customers.

Consumers become loyal to businesses that meet their needs, both internal and external, but they become committed in loyalty when businesses meet their psychological needs. In this section, I discuss the different types of loyalty so you can gain an understanding of the type of loyalty that you desire. I also show you how to attract that loyalty by being able to recognize and meet the psychological needs of your customer.

## Why consumers are loyal: Five very different reasons

By understanding the following five types of loyalty, you can easily identify your customers accordingly:

- ✔ **Committed loyalty:** This is the type of loyalty that you want to achieve. Consumers in this category have a positive commitment to your business and are devoted to purchasing from you. No matter how strong the pull is, they won't be swayed by your competition. That's because these consumers have a deliberate, emotionally based commitment to you, your product, your brand, or whatever it is that they're loyal to. This committed loyalty has been created by the service they've received and the extraordinary experience they get every time they visit your business. These consumers know they don't get this from every business they patronize, but they can always count on getting it from yours. Your goal is to strive to achieve this level of loyalty from *all* of your consumers.

An example is a customer who goes to a restaurant every week, not because it's close to his house but because the service is phenomenal, the food is excellent, and he feels like part of the restaurant family.

✔ **Cost of change loyalty:** In some situations, the cost, difficulty, or hassle involved in changing companies is so great that consumers change only as a last resort — even when other solid competitors are available. An example would be a customer who has a mortgage but isn't happy with the service of his current mortgage company. He won't switch companies because the cost would be high and the hassle would be great.

✔ **Habitual loyalty:** This repeat business is the most common. As time becomes scarce for consumers, familiar routines that can be quickly accomplished with minimal thought become part of their lifestyle. Businesses with high levels of consumers who have the habitual type of loyalty may feel a misleading sense of security. The commitment consumers feel to these businesses can be quite low. An example is a consumer who uses a dry cleaning service that's a block from his house. He isn't happy with the prices and the service in his opinion isn't the best, but he'll continue to use the service because it's convenient and fits into his daily routine and habits.

✔ **Incentivized loyalty:** This type of loyalty represents customers who are incentivized for their loyalty to a business through points programs, percentages off, or cash-back options. They see the loyalty program as something that's important, and because of this perk they continue to shop at the store that offers the program. An example would be a customer who has a credit card that offers him points for every dollar he spends at a certain store. Even though the store's service is subpar, the customer won't switch because the incentive to stay is too great.

✔ **Monopoly loyalty:** This is the type of loyalty where customers have little or no choice in where they shop. Their "loyalty" is far from devoted. Instead, it's often resentful. Unfortunately, customers who have little or no choice and have monopoly loyalty are often dissatisfied. An example of monopoly loyalty would be a utility company that has gained government legislation to be the only one who provides service in a specific area. The customer has no choice but to use them.

## *Understanding what committed loyalty — the one you want — is based on*

Consumer loyalty is strengthened when a company makes an emotional connection with its customers. Recent research indicates that when a consumer connects emotionally with a product, a segment of her brain lights up — and that's a good thing. After those emotional connections are made, consumers become loyal and go from being just a "customer" to being a "repeat buyer."

The main reason that customers leave companies that they've been doing business with is because they perceive that the companies don't care about them or their needs. When customers are asked why they remain loyal to a particular company, the top answer is "because the company cared about me." This perception of being cared for is the emotional bridge between customer satisfaction and customer loyalty. In other words, loyalty is an emotional attachment that a consumer has with a company based on the consumer's subjective perception that the company is delivering the value she desires or needs at the right time and in the right form.

Creating the kind of loyalty that you desire from consumers takes meeting their psychological needs. It's about service and creating extraordinary experiences, but it's also about providing consumers with the interaction that they need to solidify the relationship — and that starts with the first purchase they make from you. I explain all this in the following sections.

### Starting with the psychology behind the initial purchase

In today's world, consumers want choices. But they also want those choices to be relevant to what they need to accomplish. Even though the reasons consumers buy vary from one consumer to another, they're all derived from four psychological needs. This is true for all businesses and industries.

As you know, in Step 1 of the decision-making process, the consumers identify a need (see Chapter 2 for more on this process). When it comes to developing the committed loyalty that you want from consumers, it's about meeting those internal psychological needs that really creates the emotional connection that consumers are looking for. Meeting a need is one thing; meeting an emotional need at the same time is what creates loyalty. (Refer to Chapter 4 for more information on meeting the emotional needs of consumers.) When you meet one of the following needs, it causes the consumer to make the initial purchase:

- The need to be understood
- The need to feel welcome
- The need to feel important
- The need for comfort

Even after the initial purchase has been made, true loyalty to you requires commitment from the consumer, because that consumer must make a conscious decision and effort to purchase from you. Customers who feel a true commitment to you are an asset to the company, because as long as you always take care of them, they will always be your customer.

### *Moving from psychology to relationship (in effect, loyalty)*

A consumer's initial purchase is his first interaction with you. This interaction determines whether he'll return. Even though he may not become a committed loyal customer on the first visit, it definitely sets the stage for whether he'll ever become a committed loyal customer of yours in the future. A committed relationship with consumers is based on the following building blocks:

- ✔ **Communication:** You and the consumers "speak the same language" and are able to understand one another. Communication is key; if consumers feel that you don't understand them or that you aren't listening to them, it could detour them from ever coming back.

- ✔ **Competence:** Consumers view your company as knowledgeable and capable. They want to be able to trust your expertise and know that what you're telling them is true.

- ✔ **Customer orientation:** The strong relationships with your customers have filtered down to other staff members. You can be the owner of the company and treat every customer with respect and great service, but if your staff members don't, they can do damage to the work that you've done. Their lack of respect can even sever the relationship. You can't be the only one in your company who understands the importance of customer loyalty, so hire carefully and provide training.

- ✔ **Equity:** You and the consumers both see equity in your exchanges, and you're also able to equitably resolve conflicts. Consumers want to know that you value them as much as they value you. They also want to feel as if you have the same interest in resolving their problems as they do.

- ✔ **Personalization:** You treat the customers as individuals. You may even know their names. Even if you don't know their names, they want to feel as if they're important to you. They don't want to just be another sale. Consumers enter businesses daily where no one pays attention to them. It's out of the norm for someone to give them the attention they're looking for, so if you can do that, you'll make them want to be loyal to you.

- ✔ **Trust:** You and the consumers both depend on each other. Consumers love to purchase from people that they can trust. If they can trust you, they will feel safe in taking your advice and getting your feedback.

# Creating a Committed Loyal Customer

Encouraging customer loyalty is a complex task. But with a few methods, you can successfully build loyalty among your customers. Success in customer loyalty is usually achieved with a combination of marketing initiatives and excellent customer service. The success formula varies from one business to another, however.

The foundations of customer loyalty are universal, so in this section, I begin with the basic relationship-building blocks you should start with as well as offer a macro perspective on the ins and outs of loyalty programs. I then discuss ways to customize your tactics to your particular target market, which you can do to make your efforts resonate even more deeply with your customers.

If you build customer loyalty that's based on your company, you'll find it easier to gain loyalty for your products. If you only build loyalty with a certain product, you risk losing business when you decide to discontinue that product. Loyalty to the company creates a forever customer; loyalty to a product creates a customer for the life of the product. So I always suggest creating loyalty from the bottom up.

## Establishing a relationship: The basics

Building relationships with your customers isn't as difficult as you may think. You simply have to treat your customers as if they truly are your strategic partners. You also need to show them that you truly care about them. You can do both of these things by focusing your efforts on developing and exemplifying the following qualities:

- ✔ **Expertise:** Be able to answer the questions that your customers have. Consumers don't want to buy from just anyone — they want to know that they can count on you to give them good solid advice and feedback.

- ✔ **Attention:** Pay attention to your customers; listen to what they want and what they have to say. By listening to what they say, you can identify their needs and hopefully provide a solution for those needs.

- ✔ **Friendliness:** Reflect a great attitude. Customers are attracted to businesses that contain happy and helpful people. Be sure to hire those staff members who can exude friendliness to your customers.

- ✔ **Flexibility:** Be flexible in order to fulfill the needs of your customers. If customers think that doing business with you is a risk, they'll reach out to your competitors.

- ✔ **Patience:** Customers don't like being pressured to purchase, so show them options and educate them, but then be patient while they make a decision.

- ✔ **Superiority:** Offer products that are of excellent quality. Do what you do, and do it well. Be superior in both products and service. Customers hate to feel like they were scammed or taken advantage of. When purchasing from you, they want to be confident that you will provide them with quality products and will back those products with superior service.

Don't just satisfy your customers. Instead, blow them away with your service. Do whatever it takes to make them happy. The out-of-the-way service may cost you in the short term, but it will pay off in the long run. Also, be aggressive but not intrusive. Be friendly, go out of your way, and put an emphasis on forming a relationship with each customer. Whatever you do, don't simply focus on sales. Sales always follow relationships.

## Adding loyalty programs to the repertoire (but not as a solo act!)

Many businesses have experimented with loyalty cards and programs as a way of increasing customer loyalty. A loyalty card or program keeps track of the purchases that a customer has made with your business. These programs differ somewhat, depending on the business that offers them. Most of the time, however, these programs offer on-the-spot discounts on selected items. The business also may offer the customer with the loyalty card a lesser price than the customer who doesn't have a loyalty card.

Here are a few of the pros of loyalty programs:

- ✔ They keep your name in front of the customer.
- ✔ They encourage increased sales and return business.
- ✔ They can provide you with valuable customer demographic information if you collect the data on purchases.

But, of course, there are cons as well. Here they are:

- ✔ Unless the reward is significant, your program may not stand out among other programs.
- ✔ Unique offers can backfire. For example, some business owners may avoid punch cards and club cards altogether and instead opt for special sales and offers for their most loyal customers. This can be a great approach, but there's always the unfortunate risk of offending customers if your special sale or offer doesn't apply to them.
- ✔ Loyalty cards and programs can seem invasive to some customers, especially if you're tracking purchasing habits.
- ✔ Loyalty programs create a loyalty that's based on your financial commitment to the consumer. This type of loyalty lasts for a very brief time when compared to consumer loyalty that's based on your product. Product-based loyalty is a much deeper commitment on the consumer's behalf.

The results of these programs are mixed. In fact, these programs can sometimes backfire by appealing too strongly to the bargain-hunting consumer. Consumers who are economically conscious often show a lower interest in incentivized programs because they prefer to purchase from the business that gives them the best offer instead of just being incentivized for the purchase. So when using these programs, you must evaluate whether you've created a reward for the loyalty of the customer or have attracted the bargain shopper instead.

If you're going to develop a program that incentivizes customers, it's a mistake to make that the only thing you do to capture customer loyalty. Incentivizing to gain customer loyalty can work in your favor, but it can also work against you by creating customers who are only loyal to you because of the incentives you give them. However, you can create an incentive program that you pair with other loyalty development initiatives, such as superior service and relationship building, and it will be a success.

## Accounting for behavioral predispositions

Consumers are all different, but they carry around many of the same predispositions. So, in order to create the customer loyalty that you desire, you must create an emotional connection with them. An emotional connection develops when the consumer becomes more involved with your business in a way that's over and beyond the normal daily transaction.

You create customer loyalty by understanding what's important to your consumers and by going out of your way to use that understanding to provide them with an extraordinary experience every time they encounter your business — whether they're purchasing a product at the time or not.

# Part VI
# The Part of Tens

The 5th Wave                    By Rich Tennant

"How about this-'It's not just CRAP, it's Mel's CRAP'? Shoot! That's no good. I hate writing copy for this client."

## In this part . . .

In this part, I share ten tips on how to enhance your
customer satisfaction with communication. These tips
require little time, but they carry a big impact. I also show
you ten super tips regarding business-to-business consumer
behavior. It's much different from business-to-consumer
behavior, so I explain how you should treat it differently.

# Chapter 20

# Ten Easy Ways to Enhance Customer Satisfaction

*In This Chapter*

▶ Improving your relationship with customers

▶ Communicating with your customers so they remember you

**C**onsumers are affected by external and internal influences that can sometimes determine how they receive you, but you can also provide a marketing influence by communicating with them. They must feel as if you have a genuine interest in them when you communicate with them. Reception can depend a lot on your approach as well as on the manner in which you do it. You won't always understand the influences that affect every consumer, but by understanding the reasons consumers behave the way they do, you can take measures to communicate with them in ways that foster a positive consumer-supplier relationship.

As you can see, long-term success in business is about developing and maintaining good customer relationships and loyalty, but who has the time? Don't worry! In this chapter, I show you ten easy ways that you can better communicate with your customers.

## Acknowledge Customers Right Away

You'd be amazed at the number of businesses you can walk into without being acknowledged. No one says hello. Your presence goes unnoticed. Don't be one of those businesses; acknowledge everyone who steps foot into your business. Greet them and move from behind the desk or counter to shake their hands. Create that first impression, because you only get one chance to do it.

# Conduct Customer Surveys

The most important tasks that customer surveys assist with are finding out what your customers want and discovering how they feel about the service they've received from you. Customer surveys also help you

- Stay innovative in product development.
- Receive external feedback about the customer service you provide.
- Increase customer retention by showing customers that you care what they think.
- Recover customers you've lost by finding out why they left and encouraging them to return by showing that you've fixed the problem.
- Obtain an advanced warning by identifying upcoming trends, performance issues, or marketing opportunities that you may be missing.

# Follow Up to Inquire about Satisfaction

When was the last time you called a customer to find out about his experience with your business? I'm not talking about telemarketing to sell something. I'm talking about a genuine telephone call that has no motive other than to talk to the customer and find out how he felt about his experience with your business. Or, if he purchased a big-ticket item, you find out how the item is working. This tip is as easy as picking up the phone. Just remember that it isn't a sales call; it's a courtesy call that carries with it a genuine interest in the satisfaction of a customer.

# Listen Intently

Talk to your customers, but don't stop there. Also be sure to listen to them. Listen intently — hear what they have to say. Your customers' opinions are valuable. By listening to them, you often can find out what they're looking for and what type of services they enjoy. You can even get to know them personally. It's important to remember that customer loyalty is created by the emotional experience they have with your business, and if you aren't listening, the emotional connection will never transpire. Strive for customer loyalty, not just customer satisfaction.

# Build an Online Presence

If you aren't online, your customers will have trouble finding you. And I'm not just talking about new customers. Your current customers need information too. You would be surprised at how many consumers use the Internet to find addresses, telephone numbers, or special items they'd like to purchase. With today's technology, it isn't enough to be in the phone book — most folks aren't using those anymore.

It's best to have a Web site that will provide consumers with information about you and the services and products that you offer. If this approach isn't feasible, at least make sure you're listed in online directories so consumers can find you when browsing the Internet.

# Keep in Touch with E-Newsletters

More than 70 percent of individuals have e-mail addresses. Are you collecting these valuable gems? If not, it's a good time to start. When you ask customers for their e-mail addresses, tell them you're collecting the addresses so you can inform them of upcoming events, specials, or new item introductions. You'd be surprised how many customers are willing to share their e-mail addresses with you.

Don't bombard customers with daily e-mail messages. If you become a nuisance, your customers may lose trust in you and your products and services.

Instead, send out quarterly or monthly updates letting customers know what's going on at your business. Keep your promise and use the newsletters to keep them informed. You may even want to include a special coupon every once in a while as a thank you.

# Make the Purchasing Process an Experience

Go out of your way to create an experience for your customers. Too many businesses today feel that they deserve to have customers served up on a silver platter. The truth is that you must earn those customers by creating an extraordinary experience for them every time.

The experience comes from the atmosphere and the friendliness of your business. You want your consumers to notice that your business is willing to go out of the way to help without making them feel as if they're a burden. Test your place of business by walking through it and experiencing what your customers experience. Make sure you're creating an experience that keeps them coming back.

# Offer Birthday Specials

Everyone loves birthday gifts, right? Of course. Consider starting a birthday program that you can use to send that special birthday offer to your customers. The offer needs to be worth their visit to your business, so make sure it has value to them. Consider offering them a discount or a free gift when they visit your business location.

Birthday programs, which are a great way to stay in touch with your customers, show that you're thinking of them on their special day. This is the kind of program that creates loyalty with your customer base, so get started today.

# Hold Special Events

If you want customers to continue coming to your business, consider holding special events; perhaps an open house, a special sale night, or a premiere of a new product. Customers love events that are designed around specific celebrations. It gives them a reason to visit your place of business and experience what you have to offer. Besides, who doesn't enjoy a celebration? Consider your target market and then develop a calendar of special events that will keep your customers coming back over and over again.

# Volunteer for a Good Cause

Besides seeing you when purchasing a product from you, customers want to see you doing good within the community. So get out there and volunteer for causes that you support. By doing so you reflect that you not only care about your business, but you care about the surrounding community. You'd be surprised how many new customers you can gain by reaching out. People love to support the businesses that support the causes that they do. You'll not only feel great about volunteering, but you can grow your business by doing it. Consider this growth an added benefit.

# Chapter 21

# Ten Special Considerations for Business-to-Business Marketing

**In This Chapter**

▶ Understanding the core differences between marketing to businesses and to consumers

▶ Marketing successfully to businesses

*P*eople often ask how business-to-business (B2B) marketing is different than business-to-consumer (B2C) marketing. After all, as most people would say, you're still selling a product to a person. That's a valid perspective, and one that's shared by many, but experience shows that the differences between these two types of marketing run deep. And those differences are important.

In the B2B market, businesses try to streamline the purchasing process in order to not only save time but also save money. So when you're dealing with businesses, you must take certain steps to move the decision-making process in your favor. By understanding what they're looking for, you can create a plan to do this.

## Value of a Sale

The cost of a sale when it comes to the business-to-business market is typically higher than with the business-to-customer market. Why? A business-to-business transaction often requires more consideration. The cost pushes the business-to-business consumer to evaluate more options in order to evaluate price and value thoroughly.

An average sales call now costs $350 to $400 when you factor in all expenses. A complex transaction may require eight to ten calls to close a sale. Plus you have to add in the advertising and marketing expenses needed to generate inquiries and qualify leads. The initial transaction value is measured in hundreds or thousands of dollars, and the likelihood of ongoing sales is quite high. As a result, the lifetime value of a B2B customer can span many years and add up to hundreds of thousands of dollars — if not millions.

Use this information to compute the true profitability of each of your B2B accounts. Doing so will assist you in determining the true profitability when all selling costs are factored in.

# Size of Your Target Market

In a B2C market, you typically have a larger target market than you do when dealing with a B2B market. Your B2B target market is small and focused. You have less wiggle room, and you're typically required to stay within that focused target market. Consumer markets are measured in the millions, but only a few B2B firms have customer bases in the thousands.

However, with that being said, don't confuse potential revenue with the number of potential customers. B2B markets may be smaller and more concentrated in terms of number of prospective customers, but not necessarily in sales potential. Your marketing can be more condensed and better targeted, but your message needs to really appeal to the markets in order to gain their business. In other words, you'll have less opportunity for trial and error of your marketing message.

# Complexity of the Buying Process

With a business-to-consumer market, you're typically dealing with a single-step buying process. You're trying to convince an individual — the same individual who considers the options, makes the decision, and pays the bill. The same isn't true with most business-to-business transactions. You're often dealing with multiple individuals and sometimes even large committees, which could mean that you have to deal with different personalities. B2B sales organizations are characterized by well-paid field sales people, distributors, and business partners or independent representatives who aren't engaged only in the selling but in the fulfillment of the product or service.

As a result, B2B companies use marketing to educate various players in the target audience because the decision to purchase is usually a multistep process involving more than one person. Marketing activities are usually the first step in a longer, integrated touch campaign that may include direct mail, telemarketing, webcasts, newsletters, and follow-up by sales representatives who will discuss the business's requirements in more detail and move the prospect through the sales cycle.

# Challenge of Identifying the Decision Maker

Ultimately, your goal is to get to the decision maker. If you don't follow the chain of command within the business, you could lose the sale for not considering the proper people. Each person has a specific role in the decision-making process and a duty to judiciously compare all the options. The selling proposition is complex and the risk of a wrong decision is high and long lasting. As the marketer you have the added responsibility of correctly identifying the roles within that buying committee in order to identify the decision maker — and this is sometimes difficult to do.

# Duration of the Sales Cycle

The sales cycle for a B2B transaction typically takes much longer than a B2C sale. It's not unusual to have a six-to-nine month buying cycle involving five to ten people as both decision makers and influencers. A long sales cycle can cost you money, time, and effort before a sales is ever closed. It can sometimes cause frustration in the process as well. If a company isn't prepared from a revenue standpoint, its success may be affected.

# Importance of Reason in Decision Making

Purchase decisions within a business-to-business market are made rationally rather than emotionally. A business must evaluate the business value and make a determination on the purchase. So it's rare to have an impulse purchase within a B2B marketplace. On the other hand, emotions play a huge role in purchasing patterns during business-to-consumer transactions.

Take the decision-making process for example. Sure, most families consult on houses and cars, but no one ever gets fired for making an impulse buy while in the line at the grocery store. In fact, creating the interest that drives an impulse sale is one of the core tenants of B2C marketing. This isn't the case in B2B marketing.

# Motivation to Purchase

Fundamentally, B2B motivations to purchase are about addressing a point of pain and economic impact that will increase revenue or decrease costs. The consumer, on the other hand, is motivated to purchase by an emotion that's triggered as a result of identifying a need.

The business buyer makes a logical decision to purchase; there's little to no personal emotion involved. The organizational buying process is often driven by systematic procedures and purchasing systems that must be followed. The business buyer wants or needs to buy products or services to help her company stay profitable, competitive, and successful. As a marketer, you must understand that organizational buyers have to operate within the confines of their organizational procedures, so it's your job to fully understand these procedures.

# Distribution of Products

Consumers demand a variety of distribution channels for convenience. However, it's unlikely that you'll find business-to-business offerings in the local market. Convenience is of less importance in B2B transactions. In fact, most B2B products must be preordered and sometimes even produced specifically for a company. This process takes time, which means that the order must be preplanned. If you're marketing to the B2B market, you must ensure that you're getting the proper materials to businesses. This way, when they order your product, they know that you're a supplier. After all, the chances of business owners browsing the local market are pretty slim.

# Thirst for Knowledge

Consumers don't like to be handed five-page pamphlets on your products, but B2B buyers are different in this respect. They have a thirst for knowledge. They're information seekers who are constantly looking for information or advice that will help them increase profitability and enhance their careers. So, obviously, when you're creating your marketing collateral for B2B markets, you can be more in depth. If you provide them with information that's helpful, interesting, and relevant to their concerns and needs, they'll read it. Consumers are the exact opposite, however; they don't want to work to understand your benefits. Instead, the benefits must be clearly pointed out.

# Frequency of Negotiation

You can sell a consumer with little to no negotiation; as long as he feels like he's getting value, you're set. Consumers simply don't like to haggle. When it comes to the B2B market, however, be prepared. You will negotiate on cost, service plans, and delivery of your product. The buyer in the B2B market isn't the only one who needs to feel as if he has received the higher end of value from the deal; he also must prove it to the others in the chain of command. So be sure to go into a B2B market transaction prepared to negotiate. If you don't, it's very likely that you'll lose the sale.

# Appendix

# Glossary

● ● ● ● ● ● ● ● ● ● ● ● ● ● ● ● ● ● ● ● ● ● ● ● ● ● ● ● ● ● ● ● ● ● ● ● ● ● ● ● ● ● ● ● ● ● ● ● ● ● ● ● ● ● ● ● ●

*M*arketing terms can seem confusing since so many look and sound alike but carry different meanings. So to help you get everything straight, in this glossary I combine some common terms used in consumer behavior and marketing. I also include some not-so-common terms that you're likely to come across.

This glossary gives you a great reference as you read through the discussions in this book. And even when you finish this book, I think you'll find this to be a resource you refer to often.

**actual self:** Pertains to the self-concept that's reflective of how an individual actually is today.

**ad copy:** The printed text or spoken words in an advertisement.

**advertising allowance:** Money provided by a manufacturer to a distributor for the purpose of advertising a specific product or brand.

**advertising budget:** Money set aside by the advertiser to pay for advertising. A variety of methods are available for determining the most desirable size of an advertising budget.

**advertising plan:** An outline of the goals an advertising campaign should achieve. The plan also summarizes how to accomplish those goals and how to determine whether the campaign was successful in obtaining the goals.

**advertising research:** Research conducted to improve the efficacy of advertising. It may focus on a specific ad or campaign, or it may be directed at a more general understanding of how advertising works or how consumers use the information in advertising.

**affiliate:** The publisher or salesperson in an associate or affiliate marketing relationship. The affiliate gives wider distribution to the affiliate merchant's products in return for compensation based on performance.

**affiliate marketing:** Revenue sharing between advertisers/merchants and publishers/salespeople, whereby compensation is based on performance measures, typically in the form of sales, clicks, registrations, or a combination of any of these.

**attitude:** The lasting general evaluation of something a consumer experiences, including how he feels about it and what he believes.

**banner ad:** A graphical Web advertising unit, typically a large headline or title extending across the full page width, which often measures 468 pixels wide and 60 pixels tall.

**brand:** A name, term, design, symbol, or any other feature that identifies one seller's good or service as distinct from those of other sellers. A brand, which is also known in legal terms as a trademark, may identify one item, a family of items, or all items of that seller.

**business-to-business marketing:** Marketing that's directed to other businesses rather than to consumers. Also known as B2B marketing.

**business-to-consumer marketing:** Marketing that's directed to consumers rather than to businesses. Also known as B2C marketing.

**channel of distribution:** An organized network of agencies and intermediaries that, in combination, perform all the marketing functions required to move goods and services from producer to end customers. Channels of distribution are also known as marketing channels.

**cognitive dissonance:** The regret a consumer faces after a purchase. Also commonly known as buyer's remorse.

**consumer behavior:** The study of individuals and the activities they participate in to satisfy their realized needs. The satisfaction comes from the processes used in selecting, securing, and using products or services.

**consumer misbehavior:** Consumer behavior that violates laws or generally accepted norms of conduct in today's society.

**core market:** The largest market that your product or service appeals to.

**cost efficiency:** For a media schedule, the relative balance of effectively meeting reach and frequency goals at the lowest price.

**cost per inquiry:** The cost of getting one person to inquire about your product or service. This is a standard used in direct response advertising.

**cost per rating point (CPP):** The cost, per 1 percent of a specified audience, of buying advertising space in a given media vehicle.

**cost per thousand (CPM):** The cost, per 1,000 people reached, of buying advertising space in a given media vehicle.

**creative strategy:** An outline of an advertisement, showing what message should be conveyed, to whom it should be directed, and with what tone. This strategy provides the guiding principles for the copywriters and art directors who are assigned to develop the advertisement.

**culture:** The all-encompassing force that helps to form an individual's personality, which in turn is the key determinant of consumer behavior.

**DAGMAR:** A process of establishing goals for an ad campaign so it's possible to determine whether the goals have been met. The acronym stands for Defining Advertising Goals for Measured Advertising Results.

**deceptive advertising:** The Federal Trade Commission (FTC) defines this as being a representation, omission, act, or practice that's likely to mislead consumers who are acting reasonably under the circumstances. To be regulated, however, a deceptive claim must also be material. *See materiality.*

**demographics:** Basic objective and descriptive classifications of consumers, such as their age, sex, income, education, size of household, and ownership of home. This doesn't include classification by subjective attitudes or opinions of consumers.

**direct mail:** Marketing communications delivered directly to a prospective purchaser via the U.S. Postal Service or a private delivery company.

**direct marketing:** Sending a promotional message directly to consumers rather than through a mass medium, such as radio, television, newspapers, and billboards. This type of marketing includes methods such as direct mail and telemarketing.

**emotions:** Temporary state of consumers that reflects current changes in motivation, often triggering a change in behavior.

**Federal Communications Commission (FCC):** The federal agency responsible for regulating broadcast and electronic communications.

**Federal Trade Commission (FTC):** The federal agency that's primarily responsible for regulating national advertising, promotion, and competitive business practices, among other things.

**fixed-sum-per-unit method:** A method of determining an advertising budget, which is based directly on the number of units sold.

**flat rate:** A media rate that allows for no discounts.

**focus group interview:** A research method that brings together a small group of consumers to discuss a product or advertisement under the guidance of a trained interviewer.

**four Ps:** The four main components of marketing strategy, which include product, price, place (distribution), and promotion.

**groups:** Represents two or more individuals that share a set of norms, values, or beliefs. The members of a group have a collective identity, interact with one another, and share a common goal or interest.

**high-involvement purchase:** A purchase that involves a high-priced product or service and carries a great deal of personal risk.

**ideal self:** Pertains to the self-concept that represents how an individual would like to be.

**integrated marketing communication (IMC):** A management concept that's designed to make all aspects of marketing communication — such as advertising, sales promotion, public relations, and direct marketing — work together as a unified force instead of each working in isolation.

**key success factors:** The factors that are a necessary condition for success in a given market.

**lifestyle:** Individual function of the motivations, knowledge, attitudes, behaviors, beliefs, opinions, demographic factors, and personality of an individual.

**low-involvement purchase:** A purchase that involves a lower-priced product or service and that carries less personal risk.

**marginal analysis:** The technique of setting the advertising budget by assuming the point at which an additional dollar spent on advertising equals additional profit.

**market segmentation:** The division of a market using a strategy that's directed at gaining a major portion of sales within a subgroup in a category rather than gaining a more limited share of purchases by all category users.

**market share:** The percentage of a product category's sales in relation to the entire market — in terms of dollars or units — that's obtained by a brand, line, or company.

**marketing mix:** The interaction of the elements of a product's or service's marketing efforts, including product features, pricing, packaging, advertising, merchandising, distribution, and marketing budget.

**market research:** The systematic gathering, recording, analyzing, and use of data relating to the transfer and sale of goods and services from producer to consumer.

**materiality:** The importance of an advertisement to consumers. The Federal Trade Commission theoretically won't regulate a deceptive advertisement unless the deceptive claim is also material, or important, rather than trivial.

**media strategy:** A plan of action by an advertiser for bringing advertising messages to the attention of consumers through the use of appropriate media.

**motivation:** Represents the persistent need that stirs up and stimulates long-term goals within a consumer.

**motivation research:** Research used to investigate the psychological reasons that individuals buy specific types of merchandise or why they respond to specific advertising. This research helps you determine the base of brand choices and product preferences.

**National Advertising Division (NAD) of the Council of Better Business Bureaus:** The organization that serves as a major self-regulatory mechanism for advertising.

**national brand:** A nationally distributed product brand name. The product draws a distinction with regional brands and local brands.

**nonprofit marketing:** The marketing of a product or service in which the offer itself isn't intended to make a monetary profit for the marketer.

**norms:** The rules of behavior that are part of the ideology of a group. Norms tend to reflect the values of a group and categorize actions as proper or inappropriate. They also set forth rewards for adherence and punishment for nonconformity.

**objective:** A desired or needed result to be achieved by a specific time. An objective is broader than a goal, and one objective can be broken down into a number of specific goals.

**penetrated market:** The actual set of users actually consuming the product or service.

**per inquiry:** An agreement between a media representative and an advertiser in which all advertising fees are paid based on a percentage of all money received from an advertiser's sales or inquiries.

**perceived risk:** A functional, psychosocial, physical, or financial risk a consumer feels that she's taking when purchasing a product.

**percent-of-sales method:** The method of determining an advertising budget based on an analysis of past sales as well as a forecast for future sales.

**perception:** Represents how a consumer processes and interprets information. It's the way consumers see the world around them.

**persuasion process:** The process used by advertising to influence audience or prospect attitudes, especially purchase intent and product perception by appealing to reason or emotion.

**potential market:** A set of consumers who profess some level of interest in a designed market offer.

**primary research:** Research that's conducted directly from your own consumers or potential consumers.

**private self:** Represents the self-concept that an individual intentionally keeps hidden from the public.

**product differentiation:** The development of a unique product difference with the intent to influence demand by gaining a competitive advantage based upon this difference.

**product life cycle:** A marketing theory suggesting that the sales revenue and profit curves of all products or brands tend to follow a predictable pattern and sequence of stages, including introduction, growth, maturity, and sales decline.

**product positioning:** The consumer perception of a product or service as compared to its competition.

**promotion:** All forms of communication that call attention to products and services by adding extra values toward the purchase. Includes temporary discounts, allowances, premium offers, coupons, contests, and sweepstakes.

**promotional mix:** The use of several different types of communication to support marketing goals, including advertising, personal selling, publicity, and sales promotions.

**psychographics:** A term that describes consumers or audience members on the basis of psychological characteristics initially determined by standardized tests or criteria.

**psychological segmentation:** The separation of consumers into psychological characteristic categories on the basis of standardized tests or criteria.

**public self:** Represents the self-concept that an individual puts forth to the public.

**publicity:** A type of public relations in the form of a news item or story that conveys information about a product, service, or idea in the media. Publicity is a form of nonpaid promotion.

**qualitative research:** A method of advertising research that emphasizes the quality of meaning in consumer perceptions and attitudes. Examples of this research include in-depth interviews and focus groups.

**quality control:** An ongoing analysis of operations to verify goods or services, to meet specified standards, or to better answer customer or user complaints.

**quantitative research:** A method of advertising research that emphasizes measurement of incidence of consumer trends within a population.

**questionnaire:** A document that's used to show the questions (and order of the questions) that a researcher should ask a consumer about a product or service. It sometimes lists the alternative responses that are acceptable.

**reference group:** A group of people or an organization that an individual respects, identifies with, or aspires to join. Examples of these groups include membership or associative groups.

**secondary research:** Research that a company collects indirectly from various outside sources.

**self-concepts:** The mental image or perception that one has of oneself. A person can have four self-concepts: ideal self, actual self, public self, and private self.

**sociocultural:** Relating to both social and cultural matters.

**strategic market planning:** The planning process that yields decisions regarding how a business unit can best compete in the markets it elects to serve.

**subculture:** A group of people that shares specific values within a culture.

**subliminal perception:** An advertising message presented below a consumer's threshold of consciousness. A visual or auditory message that's allegedly perceived psychologically but not consciously.

**target audience:** A specified audience or demographic group for which an advertising message is designed.

**target market:** A group of individuals whom collectively are intended recipients of an advertiser's message.

**target market identification:** The process of using income, demographic, and life style characteristics of a market and census information for small areas to identify the most favorable locations to market a product or service.

**unique selling proposition:** The unique product benefit that a competitor's product or service can't claim when offered to the prospective customer in an exchange transaction.

**values and lifestyles (VALS) research:** A research method that psychologically groups consumers based on certain characteristics, such as their values, lifestyles, and demographics.

**vehicle:** A specific channel or publication for carrying an advertising message to a target audience. For example, a medium may be magazines; the vehicle for that medium would be *Time Magazine*.

**word-of-mouth advertising:** Advertising that occurs when customers share information about products or promotions with friends.

# Index

## BUSINESS, CAREERS & PERSONAL FINANCE

**Accounting For Dummies, 4th Edition***
978-0-470-24600-9

**Bookkeeping Workbook For Dummies†**
978-0-470-16983-4

**Commodities For Dummies**
978-0-470-04928-0

**Doing Business in China For Dummies**
978-0-470-04929-7

**E-Mail Marketing For Dummies**
978-0-470-19087-6

**Job Interviews For Dummies, 3rd Edition*†**
978-0-470-17748-8

**Personal Finance Workbook For Dummies*†**
978-0-470-09933-9

**Real Estate License Exams For Dummies**
978-0-7645-7623-2

**Six Sigma For Dummies**
978-0-7645-6798-8

**Small Business Kit For Dummies, 2nd Edition*†**
978-0-7645-5984-6

**Telephone Sales For Dummies**
978-0-470-16836-3

## BUSINESS PRODUCTIVITY & MICROSOFT OFFICE

**Access 2007 For Dummies**
978-0-470-03649-5

**Excel 2007 For Dummies**
978-0-470-03737-9

**Office 2007 For Dummies**
978-0-470-00923-9

**Outlook 2007 For Dummies**
978-0-470-03830-7

**PowerPoint 2007 For Dummies**
978-0-470-04059-1

**Project 2007 For Dummies**
978-0-470-03651-8

**QuickBooks 2008 For Dummies**
978-0-470-18470-7

**Quicken 2008 For Dummies**
978-0-470-17473-9

**Salesforce.com For Dummies, 2nd Edition**
978-0-470-04893-1

**Word 2007 For Dummies**
978-0-470-03658-7

## EDUCATION, HISTORY, REFERENCE & TEST PREPARATION

**African American History For Dummies**
978-0-7645-5469-8

**Algebra For Dummies**
978-0-7645-5325-7

**Algebra Workbook For Dummies**
978-0-7645-8467-1

**Art History For Dummies**
978-0-470-09910-0

**ASVAB For Dummies, 2nd Edition**
978-0-470-10671-6

**British Military History For Dummies**
978-0-470-03213-8

**Calculus For Dummies**
978-0-7645-2498-1

**Canadian History For Dummies, 2nd Edition**
978-0-470-83656-9

**Geometry Workbook For Dummies**
978-0-471-79940-5

**The SAT I For Dummies, 6th Edition**
978-0-7645-7193-0

**Series 7 Exam For Dummies**
978-0-470-09932-2

**World History For Dummies**
978-0-7645-5242-7

## FOOD, GARDEN, HOBBIES & HOME

**Bridge For Dummies, 2nd Edition**
978-0-471-92426-5

**Coin Collecting For Dummies, 2nd Edition**
978-0-470-22275-1

**Cooking Basics For Dummies, 3rd Edition**
978-0-7645-7206-7

**Drawing For Dummies**
978-0-7645-5476-6

**Etiquette For Dummies, 2nd Edition**
978-0-470-10672-3

**Gardening Basics For Dummies*†**
978-0-470-03749-2

**Knitting Patterns For Dummies**
978-0-470-04556-5

**Living Gluten-Free For Dummies†**
978-0-471-77383-2

**Painting Do-It-Yourself For Dummies**
978-0-470-17533-0

## HEALTH, SELF HELP, PARENTING & PETS

**Anger Management For Dummies**
978-0-470-03715-7

**Anxiety & Depression Workbook For Dummies**
978-0-7645-9793-0

**Dieting For Dummies, 2nd Edition**
978-0-7645-4149-0

**Dog Training For Dummies, 2nd Edition**
978-0-7645-8418-3

**Horseback Riding For Dummies**
978-0-470-09719-9

**Infertility For Dummies†**
978-0-470-11518-3

**Meditation For Dummies with CD-ROM, 2nd Edition**
978-0-471-77774-8

**Post-Traumatic Stress Disorder For Dummies**
978-0-470-04922-8

**Puppies For Dummies, 2nd Edition**
978-0-470-03717-1

**Thyroid For Dummies, 2nd Edition†**
978-0-471-78755-6

**Type 1 Diabetes For Dummies*†**
978-0-470-17811-9

---

## INTERNET & DIGITAL MEDIA

AdWords For Dummies
978-0-470-15252-2

Blogging For Dummies, 2nd Edition
978-0-470-23017-6

Digital Photography All-in-One
Desk Reference For Dummies, 3rd Edition
978-0-470-03743-0

Digital Photography For Dummies, 5th Edition
978-0-7645-9802-9

Digital SLR Cameras & Photography
For Dummies, 2nd Edition
978-0-470-14927-0

eBay Business All-in-One Desk Reference
For Dummies
978-0-7645-8438-1

eBay For Dummies, 5th Edition*
978-0-470-04529-9

eBay Listings That Sell For Dummies
978-0-471-78912-3

Facebook For Dummies
978-0-470-26273-3

The Internet For Dummies, 11th Edition
978-0-470-12174-0

Investing Online For Dummies, 5th Edition
978-0-7645-8456-5

iPod & iTunes For Dummies, 5th Edition
978-0-470-17474-6

MySpace For Dummies
978-0-470-09529-4

Podcasting For Dummies
978-0-471-74898-4

Search Engine Optimization
For Dummies, 2nd Edition
978-0-471-97998-2

Second Life For Dummies
978-0-470-18025-9

Starting an eBay Business For Dummies,
3rd Edition†
978-0-470-14924-9

## GRAPHICS, DESIGN & WEB DEVELOPMENT

Adobe Creative Suite 3 Design Premium
All-in-One Desk Reference For Dummies
978-0-470-11724-8

Adobe Web Suite CS3 All-in-One Desk
Reference For Dummies
978-0-470-12099-6

AutoCAD 2008 For Dummies
978-0-470-11650-0

Building a Web Site For Dummies,
3rd Edition
978-0-470-14928-7

Creating Web Pages All-in-One Desk
Reference For Dummies, 3rd Edition
978-0-470-09629-1

Creating Web Pages For Dummies,
8th Edition
978-0-470-08030-6

Dreamweaver CS3 For Dummies
978-0-470-11490-2

Flash CS3 For Dummies
978-0-470-12100-9

Google SketchUp For Dummies
978-0-470-13744-4

InDesign CS3 For Dummies
978-0-470-11865-8

Photoshop CS3 All-in-One
Desk Reference For Dummies
978-0-470-11195-6

Photoshop CS3 For Dummies
978-0-470-11193-2

Photoshop Elements 5 For Dummies
978-0-470-09810-3

SolidWorks For Dummies
978-0-7645-9555-4

Visio 2007 For Dummies
978-0-470-08983-5

Web Design For Dummies, 2nd Edition
978-0-471-78117-2

Web Sites Do-It-Yourself For Dummies
978-0-470-16903-2

Web Stores Do-It-Yourself For Dummies
978-0-470-17443-2

## LANGUAGES, RELIGION & SPIRITUALITY

Arabic For Dummies
978-0-471-77270-5

Chinese For Dummies, Audio Set
978-0-470-12766-7

French For Dummies
978-0-7645-5193-2

German For Dummies
978-0-7645-5195-6

Hebrew For Dummies
978-0-7645-5489-6

Ingles Para Dummies
978-0-7645-5427-8

Italian For Dummies, Audio Set
978-0-470-09586-7

Italian Verbs For Dummies
978-0-471-77389-4

Japanese For Dummies
978-0-7645-5429-2

Latin For Dummies
978-0-7645-5431-5

Portuguese For Dummies
978-0-471-78738-9

Russian For Dummies
978-0-471-78001-4

Spanish Phrases For Dummies
978-0-7645-7204-3

Spanish For Dummies
978-0-7645-5194-9

Spanish For Dummies, Audio Set
978-0-470-09585-0

The Bible For Dummies
978-0-7645-5296-0

Catholicism For Dummies
978-0-7645-5391-2

The Historical Jesus For Dummies
978-0-470-16785-4

Islam For Dummies
978-0-7645-5503-9

Spirituality For Dummies,
2nd Edition
978-0-470-19142-2

## NETWORKING AND PROGRAMMING

ASP.NET 3.5 For Dummies
978-0-470-19592-5

C# 2008 For Dummies
978-0-470-19109-5

Hacking For Dummies, 2nd Edition
978-0-470-05235-8

Home Networking For Dummies, 4th Edition
978-0-470-11806-1

Java For Dummies, 4th Edition
978-0-470-08716-9

Microsoft® SQL Server™ 2008 All-in-One
Desk Reference For Dummies
978-0-470-17954-3

Networking All-in-One Desk Reference
For Dummies, 2nd Edition
978-0-7645-9939-2

Networking For Dummies,
8th Edition
978-0-470-05620-2

SharePoint 2007 For Dummies
978-0-470-09941-4

Wireless Home Networking
For Dummies, 2nd Edition
978-0-471-74940-0

## OPERATING SYSTEMS & COMPUTER BASICS

**iMac For Dummies, 5th Edition**
978-0-7645-8458-9

**Laptops For Dummies, 2nd Edition**
978-0-470-05432-1

**Linux For Dummies, 8th Edition**
978-0-470-11649-4

**MacBook For Dummies**
978-0-470-04859-7

**Mac OS X Leopard All-in-One Desk Reference For Dummies**
978-0-470-05434-5

**Mac OS X Leopard For Dummies**
978-0-470-05433-8

**Macs For Dummies, 9th Edition**
978-0-470-04849-8

**PCs For Dummies, 11th Edition**
978-0-470-13728-4

**Windows® Home Server For Dummies**
978-0-470-18592-6

**Windows Server 2008 For Dummies**
978-0-470-18043-3

**Windows Vista All-in-One Desk Reference For Dummies**
978-0-471-74941-7

**Windows Vista For Dummies**
978-0-471-75421-3

**Windows Vista Security For Dummies**
978-0-470-11805-4

## SPORTS, FITNESS & MUSIC

**Coaching Hockey For Dummies**
978-0-470-83685-9

**Coaching Soccer For Dummies**
978-0-471-77381-8

**Fitness For Dummies, 3rd Edition**
978-0-7645-7851-9

**Football For Dummies, 3rd Edition**
978-0-470-12536-6

**GarageBand For Dummies**
978-0-7645-7323-1

**Golf For Dummies, 3rd Edition**
978-0-471-76871-5

**Guitar For Dummies, 2nd Edition**
978-0-7645-9904-0

**Home Recording For Musicians For Dummies, 2nd Edition**
978-0-7645-8884-6

**iPod & iTunes For Dummies, 5th Edition**
978-0-470-17474-6

**Music Theory For Dummies**
978-0-7645-7838-0

**Stretching For Dummies**
978-0-470-06741-3

# Get smart @ dummies.com®

- **Find a full list of Dummies titles**
- **Look into loads of FREE on-site articles**
- **Sign up for FREE eTips e-mailed to you weekly**
- **See what other products carry the Dummies name**
- **Shop directly from the Dummies bookstore**
- **Enter to win new prizes every month!**

**Separate Canadian edition also available**
**Separate U.K. edition also available**

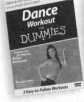